"Over many years, John Walford has been an extraordinary and energetic scholar, writer, teacher, and artist. This Festschrift is a fitting tribute to a man whose life has touched so many and in such profound ways."

Jeremy S. Begbie, Thomas A. Langford Research Professor of Theology, Duke Divinity School; author, *Resounding Truth: Christian Wisdom in the World of Music*

"Over the course of his distinguished career as an art historian, John Walford has given generations of students the gift of sight. Professor Walford has enabled us to perceive in the visible world the spiritual meanings inherent within works of art. This collection of essays displays the fruit of his labors through the work of scholars who have received his artistic insights and share his passion for close readings of visual imagery, clear expressions of doctrinal truth, and joyful experiences of aesthetic delight."

Philip G. Ryken, President, Wheaton College

"*Art as Spiritual Perception* is a rich kaleidoscope of art historical essays all centered around one common theme of increasing importance today—the way in which artists' views of the world, not least their religious beliefs, shape artistic perception and meaning. I cannot think of a more fitting tribute to the impressive work and legacy of John Walford."

Adrienne Dengerink Chaplin, coauthor, *Art and Soul: Signposts for Christians in the Arts*; former senior member in philosophical aesthetics, the Institute for Christian Studies

"It is with great delight that I herald the arrival of *Art as Spiritual Perception* in honor of Dr. Walford. James Romaine and his fellow scholars have created a fitting work in tribute to Walford and—perhaps more importantly—have added a significant new volume to the select canon of books on art and faith. This is a fantastic book. The chapter on Van Gogh alone is worth the price of admission."

Ned Bustard, editor, *It Was Good: Making Art to the Glory of God*

"This wide-ranging collection of essays by current colleagues and former students will be an encouragement and inspiration to all who love art and love God. It is a fitting testimony to the career of John Walford, whose life and work have been characterized by faithfulness to his guild, faithfulness to his students, faithfulness to his college, and above all, faithfulness to God."

Lisa DeBoer, Professor of Art, Westmont College

ART AS SPIRITUAL PERCEPTION

ART AS SPIRITUAL PERCEPTION

ESSAYS IN HONOR OF E. JOHN WALFORD
EDITED BY JAMES ROMAINE

FOREWORD BY MARLEEN HENGELAAR-ROOKMAAKER

CROSSWAY

WHEATON, ILLINOIS

Library of Congress Cataloging-in-Publication Data

    Art as spiritual perception : essays in honor of E. John Walford / edited by James Romaine ; foreword by Marleen Hengelaar-Rookmaaker.
       p.   cm.
    Includes bibliographical references and index.
    ISBN 978-1-4335-3179-8 (hc)
    1. Spirituality in art. 2. Artists—Religious life. I. Walford, E. John, 1945- honoree. II. Romaine, James, editor of compilation.
    N8248.S77A78   2012
    701'.1—dc23   2012007347

CONTENTS

LIST OF ILLUSTRATIONS   9

ACKNOWLEDGMENTS   11

FOREWORD   15
Mentoring Eyes: Hans Rookmaaker and John Walford
Marleen Hengelaar-Rookmaaker

INTRODUCTION   23
You Will See Greater Things than These: John Walford's
    Content-oriented Method of Art History
James Romaine

1   *NEOFITUS*, HE WENT TO GOD   41
The *Sarcophagus of Junius Bassus*
Linda Møskeland Fuchs

2   GOTHIC ARCHITECTURE AND "THE PURE AND   59
    NAKED SEEING OF DIVINE REALITY"
Chartres Cathedral
Rachel Hostetter Smith

3   HEAVEN COME TO EARTH   75
The Limbourg Brothers' *January* (from *Les Très*
    Riches Heures du Duc de Berry)
Matthew Sweet Vanderpoel

4   ACADEMIA'S "RELIGIOUS TURN"   91
The *Brancacci Chapel*
Matthew Milliner

5   THE SHAPE OF PLACE   109
Joachim Patinir's *Landscape with Saint Jerome*
Henry Luttikhuizen

6   THE PERCEPTION OF SPIRITUALITY   123
Hans Holbein's *The French Ambassadors*
William Dyrness

7 A LOCALIZED PROVIDENCE   137
   Pieter Bruegel the Elder's *Hunters in the Snow*
   Rachel-Anne Johnson

8 SPACE, SYMBOL, AND SPIRIT   151
   Pieter Saenredam's *Interior of the Church of Saint
       Odulphus at Assendelft*
   Jan Laurens Siesling

9 CATEGORIES FOR ART HISTORICAL METHODOLOGY   165
   Antoine Watteau's *The Dance* (*Les Fetes Venitiennes*)
   Calvin Seerveld

10 DEPARTING LIGHT   181
   Caspar David Friedrich's *Tetschen Altar* (*Cross in
       the Mountains*)
   Kaia Magnusen

11 REMEMBER THY CREATOR   193
   John Constable's *Dedham Vale*
   Anne Roberts

12 WHAT THE HALO SYMBOLIZED   207
   Vincent van Gogh's *Sower with Setting Sun*
   James Romaine

13 EVOLVING A "BETTER" WORLD   225
   Piet Mondrian's *Flowering Apple Tree*
   Graham Birtwistle

14 SPIRITUALLY CHARGED VISUAL STRATEGY   239
   Jackson Pollock's *Autumn Rhythm*
   Linda Stratford

15 THE LIBERATING MYTH   255
   Joseph Beuys's *I Like America and America Likes Me*
   James Watkins

   AFTERWORD   271
   A Portrait of E. John Walford
   Joel Sheesley

   CONTRIBUTORS   278

   INDEX   281

ILLUSTRATIONS

Young John Walford Sailing   14

Jacob van Ruisdael, *View of Haarlem*   22
    from the Dunes at Overeen

Sarcophagus of Junius Bassus   40

Nave, Chartres Cathedral   58

Limbourg Brothers, *January* (from *Les Très*   74
    Riches Heures du Duc de Berry)

The Brancacci Chapel   90

Joachim Patinir, *Landscape with Saint Jerome*   108

Hans Holbein, *The French Ambassadors*   122

Pieter Bruegel the Elder, *Hunters in the Snow*   136

Pieter Saenredam, *Interior of Saint*   150
    Odulphus Church, Assendelft

Antoine Watteau, *The Dance* (*Les Fêtes Vénitiennes*)   164

Caspar David Friedrich, *Tetschen Altar*   180
    (*Cross in the Mountains*)

John Constable, *Dedham Vale*   192

Vincent van Gogh, *Sower with Setting Sun*   206

Piet Mondrian, *Bloeiende Appelboom*   224

Jackson Pollock, *Autumn Rhythm: Number 30, 1950*   238

Joseph Beuys, *Coyote: I Like America and*   254
    America Likes Me

Portrait of John Walford: Number 2, 2009   270

ACKNOWLEDGMENTS

This is a Festschrift for Dr. E. John Walford. Dr. Walford was born February 16, 1945, in London. The son of Lt.-Col. Jack Walford and Diana Walford, nee Ralli, he married Maria Dellù, of Milan, Italy, in 1972. They have three children and eight grandchildren. He studied law in London before turning to art history. From 1969 to 1976 Walford studied under the late Professor Hans Rookmaaker at the Vrije Universiteit, Amsterdam, graduating with honors (Kandidaats). From 1976 to 1980, Walford was Speelman Fellow, at Wolfson College, Cambridge, and earned a PhD in art history at the University of Cambridge. Under the direction of the late Professor Michael Jaffé, Director of the Fitzwilliam Museum, Cambridge, he wrote his dissertation on the seventeenth-century Dutch landscape painter Jacob van Ruisdael. In 1981, Dr. Walford took a position as art historian and art department chair at Wheaton College, Wheaton Illinois, where he became a full professor in 1997. Dr. Walford retired from Wheaton College in May 2011.

Dr. Walford's publications include: *Jacob van Ruisdael and the Perception of Landscape* (Yale University Press, 1991); *Great Themes in Art* (Prentice-Hall, 2002); (With Franco Vaccaneo and Maria Walford-Dellù) *Cesare Pavese: Immagini fotografiche di David Wittig* (Pieraldo Editore, 2006); "Profile: Joel Sheesley," *IMAGE: A Journal of Religion and the Arts* (Fall 1993); "The Lost Art of Attentive Viewing, Review of John Drury's 'Painting the Word: Christian Pictures and Their Meanings' (Yale, 1999)," *Books and Culture* (May/June 2000): 34–35; "The Visibility of the Invisible: Renaissance Art and the Mediation of Belief," *Books and Culture* (July/August 2007): 38–39; "The Case for a Broken Beauty: An Art Historical Perspective," in Daniel J. Treier, Mark Husbands, and Roger Lundin, eds., *The Beauty of God: Theology and the Arts* (InterVarsity Press, 2007); and "Joel Sheesley: Twenty-Five Years of Painting," in Gregg Hertzlieb, ed., *Domestic Vision: Twenty-Five Years of the Art of Joel Sheesley* (Lutheran University Press, 2008).

Dr. Walford also produced a solo photographic exhibition and illustrated catalog essay, *Markers of Identity* (text in English & Italian), Oratorio dell'Immaculata, San Giorgio Scarampi (AT), Piedmont,

Italy: Scarampi Foundation, October 2007; and thereafter a book of Walford's digital photographs was published as *An Art Historian's Sideways Glance* (Piquant, 2008).

The contributors to this Festschrift know John Walford in many different ways. Graham Birtwistle and Jan Laurens Siesling were students with him at the Vrije Universiteit, Amsterdam, where they studied under Hans Rookmaaker. Marleen Hengelaar-Rookmaaker is Dr. Rookmaaker's daughter. Kaia Magnusen, Matthew Milliner, Rachel-Anne Johnson, James Romaine, Matthew Vanderpoel, and James Watkins were students of Dr. Walford at Wheaton College. William Dyrness, Linda Fuchs, Henry Luttikhuizen, Anne Roberts, Calvin Seerveld, Rachel Smith, and Linda Stratford are friends of Dr. Walford's. Joel Sheesley was a colleague of Dr. Walford's at Wheaton College. All of the authors have contributed their scholarship to this Festschrift in appreciation of Dr. Walford.

Young John Walford Sailing. C. 1966–1968. Photo from the collection of John Walford.

FOREWORD
Mentoring Eyes:
Hans Rookmaaker and
John Walford

MARLEEN HENGELAAR-ROOKMAAKER

Recently, when reflecting on his student days at the Free University (Vrije Universiteit) in Amsterdam, John Walford referred to the late Hans Rookmaaker, his art history professor and my father, as "the most significant man in my life."[1] Let me therefore venture to offer a few observations about the relationship between John Walford and my father, which will also allow us some significant glimpses into John's vocational life. I knew John when he was a student in Amsterdam and have followed his whereabouts from afar since then. This means that I know and understand where the art historian John comes from, because I come from that same place myself. What was foundational to John (or Johnny, as I knew him back then) was also foundational to me.

John is roughly ten years older than I, which is a big age difference when you are still in high school, as I was when John entered the scene. Indeed I looked up to this highly articulate, uncannily wise, and seemingly brilliant student of my father's. John was a bit of a long-haired hero to me, an exciting combination of a hippy and a British upperclass gentleman. While my father may have been a gift to him, John and the other foreign students who came to study with him definitely were a special gift to my father, especially since the overall climate at the Free University was quite antagonistic to Christianity. I saw how excited my father became when he was among these students and how proud he was when "they started asking all the right questions." My father loved the intimacy of John's cottage near the river Amstel when

---

[1] E. John Walford, "Hans Rookmaaker's 'Four Freedoms' and Christian Art (Part I)" (*Transpositions Symposium: The Life and Work of Hans Rookmaaker*, February 28, 2011). See http://www.transpositions.co.uk/2011/02/hans-rookmaakers-four-freedoms-and-christian-art-part-i/ and http://www.transpositions.co.uk/2011/03/hans-rookmaakers-four-freedoms-and-christian-art-part-ii/.

spending the night there after the biweekly Wednesday evening seminars with his foreign students: the spirited conversations, the laughter and the jokes, the wine and the whiskey.

Although it was providential, it is hardly self-evident that John, after already having studied law in England, would have ended up in Amsterdam studying art history in the Netherlands. My father had looked John up in London, around 1968, after John had contacted him to ask his opinion about a seventeenth-century painting. John was buying and selling paintings as a sideline in those days, being drawn to art for its aesthetic qualities. It so happened that my father appeared on John's doorstep a day early, while the house was in quite a state after a party that had ended only a few hours before. What struck John was that my father did not mind that the only drinkable liquid in the house was whiskey (at coffee time!) and that the house was a total mess. On the contrary, my father seemed to feel quite at home, staying to talk with John and look at his art collection for hours.[2] This they had in common: neither of them came from Christian backgrounds, but had come to faith in their twenties. Neither of them needed their lives to be kept straight and safe by all kinds of narrow rules; they both knew by hard experience that life without Christ was dark and dismal.

A few months later, after John had gone around museums in England with my father and his students for a week as their chauffeur, my father told him that he had a really remarkable eye for art, but that he was lacking in historical understanding. "You should see your eye as a gift of God, which you need to educate in order to make it useful in a deeper way. Come to the V. U."[3] My father, with his mentoring eyes, had seen John's potential before John had even recognized it himself. Since his conversion, John had been quite uncertain what to do with his love for art. In John's evangelical circles, art tended to be confused with idolatry. Christ, as presented to him, was "all about reading the Bible and praying and evangelizing, so that they could read the Bible and pray and evangelize, so that . . . like a machine producing a line of similar sausages . . ."[4] Studying the Scriptures, John had started to put a question mark behind this view of life, wondering if the abundance

---

[2] E. John Walford (lecture, Wheaton College, 1979).
[3] Laurie R. Matthias, "Dual Citizenship in Athens and Jerusalem: A Portrait of Professors who Exemplify the Integration of Faith and Learning at Wheaton College" (PhD diss., Regent University, 2007).
[4] Walford (lecture, Wheaton College, 1979).

of life Christ wants to offer us does not pertain to life in all its dimensions. My father echoed and confirmed these sprouting ideas. What is more, he had thought them through in their implications for his work as a Christian art historian.

During his seven years in Amsterdam (1969–1976), John was given to develop a new biblically informed and neo-Calvinist-colored perspective not only on art and art history but also on faith and life in general. John noted, "These years gradually reshaped my sense of self, my relationship to God, to others, my view of nature and the dynamics of society, as well as providing fresh grounds for cross-cultural engagement."[5] Basic to this was the emphasis my father put on the freedom God gives us to be who we are and to engage the world without fear and free from false pressures. Fundamental to this was also my father's deep affirmation of reality and our humanity. My father believed that reality is God's wonderful creation that we are given to delight and feel at home in, even though we lament and battle its brokenness. He also taught that Christ died to make us human, to reach our best God-given human potential, and to be human to all humans, serving all and rejoicing in whatever is good and wholesome. He did not hold these beliefs in a naïve way, but with discernment, testing the spirits and aware of underlying assumptions, aware of when God is affirmed or denied. For my father, this faith in Christ was not restricting; it allowed him to be open and free to explore the products of our culture.

My father died in March 1977, leaving John and the rest of us burdened with the high and lofty calling to attempt little less than changing the course of a Western world in crisis, missing our mentor, feeling alone. John had already made his next step, however, and was now working in Cambridge on his PhD dissertation on Jacob van Ruisdael and seventeenth-century Dutch landscapes, a subject also close to my father's heart. It must have been a challenge and a learning experience for John at Cambridge University, a sophisticated environment devoted to so-called neutral science, to stand for what he had learned in Amsterdam. But it also must have been a source of great joy to be able to study in depth Ruisdael's biblically informed

---

[5] E. John Walford, "Cultivating Integrative Practices of Faith and Art," 2005, http://web.mac.com/john. walford/Site/Art_%26_Theology.html.

conception of landscape painting, which perceived creation as God's second book, and to work on rich issues of representation and meaning. John left Cambridge having written a dissertation that a few years later was published as a beautiful book by Yale University Press. John had now entered the art historical arena. He had become a scholar in his own right.

Next, to my great surprise, John moved to Wheaton College, not exactly the capital of art historical activity, not exactly the place to be when devoted to Christian freedom, or so it seemed. However, John persisted, and I have a hunch that through the years he came to see that Wheaton College was actually the place he had been uniquely prepared for. His own struggle with evangelical dualism and the new hard-won vision of art and reality he had replaced it with, had made him ideally suited to deal with the questions of Wheaton College students. It also must have been beneficial to his students that their teacher's experience was larger than the Christian world only; John encouraged them to look beyond their own circle and helped them uncover the often unstated value systems that drive human thought, scholarship, and art. John became a teacher, communicating his love for art in his own passionate, energetic, and entertaining way and mentoring eyes as he educated his students to be visually discriminating. He taught future art historians as well as artists-to-be, which kept him connected to the present art world. During these years he also managed to write the book *Great Themes in Art*, a type of project that my father had considered but had not ventured to commit to paper—a textbook and introduction to Western art from a Christian perspective for a secular publisher. *Great Themes*'s thematic approach, dealing with the themes of spirituality, the self, nature, and the city for each historical period, strikes me as a distant echo of Dooyeweerd's modal aspects that were so fundamental to my father's thinking.

Trends in art history and art have changed during the course of John's career. Modernism has given way to postmodernism, which means that John found himself faced with another set of questions than those my father had sought to answer. That is to say, the problems that had clung to modernism had not really gone away but were rather injected with a deconstructive dose of relativism, pluralism, and cynicism. In this climate of confusion, with too many possibilities and too few certainties, John had to help his students make sense of the clutter of scientific trends, the chaos of art theory, and all the hard questions of identity, gender, race, rights, and self-fulfillment that are part and parcel of contemporary art and culture. Underneath all of this, however, still persisted the unsolved yet central problem of art's being put on a pedestal and accorded too high a status. That we move beyond this framework inherited from modernism can be justifiably called one of John's major concerns, as it was my father's, to which the name of John's blog, "Only Connect," testifies. He urged his students to strive for accessibility without compromising their artistic integrity and to exchange autonomy for a more serving attitude, in the hope that work would result that would be able to find its way into the wider culture as well as into the church.

One point of difference between John and my father concerned the renewed openness of the church to art. My father followed John Calvin's views on art in the church, which means that he was opposed to art in Protestant churches and cautious about the representation of religious subjects and the invisible spiritual realm. Today, religious subjects are abounding and many churches are opening their doors to art inside their buildings. Now, we tend to speak about art's using theological, sacramental, or contemplative terminology. We see art as a channel through which the truths of our faith can reach the depths of our hearts—a necessary correction to the supremacy of rationalism in earlier decades. Furthermore, art is now studied in many theology departments of Christian educational institutions. Though the present flourishing of interest in the arts can only be applauded, it is telling that all of this did only come about by lifting art to a more spiritual level and giving it a more sacred status. Perhaps the old dualism still has not left us entirely.

John's work obviously has been influenced by this turn of events, and so it should be. He testifies that the theological angle has enriched his own approach to art historical study, as the religious climate of artists illuminates their art. John, furthermore, is a champion of quality art in the church. He urges churches to take their artists seriously and encourages artists to contribute their work to the church with humility. However, though John is open to art with religious subjects, his emphasis is still on art by Christians that deals with subjects less lofty, which can be hung in homes and galleries. Moreover, as an art historian, John embodies the continuing need for art historical scholarly research and input into the relationship between Christianity and the visual arts, as his theological colleagues tend to speak about art in more theological and abstract ways.

Maybe more surprising than the differences between John Walford and my father are all the similarities. The basic ideas have stayed the same. This is due to the fact, no doubt, that my father's approach was not a closed system, but rather an instrument to get to the truth, and was as such always open to improvement, elaboration, and refinement. With the benefit of history, we can see that there are things my father did not get right. The man whose favorite line was "Let's discuss" would only have commended the correction of his views. My father was very aware that one generation builds on another and that it takes several generations to bring forth something worthwhile like a solid art historical approach or the flowering of art among Christians.

John stood on my father's shoulders, just as John's students stand on his. There are many ways in which John's work continues in that of his former students. One of his students, Matthew Milliner, has replaced him at Wheaton College. Another of John's former students, James Romaine, a professor of art history at Nyack College in New York City, has founded the Association of Scholars of Christianity in the History of Art (ASCHA). Even the book that you hold in your hand can be seen as one of the fruits of John's labour: a Festschrift written by a large number of Christian art historians, several of whom were John's own students. These are developments of which my father could only have dreamed. Over the last thirty years, has progress been made? The answer, thanks be to God, can only be yes.

Jacob van Ruisdael, *View of Haarlem*. Late 1660s. Oil on canvas, 24 1/2" x 21 3/5". Kunsthaus, Zurich.

INTRODUCTION
You Will See Greater Things than These: John Walford's Content-oriented Method of Art History[1]

JAMES ROMAINE

John Walford's art historical methodology may be described as seeing in pursuit of meaning. As evidenced in *Jacob van Ruisdael and the Perception of Landscape* (Yale University Press, 1991) and *Great Themes in Art* (Prentice-Hall, 2002), he examines the artwork as a consummation of a process of perception by which invisible and inherent content is made manifest. Through a careful study of the art object's formal and iconographic elements, as well as the historical, social, and religious context in which the work was created, Walford perceives and describes this essential significance. As a writer and educator, he has modeled this content-oriented method[2] of perception, opening up a world of visual pleasure, intellectual contemplation, and spiritual substance to his readers and students.

In the introduction to *Jacob van Ruisdael and the Perception of Landscape*, which is based on his Cambridge University doctoral dissertation, Walford simultaneously describes the monograph's objective and defends his own methodology. Although Walford does not draw direct correspondence between his own methodology and the creative process of perception that he ascribes to Ruisdael, he does address both with the same vocabulary. Walford argues that we can discover an artist's mindset and method by examining his or her process of motif selection and method of representation. It may also be possible to learn something about a scholar by considering the subjects and methods of his scholarship. While there is not always an affinity between a scholar's own worldview and that which he imputes to his artistic

---

[1] This essay's title is taken from John 1:50.
[2] This content-oriented method is distinguishable from form-, iconographic-, context-, biographic-, and market-oriented methods of art history.

subject, Walford's strategy of meaningful seeing strongly parallels what he describes as Ruisdael's process of perception.

Jacob van Ruisdael (c. 1628–1682) is widely recognized as the greatest Netherlandish landscape painter of the seventeenth century. Both Ruisdael's father and uncle were painters. Ruisdael's uncle, Salomon van Ruysdael, was and remains a highly acclaimed landscape painter. Ruisdael spent much of his artistic career in Amsterdam, after moving there in the mid-1650s. During his own lifetime, Ruisdael's art was highly valued and praised; his reputation surpassed even that of his uncle.[3]

Ruisdael was a painter of landscapes. By contrast, his predecessors, including Ruysdael, painted scenes of human activity happening outdoors. In their work, the landscape elements remained contextual to the human subject. In Ruisdael's art, the landscape becomes the subject; motifs such as trees, waterfalls, hills, and clouds, as well as architectural ruins and windmills, are the protagonists. The presence of human figures is distinctly minimized, leaving the processes of creation as the paintings' subjects. While figures appear in Ruisdael's paintings, they read in relation to the landscape.

Since there were critical and financial advantages to creating human-drama paintings, Ruisdael's daring break with convention is significant. Furthermore, since the natural motifs that Ruisdael employed had previously functioned only in supporting roles to human activity, he had to develop new compositional structures that would move them into protagonist positions.[4] He treated these motifs with a level of creative visual attention and tightness of painting such that a tree, hill, or cloud could successfully carry a painting. In this endeavor, Ruisdael's use of color, composition, and technical method correlated to the reduction of the focus on human activity in his paintings of landscapes.[5]

---

[3]Walford notes that, in understanding the value placed on Ruisdael's works, we must factor in that landscape paintings would not always match in value or prestige genre or history paintings (E. John Walford, *Jacob van Ruisdael and the Perception of Landscape* [New Haven, CT: Yale University Press, 1991], 13).

[4]Walford's Ruisdael monograph carefully traces these new motifs and composition, painting by painting.

[5]In his *Great Themes in Art*, Walford writes, "Unlike [Jan] van Goyen's sketchy, monochromatic style, Ruisdael's [method] favored greater detail, descriptive local color, and firmer compositional structure, all wrought with the eye of an acute observer" (E. John Walford, *Great Themes in Art* [Upper Saddle River, NJ: Prentice-Hall, 2002], 311). Compared to the "tonalist" outdoor scenes of van Goyen, Ruisdael's paintings of landscapes, such as *View of Haarlem from the Dunes at Overeen*, use color in a more developed method. In fact, Ruisdael needed color to have a more formally structural and visually active role in his paintings, since the viewer did not have a human drama to observe. (In the twentieth century, the Dutch artist Piet Mondrian would find color's inherent substance and movement to be all that he needed, even dispensing with motifs such as trees from his paintings.)

The prominence Ruisdael gave to nature was unprecedented and unique in his time.[6] Even Ruisdael's most talented student, Meindert Hobbema, a first-tier painter of the "golden age," failed to succeed Ruisdael as a true painter of landscapes. Hobbema's paintings, when they don't distinctly feature figures, often include domestic cottages and villages as surrogates for human activity in a way that is foreign to Ruisdael's art. It would not be until the nineteenth century that artists would again address the landscape as the dominant subject of paintings such as we find it in Ruisdael's art.

In the 1660s, Ruisdael, at the height of his talents and success, developed a method of landscape painting, exemplified by *View of Haarlem from the Dunes at Overeen* (late 1660s), that Walford describes as "richer in colour, more brilliantly illuminated and more expansive" as well as "more refined, diffuse, and less melodramatic in its concentration . . . combined with a warmer palette" than his previous work.[7] In *View of Haarlem* Ruisdael applied this "unprecedented force and majesty" to a motif, a vision of Haarlem from the dunes, that he had initially developed a decade earlier.[8]

The work's title is somewhat misleading since Haarlem, where Ruisdael was born, is just discernible in the distance. This spacious painting's most prominent motifs are clouds, fields, and the sunlight that connects them. Irregular patterns of light and shadow play over the geometric organization of the linen-bleaching fields. Much of this land had been reclaimed from the sea, and the viewer stands on the dunes that hold that water back. *View of Haarlem* is filled with signs of protection and prosperity that the Dutch credited to God's providence. On the horizon stands the church of Saint Bavo, where Ruisdael would be buried in 1682; its spire connects earth and heaven.

In looking at *View of Haarlem*, one is struck by its rich visual detail. Ruisdael has achieved a highly convincing effect of time and place. The cumulous clouds are depicted with meteorological accuracy. The famous linen-bleaching fields are laid out with precision. The viewer has a sense of arriving at a fortuitous moment when the weather is

---

[6] An uninhabited landscape would have gone against contemporary conceptions of creation that found its meaning in relation to the wisdom and majesty of the Creator and the human beings to whom he entrusted creation.

[7] Walford, *Jacob van Ruisdael*, 120.

[8] Ibid.

changing from overcast to sunshine. He or she is made to feel as if being, at once, a local (someone who belongs to this landscape) and a traveler who is encountering this sight for the first time.

However, as Walford observes, "The more closely an image approximates to natural appearances, the more easily one can overlook the modes of perception that inevitably influence the transformation of landscape into art."[9] In fact, *View of Haarlem* is calculatingly composed and harmoniously combined, a constructed scene based on acute observation of the place. Although Ruisdael demonstrates a sensitivity to the effects of light that anticipates nineteenth-century artists such as John Constable and Claude Monet, this is not a painting done *en plein air*, as its size (twenty-four and a half by twenty-one and three-fifths inches) would have been prohibitive of being painted outdoors. Without departing from the impression of naturalism, Ruisdael constructs a composition of areas of light and shadow, which lead the viewer first across the fields and then through the clouds. The compositional structure of *View of Haarlem*, by which Ruisdael brought together elements, observed and invented, in one unified vision, may be called *coherence*. This method, like the vision of Haarlem that it describes, emphasizes order and interconnectedness. In this work, Ruisdael employs the inherent character of painting to structure and cleave its parts into one seamless whole and unified work.

This painting's distinctly vertical format cultivates a more complex and nuanced play between the sky, which occupies two-thirds of the painting, and the landscape. *View of Haarlem* is painted from a high vantage point overlooking creation. This panoramic view is unusual in Ruisdael's work. Most of his works are painted from a lower vantage point that more firmly situates the viewer on the ground and in the scene. The implied position in *View of Haarlem* neither has the detachment of topographic mapping of the landscape nor is it painted from within the space. Ruisdael has found a place, from the dunes, that suggests an overlooking presence without dislocating the viewer from the landscape. A great deal of this work's success depends on the selection of this point of view.

Just as Ruisdael carefully orchestrated the viewer's position in *View of Haarlem*, scholars have carefully developed various approaches to

---

[9] Ibid., 15.

engage his art. Some of the methods employed by scholars in their discussions of Ruisdael have had the effect of reducing him. For Seymour Slive, Ruisdael is an interior decorator, a painter of skillfully composed but meaningless images that might have adorned the parlors of Dutch merchants and are now in art museums for our viewing pleasure.[10] Svetlana Alpers describes Ruisdael as a technically masterful transcriber of topography.[11] John Walford's emphasis on the content of Ruisdael's art engages the Dutch painter as a creative person, someone who means to communicate with the viewer.[12]

Noting that Ruisdael's pictorial naturalism disguises his creative and critical perception, Walford writes,

> a painted landscape, however realistic in appearance, is never a pure copy of nature and therefore can never be rendered value free. Implied in the artist's choice of motifs and his pictorial representation is a certain view of reality.[13]

Walford calls Ruisdael's process "selective naturalism," an interpretive method evidenced in the artist's motif selection and manner of representation. Ruisdael's landscapes evidence an active, critical, and self-conscious process of drawing out inherent and essential meaning found in the motif. The work's semblant spontaneity is the consequence of visual and intellectual composition.

Walford argues that Ruisdael's selective naturalism was consistent with widely held conceptions of nature in the seventeenth-century Netherlands. Thus Ruisdael's painting demonstrates a "contemporary" method of seeing "the essential character of things, including their meaning and significance."[14] This perception of landscape distinguished between, without dividing, creation's "natural," i.e., visible, and its "characteristic," i.e., invisible, qualities. Referencing the painter Karel van Mander,[15] Walford explains, "Van Mander distinguished the

---

[10] Seymour Slive, *Dutch Painting: 1600–1800* (New Haven, CT: Yale University Press, 1995).

[11] Svetlana Alpers, *The Art of Describing: Dutch Art in the Seventeenth Century* (Chicago: University of Chicago Press, 1983).

[12] In elevating the artist, Walford also elevates the viewer. If Ruisdael is merely a decorator or transcriber, the viewer is merely a consumer. However, if Ruisdael's art visually communicates a spiritual perception of the world, that content-embodying painting addresses the viewer as a critically and creatively thinking spiritual being.

[13] Walford, *Jacob van Ruisdael*, 16.

[14] Ibid., 18.

[15] Karel van Mander (1548–1606) lived in Haarlem from 1583 to 1603. The teacher of Frans Hals, van Mander may be considered a founder of visual arts in Haarlem. Beyond Haarlem, van Mander's *Schilder-*

visible world (life) from Nature so that while he considered empirical observation of the visible world essential, it is insufficient as a means to know the essence of Nature."[16] Walford, still writing about van Mander, adds, "In order to represent things in a *natural* and *characteristic* way, the artist must therefore learn to discern and select from life. He must combine observation and understanding in order to be true to the essence and not just the appearance of things."[17]

Ruisdael's method of "selective naturalism" was rooted in this cultural/religious context. Walford remarks,

> Selective naturalism may thus embody a religious and contemplative attitude towards observed reality. . . . This intertwining of material and spiritual levels of reality is typical in Dutch seventeenth-century thought and in contemporary artistic practice.[18]

Turning to a critical investigation of "selective naturalism" as a creative method, Walford notes that it

> is conditioned by the many factors that make up [Ruisdael's] working context, including the artist's personal temperament, prevailing artistic conventions, and other cultural values. Together these provide a conceptual framework that shapes the artist's perception and representation of nature.[19]

Although, in Ruisdael's case, we know more about his historical context than about his character, Walford argues that selective naturalism inevitably depends on both equally.

Of the historical, cultural, social, and economic factors impressing themselves upon Ruisdael, Walford is particularly sensitive to the religious environment in which the artist worked. Walford finds evidence in Ruisdael's landscapes of a seventeenth-century Dutch paradigm that was profoundly shaped by Reformed Calvinism. Walford observes, "Contemplation of the creation as divine revelation was of paramount importance in the seventeenth century"; contemporary Dutch writers, such as Constantijn Huygens and H. L. Spiegel, referred to nature as

---

boeck (*Painter Book*), published in 1604, became an inspiration for many artists of the "golden age" of Dutch painting.
[16] Walford, *Jacob van Ruisdael*, 18.
[17] Ibid. (emphasis mine).
[18] Ibid.
[19] Ibid., 16.

"God's second book of revelation."[20] This view was supported both by contemporary interpretations of the Bible and by the most influential confession of faith of that time.[21] Walford notes, "Exhortation to contemplative delight in the visible world was instilled by the influential *Confession of Faith* and *Catechism* of the Netherlands Reformed Churches. They were the subject of weekly evening sermons and were taught in all schools, so penetrating the entire society."[22] Did Ruisdael attend these sermons or share these beliefs? There is little specific documentation of Ruisdael's religious practices except that, on June 14, 1657, he made a profession of faith and applied to be baptized in the Calvinist Reformed Church.[23]

This Reformed paradigm and its attitude toward creation are furthermore evidenced in the writings of the seventeenth-century Dutch poet Hubert Kornelisz Poot, who described nature as "God's landscape painting."[24] God is described as the original, perfect, and providential artist, whose work is copied by human artists. Reflecting on how nature was described by preachers and poets, Walford adds, "It is perhaps significant that representation of the ordinary Dutch landscape is given an ideological value just at the time when it was receiving greater attention from landscape painters."[25]

Walford argues that Ruisdael's process of "selective naturalism" was characterized by a sensitivity to the corruption and changeability of the visible world as well as a faith in the providence of God.[26] Walford writes, "there is a sense of order, of well-being, and of everyday activity, and, in the landscapes of Ruisdael and others, a peaceful harmony between man and his environment despite a prevailing consciousness of the ultimate transience of life."[27]

Perhaps the natural motif that is at once most fleeting and infinite is light. Walford states, "Light-beams, as an image of divine

---

[20] Ibid., 19.
[21] Ibid., 20.
[22] Ibid.
[23] Walford explains Ruisdael's application to be baptized at age twenty-nine by noting that the painter had been raised in a Mennonite family, which, unlike the Reformed Church, did not practice infant baptism. Thus it can be surmised that, in 1657, Ruisdael converted to Calvinism. Walford dismisses any suggestion that Ruisdael made this conversion for anything other than personal reasons and notes that this conversion did not provide Ruisdael with any particular advantages or mark any notable change in his art (Walford, *Jacob van Ruisdael*, 8).
[24] Ibid., 23.
[25] Ibid., 25.
[26] Ibid., 29.
[27] Ibid., 20.

providence breaking into a darkened world, are a commonplace of seventeenth-century religious art, not least that of Rembrandt [van Rijn]. It is not surprising therefore that when religious subjects were given a landscape setting, it is with such light-beams that the idea of grace is conveyed."[28] Still discussing paintings with religious subjects, Walford notes,

> The manner in which the landscape is represented in these paintings contributes to their meaning. The significance of the lighting in them is made explicit by their religious subject matter. But this expressive potential was also exploited in landscapes that contain no religious subject, yet, as landscapes, are probably intended both for aesthetic delight and religious contemplation.[29]

In *View of Haarlem*, Ruisdael employs light as a sign of God's providential blessing on Haarlem, which had adopted Calvinism around 1580, and on its surroundings. The land reclaimed from the sea, cultivated fields, and bleached linens all call attention to humanity's divinely given charge to cultivate and fill the earth. Yet all of these actions and events take place within the delicate balance of forces, from sunlight to flooding, that are beyond human control. The work speaks to our ultimate dependence on the providence of God. The clouds that fill the sky and overtake the viewer suggest that, although we may be situated above the landscape, there is a realm still higher than our own. This recalls promises kept and promises of even greater things to come. Ruisdael's *View of Haarlem* may be read as visual description of God's provident direction revealed both in nature and in human activity, a distinctly Reformed theme and one that would have resonated with seventeenth-century Dutch viewers, who believed that their recent political, economic, and religious freedom was divinely ordained.

Walford acknowledges that the assertion that a work such as Ruisdael's *View of Haarlem* is more meaningful than it might first appear raises "a host of questions concerning how meaning is embodied."[30] Combining an observation of nature with a selection of inherently significant motifs, Ruisdael practiced what Walford calls "a contemplative

---

[28] Ibid., 39.
[29] Ibid., 40.
[30] Ibid., 1.

mode of perception,"[31] the consequence of which is visual delight, intellectual meaning, and spiritual power.

Walford's approach recognizes the work of art as a visual realization, through motif and method, of inherent meaning. This has consequences for understanding the role of the scholar, or viewer, who seeks to understand and critically engage that meaning. It would follow that Walford's method of meaning-oriented seeing would require a selection of subject, observational study of that object's visual elements, and commentary, informed by contextual knowledge gained through research.[32] Sensitive to the dangers of subjective personal interpretations, Walford describes this "attempting to grasp, where possible, how such pictures were perceived in their own time" as a "control of our reading."[33] A content-oriented method of art history is not an open license to speculation. These readings must be grounded in the evidence of the art object and the product of research.

In addition to challenging formalist methods, Walford also addressed methods of art history that focused on iconographic decoding. Walford warned, "The tendency in current criticism is to accentuate one of the two extremes: while some writers see Dutch landscape painting in terms of pure depiction and aesthetic delight, others have confronted this with an iconological approach, in an attempt to retrieve whatever meaning or association may be embedded within Dutch landscapes."[34] If Walford was critical of Slive's emphasis on aesthetic delight and Alpers's emphasis on art as depiction, he was equally sensitive to the problem of over-reading visual motifs as an accumulation of codes whose didactic meaning can be solved.

Walford argues,

> In seeking to identify which elements of the landscape aroused religious reflection and how this is manifest in art, the basic premise is that selective naturalness implied a depiction of the essence of nature as then understood. Dutch landscapes are therefore best approached not so much as bearers of narrative and emblematic meanings, but rather as images reflecting the fact that the visible world was essen-

---

[31] Ibid., 3.
[32] When, as John Walford's student at Wheaton College, I expressed an interest in pursuing art history as a profession, he asked me if I 1) enjoyed going to the library and 2) could see connections between things. In fact, Walford's own scholarship is marked by a careful attention to the art object and extensive research.
[33] Walford, *Jacob van Ruisdael*, 17.
[34] Ibid., 16–17.

tially perceived as *manifesting inherent spiritual significance.* Concern with aesthetic delight and the presence of meaning are not therefore seen as mutually exclusive but rather as intimately related. If the landscape painter was concerned that his viewer should be inspired by visual sensation to deeper contemplation, we may expect that this would be directed by certain stimuli. These would derive both from the sheer beauty and order within the image itself and also from elements which emphasize the essential character and significance of the visible world.[35]

If the work of art embodies themes, already pregnant with meaning, which the work visualizes and infuses with new life, the role of the scholar, as interpreter, is to read these visual elements and contextualize them.

In his Yale University Press–published monograph, Walford rightly frames his method of perception in relation to other art historical strategies. However there is, in fact, a more significant influence on his approach and a more fitting paradigmatic framework by which to understand its importance. That is the effect of his mentor Hans Rookmaaker and Walford's own contribution to the development of a Reformed Protestant paradigm of art history.

Before pursuing a PhD at Cambridge University, Walford studied art history with Rookmaaker at the Free University in Amsterdam. In an essay entitled "Hans Rookmaaker's 'Four Freedoms' and Christian Art," Walford wrote, "Rookmaaker had taught me to see and respond to the world from a totally fresh perspective, one informed not so much by my British, secular, and upper-class education, but one informed by Scripture, as filtered through the Dutch Reformed tradition."[36] With Rookmaaker's mentorship, Walford developed a conception of vocation and adopted a content-oriented method of art history consistent with Dutch Neo-Calvinism.[37]

This Reformed persuasion, which originated out of forces that also shaped Ruisdael's religious context, views creation as ordered by the sovereign will and wisdom of God in fulfillment of his covenant with Adam. It also holds that art making and the vocation of art history,

---

[35] Ibid., 29 (emphasis mine).
[36] E. John Walford, "Hans Rookmaaker's 'Four Freedoms' and Christian Art," http://www.transpositions. co.uk/2011/02/hans-rookmaakers-four-freedoms-and-christian-art-part-i/.
[37] For a thorough and critical discussion of Dutch Neo-Calvinist theology and the arts, see Jeremy Begbie's *Voicing Creation's Praise: Towards a Theology of the Arts* (Edinburgh: T & T Clark, 2000).

like all human activity, operate under the lordship and providence of God. Motivated by this faith and confident in divine ordination, Dutch Neo-Calvinists encourage an active participation in all fields of society.

To understand the Neo-Calvinist paradigm that informed Walford's maturation, it is helpful to note the influence of Abraham Kuyper, who founded the Free University in 1880. Believing in the universal authority of God over all of creation and culture, Kuyper encouraged Christians to involve themselves in every field of society. While many Christians profess belief in the sovereignty of God over all of creation, too often they have done so from the seclusion of religious institutions and communities. In founding a university, a learned environment in which scholars such as Walford could develop, Kuyper asserted a faith and theology that was both intellectually sound and culturally active.

Kuyper, perhaps to the surprise of those who might suppose that a Calvinist-influenced theology would not value the visual arts, championed art "as one of the richest gifts of God to mankind."[38] In the fifth of his *Lectures on Calvinism*, delivered at Princeton Theological Seminary in 1898, Kuyper stated, "Understand that art is no fringe that is attached to the garment, and no amusement that is added to life, but a most serious power in our present existence." Art, for Kuyper, was not an activity separate from the rest of creation and culture; it was an activity of both imminent and eternal consequence. Kuyper argued that artistic activity has been sustained by and is evidence of common grace, as manifested in the beauty and harmonies of nature. God's sovereignty is, according to Kuyper, manifested in the inherent and unfaltering laws of creation that frame all of life. He observed, "Art reveals ordinances of creation which neither science, nor politics, nor religious life, nor even revelation can bring to light."

As Kuyper argued that the visual arts held a central place in human experience, he also believed that religion, specifically Calvinism, held an important and constructive role in the history of art.[39] Passing over the facts that John Calvin did not value the visual arts and that the adoption of Calvinism, in many instances, led to iconoclasm as not

---

[38] Abraham Kuyper's *Lectures on Calvinism* is available on the web at http://reformationfiles.com/files/displaytext.php?file=kuyper_lecturescalvinism.html#lecture5. All my quotations of Kuyper are from this site. For a print edition, see Abraham Kuyper, *Lectures on Calvinism* (Peabody, MA: Hendrickson, 2008).

[39] Although Kuyper's argument is not entirely convincing, it nevertheless represents a perspective that is relevant to the discussion of a Reformed understanding of art and art history.

relevant to the question, Kuyper contended that Calvinism, in fact, "encouraged the emancipation of art. . . . as a consequence of its world- and life-view." Calvinism, Kuyper asserted, not only released the visual arts from the dictations of ecclesiastical and princely patronage; more importantly, it rescued art from the demands, placed there by the Greeks, that it be imitative of nature. Furthermore, he stated that this creative liberty found maturity in the art of the seventeenth-century Netherlands.

Addressing an issue pertinent to Ruisdael's landscapes, Kuyper asks if the artist, freed by Calvinism, should be an imitator of nature's appearances. He answered,

> if you confess that the world once was beautiful, but by the curse has become undone, and by a final catastrophe is to pass to its full state of glory, excelling even the beautiful of paradise, then art has the mystical task of reminding us in its productions of the beautiful that was lost and of anticipating its perfect coming luster. . . . Calvinism honored art as a gift of the Holy Ghost and as a consolation in our present life, enabling us to discover in and behind this sinful life a richer and more glorious background. Standing by the ruins of this once so wonderfully beautiful creation, art points out to the Calvinist both the still visible lines of the original plan, and what is even more, the splendid restoration by which the Supreme Artist and Master-Builder will one day renew and enhance even the beauty of His original creation.[40]

The responsibility of the artist is, according to Kuyper, not to imitate nature's appearances but to see in nature's present state of being the ordinances of God. Kuyper said, "it is the vocation of art, not merely to observe everything visible and audible, to apprehend it, and reproduce it artistically, but much more to discover in those natural forms the order of the beautiful, and, enriched by this higher knowledge, to produce a beautiful world that transcends the beautiful of nature." By "beauty," Kuyper meant harmony, a unity (in multiplicity) and the interdependence of all elements of creation and culture

---

[40] Ruins are a recurring motif in Ruisdael's art. While these ruins have been interpreted as melancholic, it is possible that Ruisdael, a convert to Calvinism, perceived creation, similarly to Kuyper, as a ruin, a once glorious structure waiting to be renewed. Thus, for a believing Christian, the ruin is not nostalgic but rather hopeful. Indeed, Ruisdael's ruins are not set in desolate landscapes but rather in lush hills, evidence of God's enduring sovereignty and grace.

under the common grace of God, who holds all things together and draws them toward wholeness.[41] It is not unreasonable to suppose that Ruisdael might have been an artist whom Kuyper appreciated.

If the Neo-Calvinist perspective that Walford brought to his vocation was philosophically rooted in Kuyperian theology, the application of Christianity to the field of art history was modeled by Rookmaaker. Beyond the profound effect of encouraging Walford to pursue a vocation in art history, Rookmaaker influenced Walford's scholarship in at least two specific ways.

First, Rookmaaker encouraged Walford to study seventeenth-century Dutch landscape painting. To this point, Dutch landscape painting of the "golden age" had been largely studied in terms of its formal and iconographic elements. Rookmaaker recognized that this art visually materialized a Christian content that had been all but ignored. Rookmaaker located the origins of seventeenth-century Dutch landscape painting in "a profound respect for their land (graciously given back to them by God, so that they could live in freedom), out of a deep reverence for this divine creation, [and] out of a true love of reality and all of its beauty and uniqueness."[42] Rookmaaker also debunked the myth that these landscape painters were copyists of nature, noting, "the most natural look is achieved only by those who are experts at composition and the handling of pictorial elements."[43]

Rookmaaker esteemed seventeenth-century Dutch landscape painting, especially the work of Jan van Goyen. In the opening chapter of *Modern Art and the Death of a Culture*, probably Rookmaaker's best-known book in America, Rookmaaker used a landscape by van Goyen, in contrast with a landscape by Nicolas Poussin, to establish the centrality of content, as distinguished from (but not detached from) form and subject matter, in engaging a work of art.[44] However, while Rookmaaker had a deep and personal, if not also nationalistic, appreciation for seventeenth-century Dutch art, he disliked Ruisdael's art, which he found to be too far removed from naturalism. Rookmaaker

---

[41] Although, in a work of art, this harmony is visually manifested in the formal composition of parts, on the level of content this wholeness is the realization of perception—perception not as subjective impression but rather the recognition of the objective laws.

[42] Hans Rookmaaker, *The Complete Works of Hans Rookmaaker*, ed. Marleen Hengelaar-Rookmaaker, 5 vols. (Carlisle, UK: Piquant, 2002–2003), 4:167.

[43] Ibid., 168.

[44] Ibid., 5:11–14.

was a prolific art critic, covering such wide-ranging topics as medieval treasures, Rembrandt and the Bible, and Picasso's *Guernica*; however, he never penned a review on Ruisdael. In fact, Ruisdael functioned only as a peripheral figure in Rookmaaker's writing, a point of reference in discussion of other artists.

Second, Rookmaaker encouraged Walford to develop a content-oriented method of art history, one that was ahead of most of the field. For Rookmaaker, there was no theologically neutral content in art. All content, whether dressed in "religious" subject matter or not, was measured in terms of its biblical truthfulness. For example, a sentimental painting of Christ might, in fact, be biblically false while a painting of a nude woman, such as Rembrandt's Bathsheba, might visually present biblical truth.

Rookmaaker himself modeled this content-oriented method of looking at art for its philosophical/theological meaning and consequence to the human condition. For example, in his book on Paul Gauguin, written in 1959, Rookmaaker wrote that,

> artists worthy of the name will attempt to make their work into something meaningful because it is related to their fundamental view of reality, to their view of life and the world. This . . . finds expression both in [the artist's] choice of subject, and the way in which the chosen subject is realized—in the approach, the composition and execution.[45]

Furthermore, in a 1951 essay entitled "Seventeenth-century Dutch Art: Christian Art?" Rookmaaker wrote, "We may be able to explain the choice of themes and subject matter and the way these are portrayed on the basis of the understandings and 'prejudices' of the 'Calvinists.'"[46] These passages suggest how Walford's method of "perception" was, at least in part, indebted to Rookmaaker.

Rookmaaker's influence in Walford's method is also evidenced in Walford's art history survey textbook *Great Themes in Art*. Tracing the history of Western art from prehistory to the present, each chapter is structured around four themes: spirituality, the self, nature, and the city. These themes form four points on a compass of human aspi-

---

[45] Ibid., 1:23.
[46] Ibid., 4:136.

ration and experience. They allow Walford to both address changing experience over time and stress the continuity of beingness that
ties the contemporary viewer to the ancient artist.[47] Combined with
Walford's efficient and fluid writing, as well as his content-oriented
method, this thematic structure effectively brings the work of art
to the present.[48] Walford makes a persuasive case not only that the
Doryphoros, the city plan of Constantinople, Titian's *Assumption of the
Virgin*, and Eugène Delacroix's *Tiger Hunt* are accessible to the contemporary viewer but that there is a compelling and meaning-laden
connection to be had.

Although evidence of Walford's faith is veiled in this book, it is not
absent. The title itself is bound to irritate those who believe neither in
"greatness," nor in "themes," nor in "art," but favor politically correct
pluralism; who insist that there is no knowable metanarrative; and who
prefer terms such as "visual culture." Walford's concepts of "great,"
"themes," and "art" are all distinctly rooted in a Reformed paradigm of
the sovereignty of God. In fact, all three concepts may be found in the
book of Genesis. The notion of "greatness," that anything might rightly
be called "great," ultimately demands that there be someone who is
"great." Walford's Reformed belief holds that only God is truly and
absolutely "great." Our human striving for "greatness," as evidenced
in art, is part of our longing for God and an echo of our being created
in his image. Aside from a belief in God, there is no justification for a
discussion of "greatness."

From a Neo-Calvinist perspective, "themes" is also a concept that
finds its foundation in the Bible. The comprehension of narrative is
rooted in our experience of time. However, a meaningful or directed
metanarrative originates in something outside of time. A Reformed
faith holds that, from eternity to eternity, the narrative of human

---

[47] At the same time, this thematic structure's lack of flexibility creates both gaps in and repetition of content that limit the book's usefulness as an educational text.

[48] In this, once again, Rookmaaker's influence may be discerned. In his introduction to the collected works
of Hans Rookmaaker, Graham Birtwistle, himself a contributor to this book, wrote, "Rookmaaker certainly preferred to write in an easily accessible mode. . . . But his use of ordinary language reflected more
than just personal preference or a concession to his readers; it was intimately linked to one of his deepest
teachings. Throughout his writings runs the insistent theme that reality is God's creation and as such is
neither strange nor incomprehensible to man. Rookmaaker taught that to know and experience reality as
God intends us to do, it is not necessary to approach it as a puzzle that can only be solved theoretically or
scientifically, or as a secret that is hermetically locked from the common gaze" (Graham Birtwistle, "H. R.
Rookmaaker: The Shaping of His Thought," in Rookmaaker, *Complete Works*, 1:xix). Both stylistically and
philosophically, Walford's writing in *Great Themes* follows this same belief in the knowability of God and,
by him, the knowability of creation and created things.

beingness is under the providence of God. For the Neo-Calvinist, this is the "greatest theme." Walford's four "great themes" each extend from an experience within that narrative. If there is no narrative and no director, there are no themes, only illusions.

Finally, as has already been discussed, a Neo-Calvinist concept of "art" is founded on an understanding of each human being as a creative and unique person. An alternative view, which holds that human identity and experience are culturally constructed, prefers the term "visual culture." The Genesis narrative describes God as a creative being who created human, creative beings in his image. According to this narrative, there can be no "art" without a creative individual and a point of origin for the creative impulse.

The concepts of "great," "themes," and "art" each relate to Walford's content-oriented method. These terms, further developed by Walford's four specific themes, are the conduits for a discussion of art, and potentially all of life, as meaningful. In his book on Ruisdael, Walford argued, "Besides giving aesthetic delight [Dutch landscape painting] also invites contemplation of the meaning of things."[49] Similarly, this method evidenced in Walford's own scholarship, to recognize the inherent significance of the visible world, has been both a gift of enchantment in what we can see and the occasion to imagine even greater things than these.

---

[49]Walford, *Jacob van Ruisdael*, 20.

Sarcophagus of Junius Bassus, Rome. C. A.D. 359. Marble, 4' x 8'. Grottoes of Saint Peter, Vatican, Rome. Photo: Scala/Art Resource, NY.

1

NEOFITUS,
HE WENT TO GOD
The *Sarcophagus of Junius Bassus*

LINDA MØSKELAND FUCHS

The sarcophagus of Junius Bassus, who died August 25, A.D. 359, is one of the best preserved, most finely carved and most iconographically rich examples of fourth-century Christian funerary art.[1] As John Walford observed, "Telling stories through relief carving was an invaluable artistic legacy of classical antiquity to the Church."[2] The sarcophagus of Junius Bassus, like much of early Christian art, draws imagery from Old and New Testament narratives for commemorative purposes. Its innovative development and arrangement of subjects imply thoughts of the death, resurrection, and ascension of Christ. It is designed to edify the viewer. The scenes highlight Christ's glorification and majesty and exult in his victory over death, which offers reconciliation to God and resurrection to each one who follows Christ.

Roman burial customs had begun a significant change near the beginning of the second century: interment in a costly stone coffin began to replace the custom of depositing the deceased's cremated remains in funerary urns. A sarcophagus (meaning "flesh eater")[3] was prepared by carving out the interior of a marble block and embellishing the exterior with carved imagery and/or inscriptions. The city of Rome became the center for sarcophagus carving in the western half of the Roman Empire, and held this position until the middle of the

---

[1] The iconographic identification and interpretation of early Christian art, including the sarcophagus of Junius Bassus, remains a matter of scholarly debate. This essay attempts to critically present the identification and interpretation of the sarcophagus's face as it is most commonly understood in the existing literature. A paper by the author is in preparation to discuss the relationship of iconographical elements on the front, ends, and lid of the sarcophagus of Junius Bassus in greater detail.

[2] E. John Walford, *Great Themes in Art* (Upper Saddle River, NJ: Prentice-Hall, 2002), 124.

[3] The goal was decomposition, not preservation. Sometimes lye was added to the contents to speed decomposition. The marble of some quarries was especially effective.

fourth century. It was from the milieu of Roman wall painting and sarcophagus carving that Christian art developed, drawing on Roman principles of visual organization and some Roman motifs.

Late in the second century, Clement of Alexandria recommended choosing motifs meaningful to Christians when selecting a signet ring in the marketplace.[4] Similar thoughtful choices were made in the first half of the third century when some Christians selected sarcophagi with shepherds. Distinctively biblical motifs appeared in catacomb wall and ceiling painting in the first half of the third century before these motifs were carved in stone in the second half of the third century. The horizontal format of sarcophagi (not tall, but wide) and the desire to embellish the space with figures (taller than wide) led to a filling of the space with multiple scenes in lateral succession—inviting rich combinations of episodes for commemorative and/or theological purposes. However, less than ten sarcophagi (or fragments) with *multiple* biblical themes have been found at Rome and cataloged in the period before the Peace of the Church (A.D. 313).[5]

Third-century images that were distinctively Christian were drawn primarily from the Old Testament, reflecting an engagement by Christian writers with the broader Roman culture that perceived older, more venerable religious traditions as inherently more valid than newer ones.[6] Christian art began as an inadvertently subversive art, for Christianity was not a legally protected religion in the Roman Empire until the Edict of Milan declared tolerance for all religions in A.D. 313.

The second and third quarters of the third century were politically unstable, with many military coups: twenty-six emperors "for life" ruled within fifty years. This instability affected the quantity and artistic quality of some art produced at that time. For Christians, political uncertainly was compounded by occasional threats of persecution in particular locations. The visual motif of three Hebrews in the fiery furnace became a timely encouragement to those who faced a choice

---

[4]Clement of Alexandria, *The Instructor* 3.11, http://www.newadvent.org/fathers/02093.htm, accessed 7/19/2011.
[5]Giuseppe Bovini and Hugo Brandenburg, *Rom und Ostia*, vol. 1 of *Repertorium der christlich-antiken Sarkophage*, ed. Friedrich W. Deichmann (Wiesbaden: Franz Steiner; Deutsches Archäologisches Institut, 1967), incl. no. 35 (Vatican Jonah sarcophagus), no. 747 (S. Maria Antiqua sarcophagus), and no. 773 (end plates).
[6]Early Christian writers wrote that "Moses is older than Homer." E.g., Tatian, *Address to the Greeks* 31, 36, 41. http://www.ccel.org/ccel/schaff/anf02.iii.ii.xxxi.html, http://www.ccel.org/ccel/schaff/anf02.iii.ii.xxxvi.html, http://www.ccel.org/ccel/schaff/anf02.iii.ii.xli.html.

between worshiping the one they perceived to be the true God, the maker of heaven and earth, and obeying the laws of their government. In general, early Christian art motifs proclaimed a positive message of hope in the face of death.

The third-century Christian preference for Old Testament images over New Testament images reflects the influence of the contemporary theological climate on creative decisions. Therefore, it is appropriate to examine not only the Bible but also the writings of second- and third-century Christian writers to interpret the figures shown.

Artists of this period reflect ties between the Hebrew Old Testament and New Testament writings, including prophetic links. Jesus referred to his own death, time-limited three-day burial, and resurrection as the "Sign of Jonah." Jonah motifs predominate in Christian art *ante pacem* (before the Peace of the Church).[7] Resurrection is therefore the dominant theme in third-century funerary art, and other motifs should therefore be examined in its light.

This pattern of one thing in the Old Testament standing for another thing in the Christian era—typology—was used not only by Christian writers but also by artists, as a viable image-creation strategy to convey abstract theological concepts through the depiction of material objects and persons.[8] Abraham's sacrifice of his son Isaac, one of the motifs on the Junius Bassus sarcophagus, was recognized by many Christians as a "type" of the sacrifice of God's Son on the cross.

Also basic to understanding Christian art is another principle of biblical hermeneutics, that one should interpret the Old Testament in light of the New Testament. For example, Noah (not featured on this sarcophagus) may serve as a visual cue to concepts rich with abstract resonance, such as baptism, salvation, or resurrection, because Peter named Noah in a discussion of these ideas.[9]

The need for Christians to present their faith in ways that adapted to the sensibilities of the dominant non-Christian culture diminished after Christianity became a legal religion of the empire in 313, when the administration in power increasingly affiliated with Christian ways

---

[7] On the "Sign of Jonah," see Matthew 12:39–40. Jonah paintings are visible on a ceiling of the catacomb of Saints Peter and Marcellinus. See Walford, *Great Themes in Art,* fig. 5.2.
[8] Elizabeth S. Malbon has emphasized typology in her approach to the sarcophagus of Junius Bassus (*The Iconography of the Sarcophagus of Junius Bassus* [Princeton, NJ: Princeton University Press, 1990]).
[9] 1 Peter 3:18–21.

of thinking. Accordingly, a shift emerged in the visual repertoire. Jonah scenes were favored in the third century in part because Jonah could represent the resurrection of Christ obliquely,[10] but they comprise a small proportion of Christian imagery after the Edict of Milan in 313, when covert images became unnecessary. As Christian sarcophagi began to flourish as an art form in the fourth century, New Testament motifs were increasingly emphasized. The apostles Peter and Paul, visible on the sarcophagus of Junius Bassus, were considered patrons of the city of Rome, and were portrayed often. Jesus was openly portrayed, and the visual language developed to serve Roman emperors was borrowed to give him honor: magi from the East bow before the infant; Jesus rides into Jerusalem with the welcome due a sovereign, but humbly, on a donkey; Jesus is shown frontally enthroned, as emperors had occasionally mirrored depictions of Zeus; and Christ's victory over death is symbolized by a round trophy wreath hanging on a cross stand framing his monogram, XP (*chi rho*, the first letters for Christ in Greek).

Just one generation after Christianity became legal in the Roman Empire, a prominent second-generation government official was buried in an elegant monument that displayed carefully developed Christian theology. This funerary monument visually exalts Jesus Christ, the Savior in whom the deceased, Junius Bassus, placed his hope of resurrection and fellowship in the afterlife.

Junius Bassus was born in 317, a year before his father, Junius Annius Bassus, began lengthy service as a senior official under Constantine, the first Christian emperor. Junius Annius Bassus served as praetorian prefect of Italy (318–331) and as consul when he built a secular basilica on the Esquiline Hill in Rome in 331.[11] Junius Bassus the younger became *praefectus urbi* of the city of Rome under the administration of Constantine's son and successor, Constantius II. As urban prefect, the responsibilities of Junius Bassus for administration of the city were broad, similar to those of a mayor. It is the sarcophagus of this younger Junius Bassus that remains today the only fourth-century Christian sarcophagus elaborately carved with figures that is also dated

---

[10] See Matthew 12:39–42; Luke 11:29–32.
[11] An *opus sectile* image from this basilica, with a man driving a four-horse chariot, may represent a portrait of the building's patron, Junius Annius Bassus.

by its inscription. As such, it serves as a stylistic benchmark for the dating of other sarcophagi. A lid fragment discovered in the twentieth century, inscribed with an epitaph, suggests that Junius Bassus was given a public funeral, a distinction uncommon for people outside the imperial family, but sometimes used to honor urban prefects who died in office.[12]

It is unusual to have recovered a largely intact sarcophagus for an official high in the imperial administration. To have a personalized witness to the Christian faith of such a person is rare indeed.

Questions of iconographic design in early Christian sarcophagi remain an issue of debate among scholars. The careful iconographic arrangement and high quality of execution of some sarcophagi, such as that of Junius Bassus, suggest thoughtful planning, while others seem to copy elements of previous sarcophagi with a less coherent plan. Scholars debate the relative contributions of patron and workshop to a finished design. Some Christian sarcophagi with uncarved central portrait faces may have been prepared on speculation in a workshop for any ready buyer.[13] Others, such as the sarcophagus of Junius Bassus, have unique features that set the work apart as likely to have been specially commissioned.[14]

The façade of the Junius Bassus sarcophagus features ten scenes in two rows. Across the top row, from left to right, are: Abraham's sacrifice of Isaac; Peter flanked by two unarmed men in knee-length clothing; Christ enthroned above a personification of the heavens and attended by two robed men; Christ standing before Pilate (who is in the next scene); and Pilate seated, washing his hands. Across the lower row, from left to right, are: Job seated on a dung heap and facing his wife; Adam and Eve; Christ's entry into Jerusalem; Daniel with lions (and two men with scrolls); and the arrest of Paul.

---

[12] Four of the nine public funerals known to have been granted to private individuals between the years of Augustus and Trajan were given to city magistrates who died in office. See Alan Cameron, "The Funeral of Junius Bassus," *Zeitschrift für Papyrologie und Epigraphik* 139 (2002): 288–292. See also Massimiliano Vitiello, "*Neofitus iit ad deum*: Some observations on the sarcophagus of Junius Bassus," *Studies in Latin Literature and Roman History* 13 (2006) [Bruxelles]. This article emphasizes inscriptions on the body and lid of the sarcophagus, and the implications thereof. Iconography of the central axis is mentioned as background for this discussion.

[13] E.g., the *lenos* (tub-shaped sarcophagus) at S. Maria Antiqua (Bovini and Brandenburg, *Repertorium*, no. 747). This is datable to the middle of the third century.

[14] These unique features include six spandrel scenes with sheep enacting biblical scenes portrayed since the third century. Also, while eagles occasionally adorned the central niche of a single-story column sarcophagus (a niche highlighting the person or work of Jesus), there are no sarcophagi other than the Junius Bassus sarcophagus that have eagles over more than one niche.

These ten scenes are organized within two stories of columns. On both the upper and lower levels, the outer pairs are enriched by spiral fluting, a common embellishment on Asiatic sarcophagi.[15] On the Junius Bassus sarcophagus, the fluting of the outer pairs descends toward the center of the sarcophagus. On the inner pairs of spiral-fluted columns, the direction is reversed, with flutes rising upward toward the center. When repeated on two levels, this generates a sense of movement up and down, appropriate to artwork that deals with concepts of moving from the realm of earth to the heavens. The most elaborately carved columns on the Junius Bassus sarcophagus, the central pairs, are covered with grapevine scrolls inhabited by *putti*—bare infants that in the broader Roman culture suggest general joy and festivity. The vine scroll columns highlight the central scenes between them, and, within the Christian context, imply Eucharistic associations.

The general format of the Junius Bassus sarcophagus is drawn from column sarcophagi that were first developed in Asia Minor. However, the lavish use of two stories of columns on the sarcophagus of Junius Bassus was repeated only once on a Christian sarcophagus.[16] The columnar framework on the front of the Junius Bassus sarcophagus has often been approached as a grid into which ten scenes are inserted, not unlike characters before a *scenae frons*, a stone stage set building used for Greek theaters. Initially, writers describing early Christian sarcophagi sought to identify individual scenes. In the twentieth century, scholars began to build on these identifications by seeking meaning in the relationship of various motifs.[17]

---

[15] M. Lawrence, "Additional Asiatic Sarcophagi," *Memoirs of the American Academy in Rome* 20 (1951): 120, fig. 1; 121, fig. 2; 135, fig. 19; 136, fig. 20; 140, fig. 26; 148, fig. 35.

[16] Only one other two-tiered columnar sarcophagus is known to exist, and it is later than the Junius Bassus sarcophagus. See Marion Lawrence, "Columnar Sarcophagi in the Latin West: Ateliers, Chronology, Style," *Art Bulletin* 14/2 (June 1932): 128; no. 70. Two levels are not unusual on frieze sarcophagi. Single-tier columnar sarcophagi do flourish in the 370s and into the fifth century, principally in Gaul but also in Rome. The columnar arrangement seems to have arrived from Asia Minor via the sea and Marseille in Gaul, possibly before it arrived in Rome. See Lawrence, "Columnar Sarcophagi," 103–106, on the development of trade between Syria and Gaul.

[17] Significant literature on the Sarcophagus of Junius Bassus includes: Anton de Waal, *Der Sarkophag des Junius Bassus in den Grotten von St. Peter* (Rome: Buchdruckerei der Gesellschaft des Göttlichen Heilandes, 1900); Friedrich Gerke, *Der Sarkophag des Iunius Bassus* (Berlin: Gebr. Mann, 1936); Karl Schefold, "Altchristlichen Bilderzyklen: Bassussarkophag und Santa Maria Maggiore," *Rivista di archeologia cristiana* 16 (1939): 289–298; Johannes A. Gaertner, "Zur Deutung des Junius-Bassus-Sarkophages," *Jahrbuch des Deutschen Archäologischen Instituts* 83 (1968): 240–264; G. Daltrop, "Anpassung eines Relieffragmentes an den Deckel des Iunius Bassus Sarkophages," *Pontificia Accademia romana di archeologia, Rendiconti* 51/52 (1978/1980): 157–170; H. von Campenhausen, "Die Passionssarkophage: Zur Geschichte eines altchristlichen Bildkreises," *Marburger Jahrbuch* 5 (1929): 39–85; M. Lawrence, "Columnar Sarcophagi in the Latin West: Ateliers, Chronology, Style," *Art Bulletin* 14 (1932):103–185.

The Junius Bassus sarcophagus is one of the first two examples of a group of about twenty mostly single-story column sarcophagi known as "passion sarcophagi."[18] Passion sarcophagi depict events leading up to the death of Christ on the cross, but the actual crucifixion of Christ does not appear until the fifth century. Passion sarcophagi are characterized by the inclusion of several figures that appear with varying frequency—Christ, Pilate, Peter and Paul.[19]

Roman figured sarcophagi of the third and fourth centuries were most commonly composed in one of two formats: The iconography was arranged either in narrative sequence from left to right (as in Roman frieze sarcophagi and Latin writing), or symmetrically around a strong central axis. The sequential left-to-right mode does not suit the Junius Bassus sarcophagus, for a left-to-right reading in the upper register would place Christ's trial before Pilate after his glorification in heaven (which is at center). In the lower register, a left-to-right reading would incongruously have Job preceding Adam and Eve, and Christ's entry into Jerusalem before Daniel. The second arrangement, with a strong central axis, is a better strategy for reading the Junius Bassus sarcophagus.

This composition's central axis features two scenes of Christ's kingship: his entry into Jerusalem and his eternal enthronement in

---

More recent studies include Malbon, *Iconography of the Sarcophagus of Junius Bassus*; and Alice Christ, *The Sarcophagus of Junius Bassus: Patron, Workshop, and Program*, 3 vols. (PhD diss., University of Chicago, 1992) (681 pages), the basis for her much anticipated forthcoming work *The Sarcophagus of Junius Bassus: Making and Meaning* (University of Wisconsin Press). Malbon's interpretation has emphasized typology and sacraments, while Alice Christ has contributed excellent formal analysis and observation of genealogies of type traditions among Passion sarcophagi.

On the two epitaphs, see Alan Cameron, "The Funeral of Junius Bassus," *Zeitschrift für Papyrologie und Epigraphik* 139 (2002): 288–292. On the organization of the physical framework, see Jaś Elsner, "Framing the Objects We Study: Three Late Roman Boxes from Italy," *Journal of the Warburg and Courtauld Institutes* 71 (2008): 21–38.

For important general considerations concerning the interpretation of early Christian motifs, see Sister Charles Murray, *Rebirth and Afterlife: A Study of the Transmutation of Some Pagan Imagery in Early Christian Funerary Art* (Oxford: B.A.R., International Series, 1981). Murray rightly critiques the reading of each image sign as having a single simple meaning and sees polyvalence in many Christian motifs, which, she aptly says, are to be read according to their surrounding visual context. She is responding to work done in the manner of André Grabar, who saw in episodes of rescue from danger "salvation" as the theme for most motifs in early Christian art. See André Grabar, *Christian Iconography: A Study of Its Origins* [A. W. Mellon Lectures in the Fine Arts, 1961; National Gallery of Art, Washington, DC] Bollingen Series 35/10 (Princeton, NJ: Princeton University Press, 1968).

[18] A columnar sarcophagus with passion themes that appears in Gaul as early as the 350s is from Saint-Maximin. See Lawrence, "Columnar Sarcophagi," 111, no. 4, fig. 7. However, it is from approximately A.D. 360–400 that the genre flourishes, with at least four times as many having been found in Gaul as in Rome. See Lawrence, "Columnar Sarcophagi," 105–106.

[19] Von Campenhausen first delineated the grouping of Passion sarcophagi. He defined them as including Christ before Pilate *or* martyrdoms of Peter or Paul. (von Campenhausen, "Die Passionssarkophage"; see also Alice Christ, *Sarcophagus of Junius Bassus*, 350–409).

heaven. In the lower level, Christ rides a donkey and is acclaimed by people gathering branches to strew on the road before him.[20] The story of Jesus riding into Jerusalem on a donkey, the Triumphal Entry, is characterized in all four Gospels as the approach of a king.[21] Erich Dinkler and others have observed that depictions of Christ's entry into Jerusalem resemble *adventus* ("arrival") iconography of Roman art that depicts the formal entrance of an emperor into a city.[22] After Emperor Constantine legalized Christianity within the Roman Empire, the Christian visual repertoire increasingly included imperial iconography, which became a useful means of conveying the dominion of God.

Above this scene of Jesus assuming kingship on earth, he exercises kingly dominion in heaven as he sits enthroned above Caelus, a personification of the sky. Christ enthroned above Caelus is an uncommon scene. Of six known examples on sarcophagi (all from the second half of the fourth century), only one preserves both Christ and Caelus. That sarcophagus, Lat. 174,[23] seems on stylistic grounds to be later than the Junius Bassus sarcophagus. Marilyn Stokstad's statement that the Junius Bassus sarcophagus contains what may be the first instance of Christ enthroned in majesty above the heavens may very well be correct,[24] but there is a precedent for the authoritative seated frontal pose of Christ. On a polychrome funerary plaque fragment from the second half of the third century, which is now in the Terme Museum of Rome, Jesus is seated frontally like an enthroned Zeus (with long hair and bared chest) and seems to be teaching small figures seated before him, perhaps illustrating the Sermon on the Mount.[25] Caelus on the sarcophagus of Junius Bassus may be drawn from the breastplate of the statue of Augustus of Primaporta, near the neck. The youthful, beardless Christ above Caelus holds a scroll and is flanked by two bearded male attendants, the one at left holding a rolled scroll. The men on either side of Christ have sometimes been identified as Peter and Paul. However, the figure identified as Paul, to the right of Christ,

---

[20] Matthew 21:1–10; Mark 11:1–10; Luke 19:28–44; John 12:12–19.

[21] Matthew 21:5; Mark 11:10; Luke 19:38; John 12:13, 15.

[22] Erich Dinkler, *Einzug in Jerusalem: Ikonographische Untersuchungen im Anschlüß an ein bisher unbekanntes Sarkophagfragment*, Arbeitsgemeinschaft für Forschung des Landes Nordrhein-Westfalen: Geisteswissenschaften, Heft 167 (Opladen: Westdeutscher, 1968), 48.

[23] Bovini and Brandenburg, *Repertorium*, no. 677.

[24] Marilyn Stokstad, *Medieval Art*, 2nd ed. (Boulder, CO: Westview, 2004), 22.

[25] Bovini and Brandenburg, *Repertorium*, no. 773b, depicts Jesus teaching, styled as Zeus enthroned.

does not have the high forehead or balding head commonly associated with Paul, and evident on the figure of Paul in the lower right niche of the sarcophagus.

To the right of Christ in heaven, two niches portray Jesus apprehended and his trial before Pilate. The trial before Pilate suggests the death of Jesus—the sacrifice of his life for the sin of all people—in a way that eschews violence. This avoidance of depicting his death may reflect respect for the Lord, or sensitivity to the killing of some Christians for their faith as recently as the previous generation, or deference to the sensibilities of the recently bereaved. Pilate appeared on the "Two Brothers" frieze sarcophagus, perhaps as early as the second decade of the fourth century, and on column sarcophagi in the second half of the fourth century.[26]

The proximity of the two scenes of Christ before Pilate to the central scene of Christ enthroned may affect how these scenes are interpreted. The civil trial before Pilate followed a trial by Jewish religious authorities in which Christ "kept silent." When the high priest continued questioning him, saying, "I adjure You by the living God, that You tell us whether You are the Christ, the Son of God," Jesus replied, "You have said it *yourself*; nevertheless I tell you, hereafter you will see 'the Son of Man sitting at the right hand of power,' and 'coming with the clouds of heaven.'"[27] Christ's self-identifying statement before the Jewish leaders appears to be combined in the upper central scene of the sarcophagus of Junius Bassus.

If these upper central scene features are linked with Christ's self-identification at the pivotal moment in his trial, it is fitting to examine how the lower central scene of Christ's entry into Jerusalem on the back of a donkey further contributes to his identification. The intentional way Christ acquired the donkey and its foal, specifying that "the Lord has need of them,"[28] together with Matthew's statement that follows, suggests that Christ's approach to Jerusalem (Zion) was viewed as an enactment of that which had been previously prophesied about the coming king or Messiah:

---

[26] Bovini and Brandenburg, *Repertorium*, no. 45. Pilate's appearances before A.D. 350 at Rome are generally on frieze sarcophagi (*Repertorium*, nos. 28, 45, 387, 667), while his appearances after the mid-fourth century are on column sarcophagi (*Repertorium*, nos. 49, 189, 677, 680). The fragmentary condition of *Repertorium* no. 201 makes its dating less sure.
[27] Matthew 26:63–64; cf. Mark 13:26; Psalm 110:1; Daniel 7:13, NASB.
[28] Matthew 21:1–3.

This took place to fulfill what was spoken through the prophet:

"Say to the Daughter of Zion,
  'Behold your King is coming to you,
  Gentle, and mounted on a donkey,
  Even on a colt, the foal of a beast of burden.'"[29]

At the upper left of the sarcophagus façade is a scene of Abraham sacrificing Isaac, an Old Testament narrative often viewed as a parallel to the redemptive sacrifice of Christ. This motif flourishes most strongly in the first half of the fourth century, though it also appears shortly before and after that time.[30] This combination of sacrifice scenes emphasizes the costliness of Jesus' redemptive act to God the Father, and may imply that God empathizes with the bereaved in their moment of loss.

These paired upper end motifs—Abraham sacrificing Isaac and Christ's submitting to self-sacrifice before Pilate—share a theme of sacrifice, but the use of one niche at far left for Abraham and two niches at right for Pilate's judgment of Christ is unbalanced. The second scene from the left depicts a short-haired, bearded male in a pose similar to that of a statue of Demosthenes, a Greek orator,[31] and flanked by two men in knee-length garments. This scene has commonly been identified as the arrest or martyrdom of Peter.[32] Peter's hands are clasped together as a man behind him, at left, holds Peter's upper arm. An arrest scene could be an oblique reference to death or martyrdom,[33] and as such may function similarly to the trial of Jesus before Pilate. However, the fact that the men flanking Peter do not bear weapons makes an identification of this scene as an arrest less clear than the scene of Paul's arrest in the lower right niche, where a sword is evi-

---

[29] Matthew 21:4–5 (NASB), quoting Zechariah 9:9.
[30] Of 47 examples of the "Abraham sacrificing Isaac" motif in the Bovini and Brandenburg *Repertorium*, 39 are dated to the first half of the fourth century (nos. 7, 12, 23, 33, 39, 40, 41, 42, 44, 45, 52, 99, 112, 144, 178, 179, 187, 188, 268, 283, 385, 412, 435, 480, 622, 624, 625, 674, 693, 694, 707, 746, 771, 772, 774, 820, 840, 931, 991); 2 are dated earlier (last decade of the third century; nos. 90, 980), 3 to the third quarter of the fourth century (nos. 377, 677, 680); 1 to the end of the fourth century; 1 to the fourth century generally; 1 undated. See Bovini and Brandenburg, *Repertorium*; and Ulrike Lange, *Ikonographisches Register für das Repertorium der christlich-antiken Sarkophage, Bd. 1 (Rom und Ostia)* (Dettelbach: J. H. Röll, 1996), 2–3.
[31] See Daltrop, "Anpassung eines Relieffragmentes," 166–169, figs. 8–9; and 170, fig. 10, for hands of the Demosthenes statue, which are the most clearly retained feature evident in Peter's pose on the sarcophagus of Junius Bassus.
[32] Von Campenhausen, "Passionssarkophage"; Alice Christ, *Sarcophagus of Junius Bassus*, 350.
[33] Elsner, "Framing the Objects We Study," 31.

dent. This scene has often been perceived as an arrest of Peter prior to martyrdom, as recounted in the apocryphal *Acts of Peter*. If the scene is an arrest of Peter, but is not meant as an arrest leading to martyrdom, it could be one of three arrests—Acts 4:1–3; 5:18; or 12:3–5. The first two arrests by religious authorities might give less reason to show weapons than the later arrest by Herod.

The five scenes across the lower level of the Junius Bassus sarcophagus are framed by more elaborate architecture than those on the upper level. The alternation of arches and gables as framing elements at the top of columnar niches is a common feature on Asiatic sarcophagi. On the Junius Bassus sarcophagus, this alternation pairs the end niche characters beneath arches and the inner niche characters beneath gables. The depictions of Job and Paul share a sense of the approach of death.

Job, at far left, is uncommon on sarcophagi.[34] In early Christian literature, Job was both hailed for his character and presented as a model of Christ, particularly of his sufferings. If one considers not only what was said about Job but also what Job himself is said to have thought, the potential significance of his visible presence expands. Clement of Rome paired Job's righteousness and Abraham's humility, noting that, in the face of God's glory, Abraham said, "I am but dust and ashes."[35] Abraham is placed immediately above Job on the Bassus sarcophagus; both are viewed as positive models. Zeno of Verona spoke of parallels between Job's sufferings and Christ's passion.[36] As early Christian writers understood Septuagint readings of Job 19:25–27, Job took hope in the future work of his redeemer, a hope that focused on resurrection:[37]

---

[34] Aside from the sarcophagus of Junius Bassus and a small, single-figure fragment, at Rome, Job is positively identified by Lange on only two tree-format passion sarcophagi, which Bovini and Brandenburg date to A.D. 310–330 (see Lange, *Ikonographisches Register*, 52). Trunks of trees partially separate the scenes, as columns do on passion sarcophagi after A.D. 350. Lawrence, however, dates these same tree sarcophagi to the second half of the fourth century ("Columnar Sarcophagi," 171, nos. 71–72). Such dating would move the use of Job on the Bassus sarcophagus to a very early place in the passion sarcophagus sequence (tree type: *Repertorium*, nos. 61, 215; single-figure fragment: no. 260; Junius Bassus: no. 680).

Job is also depicted in catacomb paintings on the Via Latina (cubiculum C a), dated A.D. 300–360. See Antonio Ferrua, *The Unknown Catacomb* (New Lanark, UK: Geddes & Grosset, 1991), 154; 120, fig. 110. For an earlier painting of Job in the Catacomb of Domitilla, see Samuel Terrien, *The Iconography of Job through the Centuries* (University Park: Pennsylvania State University Press, 1996), fig. 2-3; ll. I –II.

[35] See Job 1:1 and Genesis 18:27, and references to Job and Abraham in 1 Clement 17 (c. A.D. 100).

[36] Zeno's time period (and whether there were two people by this name who were bishops) is disputed. A Zeno was bishop of Verona A.D. 362 ff. If the Tractates of Zeno were written just after the death of Junius Bassus, it is possible they reflect thinking that was current shortly before that time. See Tractate 1.15 (2.15) in *Corpus Christianorum Latinorum*.

[37] M. Philonenko believes that the *Testament of Job* is a Greek midrash on the Greek Septuagint translation of the book of Job, albeit not verse by verse (*Le Testament de Job* [Paris: Librairie d'Amérique et de'Orient

I know that my redeemer lives,
  and that in the end he will stand on the earth [dust].
And after my skin has been destroyed,
  yet in my flesh I will see God;
I myself will see him
  with my own eyes—I, and not another.
How my heart yearns within me![38]

On the Junius Bassus sarcophagus, Job is accompanied by two people. Job's wife covers her mouth with a draped hand in a gesture of mourning, befitting a sarcophagus.[39] The male in the background could be one of Job's friends who arrived to console him, but it is also possible that it is a figure of Satan from a first-century A.D. apocryphal story in the *Testament of Job*, chapter 6. Job's wife strove to bring bread to Job, even when she had run out of resources. Satan, disguised as a bread merchant, persuaded her to sell her hair for a three-day supply of bread.[40] On the sarcophagus, her head covering is prominent.

To the right of the scene of Job, Adam and Eve are tempted by the serpent, which twines around the tree of knowledge of good and evil. Having sinned and having realized their sin, they cover their nakedness in shame. In Romans 5, Paul compares Adam to Christ, the second Adam, in a discussion of death and resurrection:

> For if by the transgression of the one [the first Adam, v. 12], death reigned through the one, much more those who receive the abundance of grace and of the gift of righteousness will reign in life through the One [the second Adam], Jesus Christ.[41]

Along with Adam and Eve, Daniel was among the earliest char-

Adrien-Maisonneuve, 1968], 13; cited in P. Hervé Tremblay, *Job 19, 25–27 dans la Septante et chez les Pères grecs: Unanimité d'une tradition* [Paris: J. Gabalda, 2002], 227). In the *Testament of Job*, both Job himself and his first wife, Sitis, testify of resurrection (T. Job 4:4–10 and 40:4; cited and translated into French in Tremblay, *Job 19, 25–27*, 232–233).

[38] Job 19:25–27 (NIV).

[39] Henry Maguire makes note of a similar gesture of sorrow on a Greek fourth-century tomb relief which shows a mourner pressing her draped hand against her lips (Maguire, "The Depiction of Sorrow in Middle Byzantine Art," *Dumbarton Oaks Papers* 31 [1977]: 151, n. 147; illustrated in Margarete Bieber, *The Sculpture of the Hellenistic Age* [New York: Columbia University Press, 1961], 64, fig. 206).

[40] *Testament of Job* 6 (trans. M. R. James, *Apocrypha anecdota 2, Texts and Studies* 5/1 [Cambridge: University Press, 1897]); see http://wesley.nnu.edu/sermons-essays-books/noncanonical-literature/testament-of-job/, accessed 8/3/2011. Alice Christ noted that Bosio's engraving of the Junius Bassus sarcophagus depicts the lost stick and loaf which Job's wife extended to her husband (*Sarcophagus of Junius Bassus*, 250; citing Antonio Bosio, *Roma Sotterranea* [Rome: 1632]).

[41] Romans 5:17 (NASB); see Romans 5:12–17. The juxtaposition of Adam and Christ is also found in Corinthians 15:45.

acters depicted in third-century Christian art. These two scenes are paired on the Junius Bassus sarcophagus in gabled niches on each side of the scene of Jesus on a donkey at the beginning of Passion Week. Daniel is identified by the two lions flanking him and is accompanied by two men holding scrolls, suggesting literature. The pairing of Daniel with Adam and Eve prompts reflection on dust and mortality.[42] When God cursed Adam, he said,

> By the sweat of your face,
> You will eat bread,
> Till you return to the ground,
> Because from it you were taken;
> For you are dust,
> And to dust you shall return.[43]

The writing in Daniel 12:2 becomes a hopeful response to the curse, for it states,

> Many of those who sleep in the dust of the earth shall awake, some to everlasting life, and some to shame and everlasting contempt.

This is the hope foretold by prophets like Daniel and made possible by the second Adam, who Paul says brings eternal life.[44]

At the time of the discovery of this sarcophagus in 1595–1597, Daniel was depicted, as he often was in the third and fourth centuries, as a young nude *orant* (praying) figure with hands outstretched in prayer, between lions. A drawing published in 1773 shows this,[45] but the youth had been replaced by an older robed prophet by the time the sarcophagus was photographed in 1900.[46]

At the far right of the Junius Bassus sarcophagus, Paul has

---

[42] Malbon has noted a visible link between Adam and Eve scenes and Daniel scenes about one-quarter of the time that Adam scenes are shown in Wilpert's catalog of sarcophagi: Among 34 images of Adam and Eve on sarcophagi in the catalog, 9 are either adjacent to or arranged symmetrically with depictions of Daniel (Malbon, *Iconography of the Sarcophagus of Junius Bassus*, 61; Giuseppe Wilpert, *I Sarcophagi cristiani antichi*, 3 vols. + 2 vols. [Rome: Pontificio Istituto Archeologico Cristiana, 1929]).

[43] Genesis 3:19 (NASB).

[44] Romans 5:21.

[45] Gerke, *Der Sarkophag des Iunius Bassus*, 32. The drawing is from P. L. Dionysius, *Sacrarum Vaticanae basilicae cryptarum monumenta* (1773).

[46] The timing of this exchange of the original nude *orant* Daniel for a prophet clothed to the feet is unknown, but seems to have taken place between the publication of the drawing in 1773 and the publication of photos of the sarcophagus (with clothed Daniel) by de Waal in 1900 (de Waal, *Der Sarkophag des Junius Bassus*, pll. I-II).

traditionally been identified by a high forehead or balding pate. Some have also suggested that reeds behind Paul on the sarcophagus represent a tradition of his martyrdom at the Tiber River.[47] Paul is accompanied by soldiers in knee-length garments. The lead soldier at right bears a sword. Paul's arms appear to be bound behind him as a second soldier follows. The depiction of Paul's arrest is a discreet way of referring to his demise. Paul is well known for his equanimity in the face of death,[48] and his last letter to Timothy is rich with metaphors for death familiar in a Roman milieu, expressions that place death in a positive light:

> For I am already being poured out as a drink offering, and the time of my departure has come. I have fought the good fight, I have finished the course, I have kept the faith; in the future there is laid up for me the crown of righteousness, which the Lord, the righteous Judge, will award to me on that day; and not only to me, but also to all who have loved His appearing.[49]

It may be Paul's way of characterizing death, rather than the events specific to his own death, that will be most meaningful to the viewer of the sarcophagus.

Figures at the outer frames of sarcophagi usually face inward toward the center of the composition, as do both Job, at the lower left, and Pilate, at the upper right. When Abraham, at the upper left, looks to the left, he turns away from the action with Isaac to face the hand of God who stops him. This may be read as a dramatic twist. When Paul, in the lower right corner, walks to the right, he seems to be walking "out of the picture." This may suggest a final arrest leading to his demise.

An inscription across the top edge of the sarcophagus identifies Junius Bassus by name, death date, and occupation. It reads, "Junius Bassus, *vir clarissimus* [of senatorial rank], who lived 42 years 2 months, in his own prefecture of the city, newly baptized [*neofitus*], went to God, the 8th day from the Kalends of September, Eusebius and Hypatius,

---

[47] This characterization of how Paul died is not in the Bible. For visual associations of Paul with reeds near the marsh of the Tiber, see Malbon, *Iconography of the Sarcophagus of Junius Bassus*, 181, n. 56.

[48] "For to me, to live is Christ and to die is gain. But if *I am* to live *on* in the flesh, this *will mean* fruitful labor for me; and I do not know which to choose. But I am hard-pressed from both *directions*, having the desire to depart and be with Christ, for *that* is very much better; yet to remain on in the flesh is more necessary for your sake. Convinced of this, I know that I will remain and continue with you all for your progress and joy in the faith" (Philippians 1:21–25, NASB).

[49] 2 Timothy 4:6–8, NASB.

consuls."[50] Perhaps the most unusual part of this inscription is the poignant phrase, "*Neofitus*, he went to God." *Neofitus* resonates with multiple meanings. Literally, it meant "newly planted," and as such could play on the idea of being buried in the ground, for this elaborate sarcophagus was originally placed beneath the floor of the apse of the basilica that Constantine had built over the Vatican area graveyard and which he had dedicated to Saint Peter, for a memorial to Peter had been previously raised there.[51] More commonly, *neofitus* was used to describe someone recently converted to Christian faith. In the fourth century, it could refer to someone newly baptized.

The careful arrangement of so many biblical elements on the sarcophagus of Junius Bassus suggests a degree of theological sophistication, which contrasts strikingly with the description of Junius Bassus as "*neofitus*." The combination of these features is best explained by the intentional delay of baptism by someone well-acquainted with biblical texts. Some people deferred baptism until they were near death because they wished to go to God unstained by subsequent sin. Some felt that a life in public service could require making decisions that were not always clearly and unambiguously moral, and that because of this, it was better to defer baptism. This was quite possibly the view of Junius Bassus, who, by this interpretation, was therefore baptized when near death.

The emphasis on law and governing practices in the program of the sarcophagus of Junius Bassus is fitting for a man with a career in public service. Moses the lawgiver appears twice in the spandrels, once actually receiving God's law. Pilate is depicted in a judicial capacity; Paul is led away by soldiers or officers, likely to his demise. Christ is portrayed as a kingly ruler on earth and in heaven. The sarcophagus of Junius Bassus seems to highlight the identity of Christ and some heroes of the faith in a way that would singularly befit a man like Junius Bassus, formerly consul and then an urban prefect who died in office.

The sarcophagus of Junius Bassus invites the viewer to engage in spiritual perception that is grounded in an acquaintance with the Old

---

[50] IVN BASSVS V.C. QVI VIXIT ANNIS XLII MEN. II IN IPSA PRAEFECTVRA VRBI NEOFITVS IIT AD DEVM VII KAL. SEPT. EVSEBIO ET YPATIO COSS. Inscription translation by Malbon (*Iconography of the Sarcophagus of Junius Bassus*, 3).

[51] The argument for this placement is developed by Alice Christ, *Sarcophagus of Junius Bassus*, 100–112, esp. 100–104, 112. In modern usage, "neophyte" may refer to a religious novice preparing to take vows to join a religious community, or to someone new to a certain practice; colloquially, a "newbie."

and New Testament Scriptures by meditating on correspondences between motifs—old and new—that are physically mapped on the surface of the object. Elements of the visual vocabulary and of the grammar of contemporary Roman visual culture are combined with the newer Christian motifs to enrich the viewer's perception of his own faith and his own place in contemporary society and in the kingdom of God, where he may eagerly anticipate the company of faithful "old friends."

Nave, Chartres Cathedral. C. 1194–1220. Photo by Theo Jacobs/www.rtjacobs.nl.

2

GOTHIC ARCHITECTURE AND "THE PURE AND NAKED SEEING OF DIVINE REALITY"
Chartres Cathedral

RACHEL HOSTETTER SMITH

In the first lecture of his *Entretiens sur l'architecture* (*Lectures on Architecture*, 1858–1872), the French architect Eugène Emmanuel Viollet-le-Duc (1814–1879) addressed "how art acts upon the human senses."[1] In order to illustrate this idea he recollected a boyhood visit to the Cathedral of Notre-Dame in Paris while in the care of a family domestic, a memory that remained strong and palpable throughout his life:

> One day he took me into the church of Notre Dame, carrying me in his arms for the crowd was great. My attention was attracted by the glass of the south rose-window, through which the rays of the sun penetrated, coloured by the most radiant hues. . . . Suddenly the grand organs broke into music; to me, it was the rose before my eyes which sang. My old guide sought in vain to undeceive me; under this impression, more and more lively when I imagined that such panels of glass produced the grave tones, and such others uttered the high and piercing ones, I was seized with such great terror that it was necessary to take me out.[2]

With all of the earmarks of a conversion experience, the rationalist, secularist architect recounted his first encounter with the Gothic cathedral that may well have set him on a life course of passionate advocacy of the Gothic aesthetic in nineteenth-century France.

---

[1] From the article "Viollet-le-Duc: Music and Architecture" at http://www.cca.qc.ca/en/collection/1396-viollet-le-duc-music-and-architecture, accessed 7/25/2011.
[2] Eugène Emmanuel Viollet-le-Duc, *Lectures on Architecture*, trans. Benjamin Bucknall (New York: Dover, 1987); quoted in "Viollet-le-Duc: Music and Architecture."

Martin Bressani describes Viollet-le-Duc's experience this way:

> Very far from a romantic reverie, the experience related by Viollet-le-Duc is a tactile encounter. Like Rainer Maria Rilke's poem to the "cathedral's great window-roses" that "gripped a heart and pulled it deep into God," an experience that the poet likens to being subjected, face to face, to the unsettling wildness of a great feline, Viollet-le-Duc's childhood episode at Notre-Dame is an opening into the depth of a force the strength of which makes the young boy lose himself in otherness. If it is not, strictly speaking, a religious experience, it is essentially sacred in nature and defines an apex of possibilities.[3]

Viollet-le-Duc's response was fully consistent with the purposes of the Gothic style, which set out to transport the beholder from this temporal existence to the *aevum*, that is, the eternal time of the visionary state. In medieval Scholasticism, the *aevum* constitutes the state between time and eternity where the human soul may experience what it means to be truly one with God, perfectly whole and at peace. It entails the changelessness of being with the changeability of volition that reflects the eternal present of the next life.[4]

Nevertheless, as one of the foremost proponents of the nineteenth-century Gothic revival, Viollet-le-Duc championed Gothic architecture for its rational order. But it is commonly recognized that "beneath his evident scholarship and rationalist outlook lay a deep vein of feeling, even of irrationality, a belief in the power of art to stir emotions and evoke responses that cannot be readily analyzed."[5] Viollet-le-Duc came to believe that buildings were like living beings that speak to us. As Bressani remarks, ". . . he came to feel the monument's body endowed with its own secret life,"[6] and that he had only to tap into its source. Widely dismissed as vulgar and brutish since the Renaissance, as a result of proponents like Viollet-le-Duc, Gothic

---

[3] Martin Bressani, "Viollet-le-Duc's Optic," in *Architecture and the Sciences: Exchanging Metaphors*, ed. Antoine Picon and Alessandra Ponte (Princeton, NJ: Princeton Architectural Press, 2003), 121. The poem referenced in this passage is "The Rose Window," found in Rainer Maria Rilke, *The Rose Window and Other Verse from New Poems* (Boston: Little, Brown, 1997).
[4] See chapter 2, "Anagogy, *Aevum* and Two Later Medieval Visionary Arts," in Barbara Nolan, *The Gothic Visionary Perspective* (Princeton, NJ: Princeton University Press, 1977) for a discussion of the concept of the *aevum*.
[5] "Viollet-le-Duc: Music and Architecture."
[6] Bressani, "Viollet-le-Duc's Optic," 121.

architecture enjoyed a new popularity which has continued to the present.[7]

Significantly, the struggle to find the proper balance between reason and emotion, intellectual knowledge and experiential insight was not new but extended back to Greek antiquity and the roots of Western thought. As such, it was one of the essential issues facing Christians from the earliest days of the church. In the Middle Ages, this debate continued between the Scholastics, who advanced the view of God as one who presents himself through clear and logically discernible precepts,[8] and the mystics, who saw God as one who so far surpasses human understanding that he must necessarily reveal himself to us largely through direct and mystical experience, something that can be described only as spiritual sight. As John Walford puts it in *Great Themes in Art*, the Gothic cathedral stands at "the climax of a long tradition of creating space to express Christian faith in material form."[9]

It was, in fact, the vision of a new form of architecture that could bridge the gap between the material and the immaterial realms, articulated by the French cleric Abbot Suger of Saint Denis in the early decades of the twelfth century, that gave birth to the Gothic style. Suger described the objective of this new architecture as the *anagogicus mos*—the upward-leading way—as follows:

> Thus, when out of my delight in the beauty of the house of God—the loveliness of the many colored gems has called me away from external cares, and worthy meditation has induced me to reflect, transferring that which is material to that which is immaterial, on the diversity of the sacred virtues: then it seems to me that I see myself dwelling, as it were, in some strange region of the universe which neither exists entirely in the slime of the earth nor entirely in the purity of Heaven; and that, by the grace of God, I can be transported from this inferior to that higher world in an anagogical manner."[10]

---

[7] The term "Gothic" was first applied to the architecture of the high and late Middle Ages by the Italians in the fifteenth and sixteenth centuries, who attributed the style to the Goths. It was understood as a pejorative reference based on perceptions of the Goths as a coarse and barbaric people "whom they blamed for destroying classical art" (E. John Walford, *Great Themes in Art* [Upper Saddle River, NJ: Prentice-Hall, 2002], 158).

[8] Erwin Panofsky makes the case for the way that Gothic architectural design is understood through the lens of Scholastic thought in his well-known book *Gothic Architecture and Scholasticism* (Latrobe, PA: Archabbey, 1951).

[9] Walford, *Great Themes in Art*, 168.

[10] Suger, Abbot of Saint Denis, *Abbot Suger on the Abbey Church of St.-Denis and Its Art Treasures*, ed., trans, and annotated by Erwin Panofsky; 2nd ed. edited by Gerda Panofsky-Soergel (Princeton, NJ: Princeton University Press, 1979), 63–65.

For Suger, the church was not just a building for serving the liturgical needs of the faithful but a vessel by which humankind might be transported into the presence of the divine. And Suger and his contemporaries clearly recognized that it was sensory experience—a response to the building's material beauty and mystical effect—that provided the primary means by which this might occur.

The realization of this goal depended largely on the light and height of the structure made possible by new engineering techniques that created a space that can be truly understood only in view of the theological thought of the time. Undergirding these ideals was the fundamental belief in medieval Christian thought that it is the church, foreshadowed in the Old Testament by Noah's ark, that is the prime vehicle of redemption. So often described as a ship of souls, this second ark, whose architectural congregational space is called the *nave*, Latin for ship, stands as a vessel that must be fitted out and manned to make this journey and thereby fulfill its divinely ordained mission. The new style of architecture produced by Suger at Saint Denis, the necropolis of the French monarchy outside of Paris, quickly found a host of imitators as Gothic style swiftly spread around the Île-de-France and then throughout Europe. The Bishop of Chartres, a friend of Abbot Suger, was one of the first to adopt Gothic style—at Chartres, as early as 1145. The subsequent rebuilding of the cathedral following its destruction in a devastating fire in 1194 incorporated aspects of a more fully realized Gothic style developed at other churches in the Île-de-France, so that Chartres stands as a "paradigm" of French Gothic cathedral architecture.[11]

In *Great Themes in Art*, John Walford presents works of art and architecture as carriers of meaning that arise out of the particularity of the contexts in which they were made. The medieval cathedral was not only a center of religious and civic life but served to teach the stories and doctrines of the church and to inspire believers to deeper faith. Specifically, "the sculptural program of Chartres Cathedral presents historical events as having ultimate meaning within a theological framework that links the creation of the world, the fall of humankind into sin, their redemption through Christ, and the Last Judgment. This view of history pivots on the incarnation of Christ—in Christian

---

[11] Walford, *Great Themes in Art*, 163.

belief, the Son of God."[12] A primary theme of Walford's discussion of Gothic architecture (in which he uses Chartres Cathedral as his prime example) is the way in which the Gothic cathedral seeks to present a vision of the heavenly New Jerusalem and of God as "the Light of Lights."[13] Three engineering components—pointed arches that direct the thrust of the weight of the ceiling and vaults down onto narrow supports, ribbed vaults that provide additional strength that make possible the reduction of the bulk of the supporting structure, and external flying buttresses that counter the tremendous thrust these elements exerted on key stress points without compromising the lightness of the structural elements—made possible the height and light which made manifest these theological ideals. But beyond these two dimensions, the makers of Chartres situated aspects of the program in relation to the light and the movement of the sun to reflect their theological and cosmological significance. As Walford explains,

> On the north portals, which remain in shadow, are mostly Old Testament subjects, conceived as a lesser light, foreshadowing the brighter light of the New Testament. New Testament subjects, therefore, are clustered around the sunlit south portals. The main west portals, lit by the setting sun, reiterate elements from both Testaments, and depict the end of time. Inside the cathedral, the altar, where the life renewing sacraments are received, is at the east end, where the sun rises.[14]

Clearly, the builders of Chartres Cathedral sought to imbue every aspect of the church's fabric and furnishings with the capacity to convey meaning to those who came there.[15] This essay seeks to extend Walford's method of careful examination of the Gothic cathedral itself to investigate the *experience* of the Gothic cathedral in relation to the

---

[12] Ibid., 164.

[13] Ibid., 163.

[14] Ibid., 164.

[15] Essential studies on the Gothic cathedral and architecture include: Otto von Simson, *The Gothic Cathedral* (Princeton, NJ: Princeton University Press, 1956); Jean Gimpel, *The Cathedral Builders*, trans. Teresa Waugh (New York: Harper & Row, 1984); and Louis Grodecki, *Gothic Architecture* (New York: Electa/Rizzoli, 1978). For broad critical treatments of Gothic, see: George Henderson, *Gothic* (Harmondsworth, UK: Penguin, 1967); Andrew Martindale, *Gothic Art* (New York: Praiger, 1967); and more recently Michael Camille, *Gothic Art: Glorious Visions* (New York: Harry N. Abrams, 1996). For a selection of some of the essential primary texts, see Teresa B. Frisch, *Gothic Art, 1140–c. 1450: Sources and Documents* (Toronto: University of Toronto Press, 1987). For sources specifically focused on Chartres, see: Henry Adams, *Mont-Saint-Michel and Chartres* (Boston and New York: Houghton Mifflin, 1905); Jean Favier, *The World of Chartres* (New York: Harry N. Abrams, 1990); and Robert Branner, ed., *Chartres Cathedral* (New York: W. W. Norton, 1969).

theological currents of the time, and to better understand the spiritual impact of the practices that took place there.

In the mid-twelfth century, theologian Richard of Saint Victor (d. 1173) laid out his conception of fourfold vision in *The Mystical Ark*.[16] These four modes of seeing, as he refers to them, describe the various levels of human perception that create our understanding of the world around us, our experience of it, and their relationship to spiritual matters. The first mode of the four is the recognition of "the figures and colors of visible things in the simple perception of matter." The second moves beyond the perception of the "outward appearance" of a thing to include the "mystical significance" in it. The third involves the discovery of the "truth of hidden things . . . by means of forms and figures and the similitude of things," while the fourth and final mode entails the "pure and naked seeing of divine reality." In an article focusing on the first mode, medieval art historian Madeline Caviness writes that this last mode, which occasioned the "pure and naked seeing of divine reality," was "virtually unattainable by the artist."[17] But it is clear that Richard uses the term "seeing" to refer to intellectual comprehension and spiritual revelation as well as to physical sight. Richard drew from the *Celestial Hierarchy* of Pseudo-Dionysius and from Hugh of Saint Victor's commentary on that text when he described "anagogical" vision as a mode of experience that allows a person briefly to bridge the gap that exists between the temporal world to which we are bound in this life and the celestial realm. An examination of *experience*, however, shows that the Gothic cathedral was a context within which the objective of Richard's fourth mode of seeing was recognized *and* actively pursued. One of the primary means to achieving this was aesthetic. It is the form of the cathedral itself in combination with contemporary practice that established conditions that made possible that experience of temporary transcendence. More specifically, it is through an overload of the senses that this occurs. The three examples of this sensory overload that follow—of the approach and entry into the sacred space in relation to the form of the architecture; the qualities of chant music

---

[16] See Richard of Saint Victor, *The Twelve Patriarchs; The Mystical Ark; Book Three of the Trinity*, trans. Grover A. Zinn, (Mahwah, NJ: Paulist, 1979) for the original texts on the four modes of seeing in *The Mystical Ark*.
[17] Madeline Caviness, "'The Simple Perception of Matter' and the Representation of Narrative, ca. 1180–1280," *Gesta* 30/1 (1991): 48–64. The quotes are from page 55. Caviness has also written about the third mode, in her article "Images of Divine Order and the Third Mode of Seeing," *Gesta* 22/2 (1983): 99–120.

in the space of the cathedral; and the devotional practice of walking the labyrinth in the cathedral—effectively demonstrate this phenomenon and how it relates to the theological thought of the time.

In the twelfth century, there was a significant rise in theological literature emphasizing the importance of the spiritual experience of the believer. From the time of Eusebius in the fourth century, Christian literature had divided the whole history of the world from Adam to the Apocalypse into Six Ages. But by the twelfth century there was a shift in emphasis based upon the writings of Berengaudus (probably ninth century), Rupert of Deutz (c. 1075–1129), Hugh of Saint Victor (c. 1096–1141), Richard of Saint Victor, and Joachim of Fiore (c. 1135–1202), so that in the Sixth Age, the period following the incarnation of God in Christ, it *was* possible to *see God* "face-to-face," if only momentarily.[18] Berengaudus, for example, in his commentary on the Apocalypse, writes that, face-to-face with God at the revelation, John falls "down into himself because in comparison to God he easily perceives that he is tiny. He falls *as if dead* because in comparison to God he perceives that he is nothing."[19] This is the type of response typically attributed to figures privileged with a vision of God. Commentaries in the twelfth century indicate that others *may share in the visionary experience of John*. Moreover, they describe the way in which such accounts may serve as a medium for the experience but also caution about the limitation of that experience—which is primarily its brevity.

Richard of Saint Victor begins his commentary on John's revelation by asking how John "saw" the last things and answers with a description of his conception of fourfold vision, two levels of which are predominantly corporeal and two predominantly spiritual. Barbara Nolan summarizes Richard's description of the distinctions of these four modes in *The Gothic Visionary Perspective*:

> At the first level one merely opens his eyes to the exterior visible world. . . . The first "seeing" is corporeal, when we open our eyes to the exterior and the visible, . . . the figures and colors of visible things. [But it is] limited to the simple perception of matter, [unable]

---

[18]The discussion of these theological developments is largely drawn from Nolan, *Gothic Visionary Perspective*.

[19]Quoted in ibid., 12.

to penetrate the "occulta" (hidden). Hence, . . . it contains nothing of mystical significance. . . .

　　There is a second kind of corporeal vision of a higher order which does admit of mystical meanings. It also begins with an outward appearance or physical action, but the object perceived contains within it . . . great power of mystical significance.[20]

This would include events like Moses' vision of God in the burning bush or the identification of typological relationships between the Old and New Testaments such as Jonah's three days in the whale and Christ's three days in the grave. The third mode moves one to an internalized spiritual level, putting "the soul in touch with its end," where signs and symbols reveal "the truth of hidden things" in a more complex symbolic relationship that reveals theological truths. The fourth mode is almost entirely of the spirit. It is a visionary mode which allows for the "pure and naked seeing of divine reality."[21] According to Nolan,

　　Richard quotes Pseudo-Dionysius in order to differentiate between the third and fourth kinds of vision and he divides *anagogy* from *symbol* in the following way: "A symbol is a gathering . . . of visible forms for the demonstration of the invisible. Anagogy is the ascent or elevation of the mind for supernatural contemplation."[22]

Richard stops just short of claiming that John's *figural* revelation achieves this last mode here. However, Berengaudus's interpretation of John's initial collapse as described at the opening of the Apocalypse corresponds with Richard's description of the "pure and naked seeing of divine reality," the fourth anagogical level. Further investigation of Richard's thought indicates he believed that in the Sixth Age (which encompasses his time and ours) it is possible for the soul briefly and temporarily to achieve this mode, transcending the limitations of materiality to "see" God face-to-face.

　　In its essence, the anecdote that Viollet-le-Duc recounted regarding his boyhood experience of being overwhelmed by encountering the glory of the stained glass rose and the music of the organ at Notre Dame is precisely the kind of response one could expect of someone

[20]Ibid., 36.
[21]Ibid., 37.
[22]Ibid., 37.

encountering the fabric of the Gothic cathedral for the first time, as well as for those who engaged in the worship and other devotional practices designed for that place. By creating an overload of the senses that overwhelms and subverts their natural function of helping the human being negotiate the material world, the beholder is temporarily disassociated from the earthly, temporal realm. One is released, as it were, from a consciousness of time and space as they occur in everyday life and transported to another realm, the realm of divine reality.

An examination of the experience of the approach and entry into Chartres Cathedral demonstrates this process. From a great distance in the surrounding countryside, the pilgrim first receives a glimpse of a building of a scale that dwarfs all other structures in the city. As he draws closer, he sees that it is more magnificent than anything he would encounter in his everyday life outside of the city. As he enters the cathedral, he moves from the bright and lucid familiarity of the outside world through a narrow portal into a dark interior. Inside, it is refreshingly cool in summer and a respite from the bitter cold in winter. The deep blue and red tones that dominate the early Gothic stained glass at Chartres create a contrast so sharp that the pilgrim must halt, temporarily blinded. His sense of sight has ceased to orient him properly in space as he enters because he is in a space wholly unlike any other place in the world outside. As his eyes adjust to the dimness, he becomes aware of richly colored, glittering panels suspended, as it were, in mid-air. This progress from the bright clarity of the temporal world to the dark mystery of the sacred space effectively denies the materiality of the solid stone structure of the building, transporting him to a vision of the heavenly Jerusalem, which is described in the book of Revelation as having walls covered with jewels. In his article "Gothic Glass: Two Aspects of a Dionysian Aesthetic," John Gage convincingly argues that the dark colors of early Gothic stained glass like that at Chartres reflect the negative theology of Pseudo-Dionysius, which stands in stark contrast to the more commonly used metaphor of God as light. The Dionysian conception of God presents him as divine darkness whose presence can be made "visible" to man only through a passage into the light by which man is able to see.[23] Thus the darkly lit interior provides a glimpse of the presence of this divine darkness that is God. This

---

[23] John Gage, "Gothic Glass: Two Aspects of a Dionysian Aesthetic," *Art History* 5/1 (March 1982): 36–58.

experience is short-lived but thrusts one momentarily into the *aevum*, the "eternal time" of the visionary state. The tangible change of temperature from outside to inside this sacred precinct only contributes to the sensory stimuli that trigger this experience. The fact that the programs of most early Gothic stained glass panels read from the bottom to the top, which draws the beholders' eyes upward, only extends the anagogical experience originally conceptualized by Abbot Suger.[24]

Yet another key aspect of the experience of the Gothic cathedral is that of music. As Walford notes, "The majestic interior . . . [of the Gothic cathedral] provides a worthy setting and perfect acoustics for the Eucharist's liturgical celebration in word and music."[25] In his book *Philosophy of Art*, published in 1802–1803, Friedrich von Schelling famously stated, "Architecture is music in space, as it were a frozen music."[26] Architecture has long been recognized as sharing with music a mathematical structure. But beyond the mathematical structures that relate time and space there is a critical interdependence between music and architecture that binds them when they are brought together. Music is quite literally *shaped*, that is, it is enlarged or diminished by the specific nature of the structure and space within which it is performed. Conversely, the experience of the place—the architecture—is augmented or transformed by the sounds produced therein. Music performed in a Gothic cathedral reverberates throughout the space in such a way that the location of its source cannot easily be identified. This, in combination with the high-pitched, limited tonal range and repetitive structures of the chant, so commonly employed in worship and devotion throughout the Middle Ages, creates an ethereal, otherworldly quality. In this case, one's sense of hearing has been subverted, generating an aural experience wholly unlike other experiences of sound in the temporal world. Here, sound, which ordinarily helps us to orient ourselves in space, does not function as it should, due to

---

[24] This is especially true of the glass panels at Chartres, which exemplifies the experience of a twelfth-century French Gothic cathedral interior, because Chartres contains most of its original early Gothic glass. The residents of Chartres removed the panels and stored them in the cathedral's crypt during World War II to protect them from the bombing; unfortunately, the other major French Gothic cathedrals lost a great deal of their original glass during the war because they did not follow Chartres' example.

[25] Walford, *Great Themes in Art*, 167.

[26] This concept was popularized by the German writer Johann Wolfgang von Goethe when he used the phrase, "Architecture is like frozen music," in conversations with his personal secretary, Johann Peter Eckermann, recorded in *Conversations of Goethe with Johann Peter Eckermann* and published in 1836 (republished by Da Capo Press, 1998).

both the qualities of chant and its reverberations through the sacred space of the cathedral.

Music played a significant role in medieval thought regarding a multiplicity of concerns. Katharine LeMée writes, "In medieval times music theory informed not only musical performance, but also proportion in architecture and structure in society. It was also understood to regulate the health of the body and explain the very workings of the universe. . . . Music was the very essence of the nature of things and to sing was to align one's body with the laws of nature and one's mind and soul with the laws of God."[27] Gregorian chant, more specifically, has been shown to have qualities that stimulate our auditory sense in very particular ways.[28] Gregorian chant, which was sung not only in monastic communities as a spiritual discipline but also as part of the celebration of the mass in the great cathedrals, commonly employs melisma, the practice in which a single syllable of the text is held and sung over many notes. This often extends for such a prolonged time that the vocalists lose a conscious awareness of where they are in the lyrical content of the composition as well as of their sense of time and place. This is commonly described as an experience of sublime harmony and transcendent unity. It has also been demonstrated that both the frequencies of the voice spectrum employed in chant and the vocalizing of the vowel sounds that dominate the compositions have energizing qualities for the body that positively affect the vocalists' emotional state—widely identified as a peaceful and even euphoric spiritual experience.[29] Moreover, it is the form of the chant that ebbs and flows around a center at rest that helps create its otherworldly effect. By employing musical mirrors as the forward variant of the motive, followed by the reverse, the music maintains an overall quality of ultimate balance and dynamic equilibrium. These compositional elements, which frequently employ a limited tonal range and

---

[27] Katharine LeMée, *Chant: The Origins, Form, Practice, and Healing Power of Gregorian Chant* (New York: Random House, 1994), 21, 23.

[28] Gregorian chant is the central type of Western plainchant, a form of monophonic liturgical music. It is named after Pope Gregory I (590–604). For information on chant and Gregorian chant see: Willi Apel, *Gregorian Chant* (Bloomington: Indiana University Press, 1990); David Hiley, *Western Plainchant: A Handbook* (Oxford: Clarendon, 1995); and William P. Mahrt, "Gregorian Chant as a Paradigm of Sacred Music," *Sacred Music* 133/1 (2006): 5–14. For information on the performance of chant, see William P. Mahrt, "Chant," in *A Performer's Guide to Medieval Music*, ed. Ross Duffin (Bloomington: Indiana University Press, 2000), 1–22.

[29] LeMée describes these phenomena in some detail, in addition to recounting an interesting case study about the effects of eliminating the practice of chant on a French monastic community in the 1960s.

tonal center around which the other notes hover, allow for many variations with no clear climax or movement toward a conclusion and give the impression that it could continue "forever." In all of these ways, the chant performed in the Gothic cathedral contributes to the experience of transcendence, where one meets God face-to-face, an encounter that is often described in the theological writings of the Middle Ages.

The delicate soaring magnificence of the stone architecture that seems to deny its true weight, mass, and material substance, as well as the jeweled mysterious light of the interior are only two of the means by which the fabric of the Gothic cathedral exploits the experience of the beholder for its spiritual impact. The labyrinths embedded in the design of the floors of cathedrals at Chartres and Amiens (and many others no longer extant) signified "pilgrimage toward Jerusalem in this world and the road to Salvation in the next world." They are "a symbol of the Christian way," writes Jean Favier.[30] Although it is uncertain just when walking the labyrinth as a spiritual discipline began and whether it occurred during the Middle Ages, consideration of the practice reveals yet another means by which sensory experience commonly leads to an intense spiritual encounter. Labyrinths typically take the form of a circle or octagon and have a single opening along the outer perimeter, allowing the pilgrim to embark on the journey.[31] In a maze, which has many dead-ends and false passageways that confound and confuse one's progress, one may lose oneself, remaining indefinitely among the blocked passages searching for the way out. In contrast, a labyrinth has only one path that requires only focused concentration and persistence to reach one's goal. Whereas the goal of traversing a maze is to find the exit, the destination of the path of the labyrinth is the center, which represents the union with God at the end of one's temporal and spiritual journey. When walking the labyrinth, the pilgrim traverses a single narrow path that winds in and out, tracing hairpin turns barely wide enough for an individual person. Just remaining on the path requires a high degree of concentration. At times the trajectory of the pathway brings the pilgrim deceptively close to the cen-

---

[30] Jean Favier, *The World of Chartres* (New York: Harry N. Abrams, 1990), 26.
[31] For information on labyrinths: Penelope Reed Doob, *The Idea of the Labyrinth: From Classical Antiquity through the Middle Ages* (Ithaca, NY: Cornell University Press, 1992); and Hermann Kern, *Through the Labyrinth*, ed. Robert Ferré and Jeff Saward (New York: Prestel, 2000). For the practice of walking the labyrinth and its resurgence in recent times see Lauren Artress, *Walking the Sacred Path* (New York: Penguin, 2006).

ter only to frustrate him by turning him outward again, reflecting the realities of spiritual growth. These qualities create an experience that is nearly universally described by pilgrims as disorienting, causing a temporary loss of consciousness of the passage of time and movement through space. That this walk is frequently taken on one's knees on the cold hard stone floor requires the concentrated will of the practitioner to persist in his walk in spite of growing stiffness and intense pain from bruised and sometimes bloodied knees. This physical agony only increases the sense of disorientation by forcing attention away from that which is external to focus inward in the effort to persist.[32] Through this practice the senses have been subverted so that they no longer perform their temporal function as they would under normal conditions. Instead, they lift the pilgrim out of time so that he finds himself, after an unidentifiable period of time, miraculously at the center of the labyrinth, the goal of his walk, mysteriously at one with God. It cannot be coincidental that the size of the labyrinth at Chartres matches that of the great west rose, and that it was positioned in the nave so that, were the west façade folded down on top of it, the two would be perfectly aligned. Symbolically, the pilgrim at the center of the labyrinth meets the Christ of the Apocalypse depicted at the center of the rose, who displays his wounds as a sign of his sacrificial love of the believer.

Eriugena, the ninth-century Scottish theologian who advocated the Dionysian concept of negative analogies such as "divine darkness" for describing God, claimed that, because God is so wholly unlimited and therefore unlike anything human beings experience in their mundane temporal existence, metaphors such as frenzy, intoxication, and forgetfulness were more useful to grasp something of the true nature of God.[33] In many respects, the purpose of the Gothic cathedral, including its devotional practices, was to disconnect, one might even say to alienate, the beholder from the material world. As demonstrated by the examples discussed here, this commonly occurred by subverting the normative functioning of the senses, which were intended to orient the person effectively to his earthly environment, so that he might be

---

[32]There is an interesting correlation between the Christian devotional practice of walking the labyrinth and ascetic practices in other religions, such as Hinduism and Buddhism, that employ cyclical repetition and the deliberate inflicting of physical pain to simultaneously stimulate and focus the practitioner's mind and spirit by way of bodily experience.

[33]Cited in Gage, "Gothic Glass," 42.

transported, albeit momentarily, to divine reality. When one recalls biblical accounts of those who have seen God face-to-face—Moses, Paul, John—the encounters are always overwhelming and sometimes physically traumatic. This effectively reflects just how far removed human beings now are from the easy communion that Adam and Eve enjoyed with God in the cool of the garden as described in the book of Genesis.

In *A Secular Age*, Charles Taylor makes this important observation:

> There are certain works of art—by Dante, Bach, the makers of Chartres Cathedral: the list is endless—whose power seems inseparable from their epiphanic, transcendent reference. Here the challenge is to the unbeliever, to find a non-theistic register in which to respond to them, without impoverishment.[34]

It is certainly possible to respond to the aesthetic qualities of a cathedral like Chartres from a position of unbelief with powerful effect, as Viollet-le-Duc's boyhood encounter with Notre Dame attests. Nevertheless, the full significance of Chartres Cathedral, and sacred buildings like it that attempt to "express Christian faith in material form," can only be grasped from the vantage point of belief that interprets experience as a means of spiritual transformation. To attempt to make sense of such a place apart from this perspective is to miss something—the very thing which is most critical for grasping its ultimate purpose, which is to provide the believer with a glimpse of God so that he might be united with him.

---

[34] Charles Taylor, *A Secular Age* (Cambridge, MA: Harvard University Press, 2007), 607. I am indebted to Jeremy S. Begbie's review essay, "Pressing at the Boundaries of Modernity," *Christian Scholar's Review* 40/4 (Summer 2011): 465, for bringing this specific quote to my attention.

The Limbourg Brothers, *January*, page from *Les Très Riches Heures du Duc de Berry*. 1413–1416. Illumination on parchment. 9 1/2" x 6". Musée Condé, Chantilly. Photo: Réunion des Musées Nationaux, Paris/Art Resource, NY.

3

HEAVEN COME TO EARTH
The Limbourg Brothers' *January* (from *Les Très Riches Heures du Duc de Berry*)

MATTHEW SWEET VANDERPOEL

The fifteenth century was famously described as the "Waning of the Middle Ages" in the title of Johan Huizinga's 1924 study.[1] In his estimation, the fourteenth century saw Europe seized by pessimism. Papal schism, outbreaks of plague, and the political conflict of the Hundred Years' War all cast a long shadow. But Huizinga suggested that as people saw this entropy all around them, they cultivated a decadent, opulent culture as counterpoint. Their spectacular art, in literary and visual media, was an example of "the decay of overripe forms of civilization."[2] While Huizinga's generally negative tone has come under criticism,[3] the period was certainly one of upheaval and uncertainty.

---

[1] Johan Huizinga, *The Waning of the Middle Ages: A Study of the Forms of Life, Thought and Art in France and in the Netherlands in the XIVth and XVth Centuries*, trans. Frederik Jan Hopman (London: Doubleday, 1924). Gail McMurray Gibson explains the original translation of the title into English: "Although Huizinga himself named the book the 'Herfsttij' or 'harvest-tide' of the Middle Ages, the English word 'waning' more accurately reflects Huizinga's point of view toward the times" (*The Theater of Devotion: East Anglian Drama and Society in the Late Middle Ages* [Chicago: University of Chicago Press, 1989], 4). A newer translation of Huizinga's work opts instead for a more neutral connotation: *The Autumn of the Middle Ages*, trans. Rodney J. Payton and Ulrich Mammitzsch (Chicago: University of Chicago Press, 1996).
[2] Huizinga, *Waning of the Middle Ages*, v.
[3] Most critics suggest that Huizinga insufficiently accounts for the ways in which late medieval cultural forms were constructively navigating new contexts in ways that would continue to impact early modern Europe. See Michael Camille, "Visionary Perception and Images of the Apocalypse," in *The Apocalypse in the Middle Ages*, ed. Richard Kenneth Emerson and Bernard McGinn (Ithaca, NY: Cornell University Press, 1992), 281: "[Huizinga's] notion of the superfluity and decadence of late medieval religious imagery needs questioning. Emphasis should instead be placed on the constant effort by artists to rethink and clarify earlier medieval models in the light of new spiritual trends." See also Heiko Oberman, *The Harvest of Medieval Theology* (Grand Rapids, MI: Baker, 2000), 5: "Deeply indebted as we are to Johan Huizinga's *The Waning of the Middle Ages*, the image of 'harvest' in our title is intentionally opposed to the connotation of 'decline' carried by the French and English translations of the Dutch 'Herfsttij,' which literally means 'harvest-tide.'"

Yet in this context, innovation also thrived. Politically, monarchs pursued more centralized governance. Economically, in the Low Countries particularly, a new market economy was helping to grow a new middle class. Theologically, lay piety movements were flourishing, and some, such as the Hussites of Bohemia, were distancing themselves from the Catholic Church. Artistically, the fifteenth century marks the emergence of the Northern Renaissance. This new approach to art moved away from the abstracted settings and forms of medieval art toward an increasingly naturalistic style of depiction. Instead of the transcendent space of most medieval religious art, Northern Renaissance art chose to incorporate religious iconography into the setting of everyday life. This effectively challenged the distinction between religious meaning and mundane life which was assumed in the medieval period. This new world, in all of its complexity, is on lavish display in illuminated manuscripts such as *Les Très Riches Heures* ("The Very Rich Hours") (1413–1416), illustrated by Herman, Paul, and Johan Limbourg (1370/1380–1416).

Works of art, such as the *Les Très Riches Heures*, provide a unique medium of perception into the beliefs of the artist, the patron, and the broader society. One specific image, *January*, from the calendar cycle of the Limbourg brothers' illuminated manuscript, *Les Très Riches Heures*, illustrates a ducal feast. This image is a display of royal magnificence and an apology for the nobility's status amid the social changes around them. However, the method by which the artists, under their patron's supervision, painted this banquet reveals underlying ideas about the nobility and their place in society. By carefully viewing *January*, and trying to understand the conceptual structure that underlies the artistic composition, this claim to noble privilege can be interpreted as part of a larger belief about God's ordering of the universe. This arrangement of meaning in the image shows their patron, Jean of France, as an almost divine mediator of otherworldly blessing.

Herman, Paul, and Johan Limbourg were brothers who were active artists for French royalty from 1402 until their death in 1416.[4] The Limbourg brothers worked primarily on illuminated manuscripts, providing images to accompany the text of a given book. They were the

---

[4]Although records attest to there being five Limbourg brothers, the appellation refers to the eldest three.

nephews of Johan Maelwael, a painter who became the court artist for Philip the Bold, Duke of Burgundy. Herman and Johan became apprentices to a goldsmith in Paris, while Paul stayed in Nijmegen where he also was apprenticed to a goldsmith.[5] Likely on account of their uncle, Paul and Johan were employed by Philip the Bold to illuminate a Bible. After Philip the Bold's death, the Limbourg brothers came to work for John of France, Duke of Berry, from 1404 until their death in 1416. The brothers likely died of plague, with their magnum opus, *Les Très Riches Heures*, left unfinished.[6]

Les Très Riches Heures was an illuminated book of hours, executed for Jean of France, Duke of Berry, an uncle of Charles VI, then king of France. The Limbourg Brothers had earlier done another book of hours for the same patron, known as the *Belles Heures* (Beautiful Hours), in the years 1405–1408/1409. Perhaps owing to their success in that work, they were again commissioned by Jean of France to produce another book of hours—what would become *Les Très Riches Heures*—in 1413.

A book of hours, one of the most popular forms of devotional art in the fifteenth century, was a collection of prayers to be said at different hours of the day or, often, according to times of year or certain events. In France, most contained "the Hours of the Virgin, the seven penitential psalms, and the Office of the Dead,"[7] but they could vary widely in other regards. They provided an ideal medium for patrons to convey their wealth, in terms of the great cost in commissioning an illuminated manuscript; their Christian faith, by the devotional nature of a book of hours; and their own personal concerns, because of the flexible arrangement of prayers and events within the book.[8]

As a book of hours, the *Très Riches Heures* is primarily a devotional book. The tradition of the book of hours goes back to the medieval psalters, books containing the text of the Psalms for use in individual prayer. Around the eleventh century, psalter books began to vary from the strict biblical text, often including prayers purposed for a specific

---

[5] Gerard Nijsten, *In the Shadow of Burgundy: The Court of Guelders in the Late Middle Ages* (Cambridge: Cambridge University Press, 2004), 261.

[6] Timothy B. Husband, *The Art of Illumination: The Limbourg Brothers and the* Belles Heures *of Jean de France, Duc de Berry* (New Haven, CT: Yale University Press, 2008), 34–35.

[7] Ibid., 25.

[8] For instance, Jean of France began including images of himself and his retinue departing for a journey in later books of hours that he commissioned. This is likely the result of the murder of his brother, Louis, Duke of Orléans, while setting out on a trip (ibid., 27).

devotion (e.g., to the Virgin).[9] Books of hours were a development of this genre. They reduced the quantity of text and allowed a great deal of flexibility as to which prayers would be included. Also, they often included full images rather than the simple illuminated letters that predominate within traditional psalters.[10] A book of hours thus structured devotional material in a profoundly new way: images became the key navigational aid.

For instance, in the *Très Riches Heures*, the small image that accompanies each psalm or canticle would also have functioned as a title. The reader could browse the book, and by reference to the pictures choose a prayer to contemplate.[11] Furthermore, the images also allude to doctrines, liturgical events, and even the emotions that one ought to bear in mind when reading the accompanying text.[12] This late medieval devotional practice marks the emergence of a new form of spiritual perception: visual material has become essential to ordering and interpreting the textual material hitherto emphasized in medieval Christian devotion.

The *Très Riches Heures* expands this new perceptive structuring through the lavish illumination of a full calendar cycle. While this is not surprising—the overarching structure of most books of hours was the church calendar—[13] the *Très Riches Heures* breaks from tradition by giving each month's illumination a full page, rather than the typical small calendar scene at the top of the page with zodiacal signs fitting in the margins.[14] Often these zodiacal calendars would be less prominent than the religious images, but within this book of hours they are clearly the primary illuminations. Thus, it is these images that are meant to orient the reader for how to understand the entire book.

The centrality of the calendar ties the scenes of courtly and rural life shown therein to the liturgical calendar that structures the religious life of the church. From the outset of the *Très Riches Heures*, a mode of perception is signaled that relies on comparisons: the juxtaposition of

---

[9] Anne Rudloff Stanton, *The Queen Mary Psalter: A Study of Affect and Audience* (Philadelphia: American Philosophical Society, 2001), 65.
[10] Ibid., 67.
[11] Margaret M. Manion, "Psalter Illustration in the Très Riches Heures of Jean de Berry," *Gesta* 34/2 (1995): 156.
[12] Ibid., 157.
[13] E. John Walford, *Great Themes in Art* (Upper Saddle River, NJ: Prentice-Hall, 2002), 180.
[14] Jonathan Alexander, "Labour and Paresse: Ideological Representations of Medieval Peasant Labor," *The Art Bulletin* 72/3 (September 1990): 438.

apparently dissimilar things is generally an indication of some perceived commonality. Moreover, the calendar cycle indicates the growing practice, particularly within Northern Renaissance art, of integrating religious meaning and settings taken from everyday life. These two tendencies are not exclusive, but rather they frequently cooperate, framing theological issues such that they speak to the immediate context.

Although the Limbourg brothers were unable to complete the *Très Riches Heures*, their hand has been consistently identified in the *January* scene and most of the calendar cycle as a whole. While there is less certainty about which brother executed *January*, Edmond Pognon identified stylistic similarities among the courtly scenes throughout the *Très Riches Heures* which differed from the rural scenes.[15] Paul seems to have been the favorite of Jean of France, attested to by his receipt of extravagant gifts from Jean such as a golden ring with an emerald, two diamond rings, and even a large home in Bourges.[16] Therefore, he was most likely involved in an important scene of the duke himself, such as *January*. Nevertheless, medieval art was often a communal process performed by many craftsmen in a workshop; trying to exclusively identify only an individual with an entire page of illuminated manuscript is probably imprudent. Regardless of the impossibility of precise attribution, it is clear that the Limbourg brothers enjoyed great privilege at the court of Jean of France. Given this special position, they were exceptionally situated to illustrate the duke's sumptuous wealth in *January*.

The miniature of *January* presents the viewer with a colorful scene: the celebration of the New Year's feast in Jean, the Duke of Berry's palace. Showing the duke surrounded by golden vessels, well-dressed courtiers, and vivid tapestries, the image is most visibly a celebration of courtly wealth. Yet the image is not just any feast of the nobility but rather is remarkable in its specificity. The scene is dominated by the commanding figure of the duke himself, in a blue and gold robe, seated on the right of the image. His identity is clear: pairings of the swan and the bear—his chosen emblems—adorn both the canopy over his seat and the golden saltcellar on the table before

---

[15] Edmond Pognon, Pol de Limbourg, and Jean Colombe, *Les Très Riches Heures du Duc de Berry* (Geneva: Liber, 1987), 12–13.
[16] Husband, *Art of Illumination*, 34–35.

him.[17] Moreover, the miniature presents a clear portrait of the duke's distinctive facial features, well illustrated in numerous other portraits of Jean of France.[18] The representation of other figures in the image is so detailed that, since the emergence of scholarship on the *Très Riches Heures*, scholars have endeavored to identify numerous other portraits.[19] The lifelikeness of the individuals, the precise heraldic imagery, and even the particular association of New Year's celebrations with the French royal family all underscore an almost documentary interpretation of a certain event.

Nonetheless, other elements in the image complement this specificity by referencing broader themes. Most apparent is the zodiacal calendar above the main scene. The stars bring the heavens into the viewer's mind. What results is a geographic displacement from the main scene; the image refers to both a French royal palace and the heavens. Furthermore, the fine tapestry that hangs across the back of the hall depicts the conflict of the Trojan War.[20] Here, there is a temporal displacement, as the feasting of the duke and his entourage is spatially abutted by the long-past exploits of classical heroes. These displacements indicate a degree of universality within the image, as the ducal feast extends across other spaces and times.

This layering of disparate settings—cosmic space, long-past battlefield, and a courtly celebration—would not have been jarring to a fifteenth-century viewer. Instead it would have provided a structure for looking at the image by indicating the associations that the artist and patron had in mind concerning the subject matter. For a modern viewer, accounting for this structure and the details included therein allows a glimpse of a late medieval perception of noble authority. To elucidate this mode of viewing *January* from the *Très Riches Heures*, this essay will first consider the immediate depiction of Jean of Berry's banquet as an assertion of his noble authority. Second, it will consider the tapestry of the Trojan War as a complementary way of formulating the same meaning. Third, an analysis of the zodiacal calendar will provide another analogous source of meaning. Finally, these cooperative mean-

---

[17]Rob Dückers and Pieter Roelofs, *The Limbourg Brothers: Reflections on the Origins and the Legacy of Three Illuminators from Nijmegen* (Boston: Brill, 2009), 52.
[18]Husband, *Art of Illumination*, 26.
[19]Dückers and Roelofs, *Limbourg Brothers*, 54.
[20]Walford, *Great Themes in Art*, 180.

ings will be related to each other as part of a comprehensive apology for royal power that postures Jean of France as a conduit of heavenly goods to his subjects.

The ducal feast of *January* is a dazzling arrangement of vibrant costumes and glittering goldenware. Fine cloth, in terms of both dress and the tapestry, abounds in the scene. Even the courtiers occupied with simple tasks such as carving the meat and pouring the wine are clothed in colorful garments with complex patterning and trims. In medieval society, clothing and appearance were essential to showing occupation and status. Also, at this time, nobles in France were known for embroidering political sentiments into their clothes to designate their loyalties.[21] Wearing clothing unfitting for one's station was considered not just a faux pas but even a moral transgression, according to sermon literature from the period.[22]

Bearing distinctive robes and the tonsure is the member of the clergy (possibly a bishop)[23] seated at the table with the duke himself. While both figures mirror each other in their general positioning, a couple of contrasts demarcate the two individuals. First, the blue of the ducal robes is echoed far more frequently throughout the image than the red and white of the bishop. Second, the resolute profile of Jean of France, coupled with his fine hat, strikes a contrast with not only the bishop's tonsure but also his obeisant tilting of the head. Throughout the Middle Ages, the relationships between the church and political leaders were complex: while both recognized the authority of the other, they also frequently tried to demonstrate primacy. However at the time of *January*'s execution the Catholic church was embroiled in the Great Schism, a dispute among multiple claimants to the papacy—including one in Avignon, France, largely perceived to be a puppet of the French monarchy. Thus, the bishop's submissive posture asserts Jean of France's preeminence even over the church.[24]

This main banquet scene, a feast showing the consummate wealth

---

[21] Margaret Scott, *Medieval Clothing and Costumes: Displaying Wealth and Status in Medieval Times* (New York: Rosen, 2004) 35.

[22] Alexander, "Labour and Paresse," 445.

[23] This figure has been identified as the bishop of Chartres, Martin Gouge, but even if one is hesitant to suggest that the figures all represent specific persons of the court, it is likely that only a bishop would have the influence to be seated in such an honorable position beside Jean of France.

[24] If this identification is correct, the cleric's subordinate posture in the image would be reinforced by historical fact: Martin Gouge held political offices within Jean of France's court (see Dückers and Roelofs, *Limbourg Brothers*, 54).

of Jean of France, is a doubly arranged display of wealth. In the first instance, the feast itself would have been a carefully choreographed chance to show off wealth and power, and thus "appeal to the loyalty of [one's] followers."[25] The New Year's feast would have been a performance, a work of art in its own right. By transcribing such an event into an illuminated manuscript, a second instance of arrangement occurs. Depicting the feast allows greater flexibility in controlling the associations one makes with the banquet scene. The Limbourg brothers are able to tie in the tapestry with the main scene by careful use of repeated colors, and they are able to introduce the larger motif of the zodiacal calendar that overarches the whole piece. This doubly arranged display is thus not a simple snapshot of royal life. Instead, the viewer should be alert to resonances and nuances throughout the rest of *January*.

The tapestry along the back of the hall, illustrating the Trojan War, further declares royal privilege. To a large degree, this results from the medieval nobility's self-identification with the heroes of classical epics. The dukes of Brittany, a semi-autonomous region in the northwest of France, had appealed to the *Historia Regum Britanniae* to demonstrate their claim to royal rights. This account of the Bretons' ancestry argues that these dukes were actually the continuing dynasty of the Trojan royalty.[26] Later, Philip the Good of Burgundy, a duchy within France, created the Order of the Golden Fleece, a group of knights and nobles. One of the patrons was Jason, from the *Argonautica*, another classical hero. This order carried great prestige by showing its members' commonality with an ancient warrior.[27] Tapestries were commissioned to commemorate this order. This "portable propaganda" traveled with Philip the Good wherever he held court.[28]

Importantly, the knights riding into battle within the tapestry appear decidedly medieval. They fight between two northern European castles. They sport bright colors and even the heraldry of specific medieval royal houses. Thus, while the inscription alerts the viewer that it is, in fact, the Trojan War being shown, it would be equally clear to a con-

---

[25] Walford, *Great Themes in Art*, 179.
[26] Patrick Galliou and Michael Jones, *The Bretons* (Cambridge: Blackwell, 1991), 233.
[27] Richard Vaughan, *Philip the Good* (New York: Barnes & Noble, 1970), 161.
[28] Jeffrey Chipps Smith, "Portable Propaganda—Tapestries as Princely Metaphors at the Courts of Philip the Good and Charles the Bold," *Art Journal* 48/2 (Summer 1989): 123–129.

temporary viewer that it also represents the Hundred Years' War. The *Très Riches Heures*, made during the low point of France's power during the war, suggests that regardless of the course of the war, France's participation marked them to be the true comrades of those classical heroes in Homer's *Iliad*.

Furthermore, some elements in the main scene space establish greater continuity between the tapestry and the courtly action. Two courtiers in the foreground are conspicuous both for their spurs and for the prominent phallic objects they sport. Michael Camille has convincingly demonstrated the sexual overtones of these courtiers, most especially due to cupbearers' association with Ganymede, who served Jupiter drink during the day and more intimately at night.[29] In some ways, then, the masculine combat of the tapestry is paralleled in the sexual back and forth of the banquet. Jean of France's courtly activities become a sort of domestic parallel to the heroic exploits of the Trojan and Hundred Years' Wars.

So far, the temporal displacement between the antiquity of the tapestry and the fifteenth-century feast has been identified. Rather than a clear division, though, these two different eras are blurred both by the tapestry's medieval setting and by its continuity with the foreground scene. The Limbourg brothers' perception is of such a quality that it identifies and links similarities across time. So, although the portrait is of a particular noble, Jean of France, Duke of Berry, he is seen as inextricably bound to a noble class that persists throughout history, a noble class with a special capacity for heroism.

Finally, the zodiacal calendar shows the beginning of the New Year, as the constellation Capricorn gives way to Aquarius. Poised within this ring of the stars is Apollo, the god of the sun, riding his chariot across the heavens. The concentric semi-circles of the calendar indicate its cosmological structure. Late medieval cosmology was indebted to Ptolemy and Aristotle. In this understanding, the earth was the center of the universe. Radiating out from it was a series of rings within which spheres (e.g., the moon, the sun, a planet) revolved. Ultimately, the Trinity was postulated to reside beyond all such spheres. Yet, to the

---

[29] Michael Camille, "'For Our Devotion and Pleasure': The Sexual Objects of Jean, Duc de Berry," in *Other Objects of Desire: Collectors and Collecting Queerly*, ed. Michael Camille and Adrian Rifkin (Malden, MA: Wiley-Blackwell, 2001), 7–32.

medieval mind, this cosmology reflected the arrangement of things on earth as well: "Society's concept of the origin, structure, and operation of the world was drawn almost exclusively from the Aristotelian-Ptolemaic astronomical and cosmological tradition."[30] The *January* page of the *Très Riches Heures* visually describes a universe in which heaven and earth are structurally and inseparably linked.

The connection between cosmology and people's everyday life was strengthened by the widespread belief in, and application of, astrology. Just as the arrangement of the heavenly bodies exerted influences on weather (e.g., the position of the sun governs the seasons), it was thought that the heavenly bodies also affected other earthly affairs. Medically, certain body parts were believed to be especially attuned to different zodiacal constellations (a diagram mapping constellations onto different body parts of a person appears elsewhere in the *Très Riches Heures*). Surgeons often took care to treat certain organs only under auspicious celestial arrangements.[31] Generally, astrology was predicated upon the belief in affinities between what was in the heavens and what was on earth.

These affinities could be grouped under the larger medieval heading of similitude, a relationship between two objects on the basis of a resemblance. Many iconographic associations in artwork, such as the pelican's allusion to Christ, were grounded in perceived similitudes. In this case, the pelican's alleged wounding of itself was to nourish its children. Structurally, similitude was arranged within the categories of microcosm and macrocosm. Because of the potential infinity of resemblances between objects, the microcosm was used as a limiting space for identifying these resemblances.[32] Augustine had identified the human person's rational mind as a microcosm of the Trinity itself: "A human being is an important kind of thing, being made 'in the image and likeness of God' not by virtue of having a mortal body but by virtue of having a rational soul and thus a higher status than animals."[33] Such identifications between the terrestrial and the celestial abounded throughout the Middle Ages.

---

[30] Edward Grant, *Planets, Stars, and Orbs: The Medieval Cosmos, 1200–1687* (Cambridge: Cambridge University Press, 1996), 59.

[31] Richard Kieckhefer, *Magic in the Middle Ages* (Cambridge: Cambridge University Press, 2000), 122.

[32] Michel Foucault, *The Order of Things: An Archaeology of Knowledge* (New York: Vintage, 1970), 31.

[33] Augustine, *De doctrina Christiana* (Oxford: Oxford University Press, 1995), 1.39.

Given such beliefs, likenesses between the calendar and the rest of this book of hours should be looked for. The image of Aquarius, at the top right set against a vibrant blue and gold backdrop, is mirrored in the cupbearer at the bottom left. The inclination of the cupbearer's head follows the angle of the constellation, and his blue robes with gold trim recall the backdrop of the stars. This resemblance, however, is more than visible, as Aquarius, the water bearer, was synonymous with Ganymede, the cupbearer, during the medieval period.[34] Their resemblance within the miniature indicates the artist's acute awareness of cosmic similitude.

The chariot of Apollo, in the center of the calendar, is visually dominated by the bright glowing sun, which radiates light out from it. Apollo had been, since at least the second century of the Common Era, associated with Christ. For instance, Clement of Alexandria stressed the parallels between Apollo's defeat of the dragon, Python, and Christ's victory over the serpent.[35] The similitude between divinity and light also had a firm scriptural basis. James 1:17 reads, "Every good gift and every perfect gift is from above, coming down from the Father of lights." Analogous to the way the sun gives off rays of light, God bestows gifts.

Although the golden rays of the sun in this piece visually interact with the golden implements and decoration throughout the banquet hall, the circular form of the sun is magnified in the fire screen resting behind Jean of France's head. Just as the rays are a series of lines radiating out from the sun in the calendrical image, the artist has carefully composed the feast scene in such a way that the duke's face, framed by the halo of the fire screen, becomes the focal point of numerous lines. For instance, the heads of the two attendants to the right of the fire screen are collinear with that of the duke. The plates laid out in front of the duke similarly are arranged as two lines coming out from him. The red canopy runs downward, through the rod, and directly to the duke. Even the arrangement of the various courtiers on the left forms a number of lines back to the figure of the duke, either by their positions or by their gazes. The artist has portrayed the entire feast as the literal radiance of Jean, Duke of Berry.

---

[34] Camille, "'For Our Devotion and Pleasure,'" 15.
[35] Jamie C. Fumo, *The Legacy of Apollo: Antiquity, Authority, and Chaucerian Poetics* (Toronto: University of Toronto Press, 2010), 82.

The lord was seen as the pinnacle of the medieval social hierarchy. Medieval Europe saw the ideal society as made up of three "estates": the clergy, the nobility, and laborers. The clergy were believed to safeguard society spiritually, and the nobility were expected to defend it physically. Laborers, both peasants and those in the small middle class, simply worked. Due to the nobility's incredibly disproportionate control of land and wealth, resources did tend to flow from them to the rest of the population. These somewhat static relationships began to rupture in the fourteenth century. The Black Death killed a huge portion of the population, sending peasants' wages soaring. Concomitantly, a lower population meant less demand, and less profit, for nobles selling their harvests. A growing middle class in urban centers also created new space outside of the lord's purview. While the lord may have been at the top of society, the late medieval period saw it become an increasingly uncertain position.

January, and indeed all of *Très Riches Heures*, does not show any reticence in asserting Jean of France's authority. In *Great Themes in Art*, John Walford rightly describes the *January* page as a "feudal display" of wealth,[36] but it also acts as a normative description of the ideal lord. There is no evidence of peasants' unrest or the lord's financial instability; on the contrary, *January* projects the duke as possessing and controlling all things. Numerous well-dressed individuals, including nobles and a member of the clergy, are crowded around the duke. In later months of the calendar cycle, peasants are frequently shown laboring in the shadow of one of the duke's various castles. Just as the sun radiates light, Jean of France radiates power—power over both material and human objects. Likely, the recurrence of Apollo's chariot in each month of the calendar indicates the continuing place of Jean of France as the authority in the pictorial space.

Here, the visual apology of ducal power comes to a head. Jean of France's innumerable *joyaux* throughout the main scene refute any notion of economic weakness. The crowd of individuals warming themselves at the fire—which pictorially becomes a sort of halo of the duke himself—reveals an ambiguous sense of dependence. There is a blurring of the line between the duke and fire, signaled by the unusual location of the chamberlain, who directs access to both. The duke is

---

[36]Walford, *Great Themes in Art*, 179.

a metaphorical fire in the midwinter: a source of life to those close to him. This is again echoed by the duke's large table, offering food for all at the banquet. Visually, the guests bleed into the space of the tapestry. Furthermore, Apollo, whose sun bears such visual parallels to the duke before the fire screen, rides across the heavens in each of the calendar miniatures in *Très Riches Heures*. Analogously, Jean of France's power is carried across all those different locations and months. Effectively, Jean of France is depicted as the nexus of power, not bound by space, time, or the activities of his peasants. His radiant position is shown to be as salutary, and as inevitable, as that of the sun.

By means of the clever overlay of the New Year's celebration, a tapestried image of the Trojan War, and a zodiacal calendar, the Limbourg brothers are able to celebrate the specific aristocratic lifestyle of Jean of France while appealing to a universal order to reinforce this practice. The artwork is doubly arranged; in the first place the duke reveals his own self-image, and in the second his self-image is linked to a far broader perception, that of the entire cosmos. Just as God is the ruler and provider of—both cosmologically and authoritatively—creation, so is the sun of the earth. And just as the sun governs the earth, so does the duke the rest of society.

The ideological aim of the calendar cycle as a statement of the rightness of noble luxury and the peasant labor supporting it is apparent enough. Nevertheless, what *January* illustrates is the extent to which this social logic was predicated upon a certain metaphysical understanding of the world. While the extravagant wealth carefully displayed at a midwinter's feast shows an economic claim to noble privilege (i.e., the resources to maintain noble privilege), the further translation of the duke's self-image onto the manuscript page witnesses an influx of more ambitious defenses of noble authority. The temporal displacement introduced by the tapestry offers a historical claim, which cleverly transmutes the chaos of the Hundred Years' War into a sign of Jean of France's mythic pedigree. The geographic displacement, signaled in the calendar's transcendence of earthly space, puts forward a cosmological, even theological, account of the privilege given to royalty as the source of good for their subjects.

These complementary apologies for the duke's status show the way in which similitude offered a creative intellectual space. Perception, as practiced by the Limbourg brothers in *January*, structures the resemblances among the various pictorial elements in order to construct coherent meaning. Although *January*'s careful composition shows it not to be a documentary account of late medieval courtly life, neither is it a simple piece of classist propaganda. Instead, it reveals the complexity with which the late medieval court tried to answer fundamental questions about its wealth, authority, and importance.

Given the abundance of gold and precious materials, the celestial canopy of the heavens, the similitude between the duke and God's authority, and the setting of a feast, the duke is no longer just a noble. The vivifying warmth, radiating from his halo, and the nourishment of the banquet underscore his role in sustaining all that is around him. Because of Jean of France's appeal to the theological, he has been transformed into a Christ-figure, complete with a cross formed by the intersection of canopy and rod with the molding above his head. The duke now mediates blessings to his retinue, and the feast seems less and less to be a simple New Year's celebration in fifteenth-century France. Rather, the duke, triumphantly presiding over the whole scene, now ushers in a feast that looks ahead to that in the heavenly Jerusalem. By an expert pairing of formal and iconographic elements, *January* asserts a duke whose power is such that he blurs the boundary between divine and profane and heralds the joys of heaven in his own royal celebrations.

Masolino and Masaccio, and Filippino Lippi, *The Brancacci Chapel*. Santa Maria del Carmine, Florence (15th c.). Photo: The Bridgeman Art Library.

4

ACADEMIA'S "RELIGIOUS TURN"
The Brancacci Chapel

MATTHEW MILLINER

In his profoundly influential *Lectures on Fine Art*, the nineteenth-century philosopher G. W. F. Hegel complained about the aesthetic demerits of icons: "A man's attitude to [miracle working pictures] as to something stupendous is stupid, indifferent to their character as art; . . . those that are given the greatest religious veneration are, from the point of view of art, the very worst of all."[1] Similarly, the contemporary art historian James Elkins, a cartographer of the discipline, describes entering an Italian church to see canonized Renaissance frescoes, where he encountered a plastic baby-doll Jesus wrapped in Christmas lights being venerated instead. Strangely enough, however, Elkins's complaint is the opposite of Hegel's: "How can I begin to understand the people who would rather worship a novelty light? What do they see? And for my part, could I ever worship the painting? And what do I fail to see when I lecture about the masterpiece as an example of the art of painting?"[2] Elkins's interrogations center on the limitations of his discipline: "In the art historical textbooks that discuss this church, there is no mention of the plastic Jesus, and I doubt there are any books on it except perhaps some tongue-in-cheek study of postmodern culture."[3] These two observations, from Hegel and Elkins, illustrate the recent dilation of the history of art. Whereas once art historians focused exclusively on paintings worthy of the label "art," scholars today are as likely to include anything that falls under the rubric of visual culture,

---

[1] G. W. F. Hegel, *Aesthetics: Lectures on Fine Art*, trans. T. M. Knox, 2 vols. (Oxford: Oxford University Press, 1988), 2:851. Hegel's ideal is not necessarily secular—on the contrary, his ideal in painting is an illusionistic Madonna and Child in the style of Raphael. His remark is based on the notion that illusionistic rendering, which traditional icons fail to offer, is the unique gift of painting. See Stephen Houlgate, "Hegel and the Art of Painting" in *Hegel and Aesthetics*, ed. William Maker (Albany: SUNY Press, 2000).
[2] James Elkins, *The Object Stares Back: On the Nature of Seeing* (Orlando: Houghton Mifflin Harcourt, 1997), 40.
[3] Ibid.

especially when religious in nature. This has everything to do, I believe, with what has been called academia's "religious turn."[4]

With this broadening in mind, this essay turns to Florence's famous Brancacci Chapel, located in the "Oltrarno" (beyond the Arno River) district of Florence. The Brancacci family of clothing merchants had been worshiping in the Santa Maria del Carmine, a church of the Carmelite Order, since its foundation in 1268.[5] The Brancacci Chapel, connected to that earlier church, was built by the Brancacci family in the late fourteenth century and decorated around 1425, chiefly by famed Renaissance artists Masolino and Masaccio (as well as later portions by Filippino Lippi).[6] The chief patron was the colorful figure Felice di Michele Brancacci, an adventurer of sorts with knightly aspirations, though also a man of serious personal faith.[7] The themes of the frescoes, which center on Saint Peter, are drawn chiefly from the Bible and *The Golden Legend*, resonating with Florence's Guelf tradition, which favored the papacy.[8] The innovative naturalism of the scenes, especially those of Masaccio, reflects the gritty details of Florentine urban life, and they "are universally recognized as the first mature example of early-Renaissance Italian painting and as a turning point in the history of western art."[9] The frescoes have generated a staggering amount of art historical commentary, much of it centered on distinguishing which artist painted which scene. However, the focus of the chapel, both visually and spiritually, is not the frescoes but the miraculous image of *Madonna del Popolo*, "Madonna of the people,"[10] which preceded the chapel and was later placed centrally within it.

---

[4] Perhaps the most oft-quoted remark in this respect comes from Stanley Fish: "When Jacques Derrida died I was called by a reporter who wanted to know what would succeed high theory and the triumvirate of race, gender, and class as the center of intellectual energy in the academy. I answered like a shot: religion. . . . Announce a course with 'religion' in the title, and you will have an overflow population. Announce a lecture or panel on 'religion in our time' and you will have to hire a larger hall" (Stanley Fish, "One University Under God?" *Chronicle of Higher Education*, January 7, 2005).

[5] Diane Cole Ahl, "Masaccio in the Brancacci Chapel," in *The Cambridge Companion to Masaccio*, ed. Diane Cole Ahl (Cambridge: Cambridge University Press, 2002), 143.

[6] Carl Brandon Strehlke, "The Brancacci Style and the Carmine Style," in *The Brancacci Chapel: Form, Function, and Setting*, ed. Nicholas A. Eckstein (Florence: Leo S. Olschki, 2005), 89. Masolino began the frescoes, and Masaccio probably took over when Masolino left Florence for another commission. Masaccio did not complete the frescoes either, but they were completed by Lippi in the 1480s.

[7] Dale Kent, "The Brancacci Chapel Viewed in the Context of Florence's Culture of Artistic Patronage," in *Brancacci Chapel: Form, Function, and Setting*, 53–71.

[8] Ibid., 54.

[9] Nicholas A. Eckstein, "The Brancacci Chapel: New Questions, Hypotheses and Interpretations," in *Brancacci Chapel: Form, Function, and Setting*, 1.

[10] There are other icons that have been given this title as well, such as the *Maria del Popolo* image in the Augustinian Church of *Santa Maria del Popolo* in Rome.

"[Icons] played a catalyzing role in the development of Renaissance art," explain Alexander Nagel and Christopher Wood, "and yet the importation of the icons has never been fully integrated into accounts of the art of this period."[11]

Such an integration, however, is finally occurring. The individual genius of Renaissance artists and the birth of perspective are no longer art history's overriding concerns. Instead, attention has shifted to the *Madonna del Popolo* icon and the religious motivations of the Carmelite Order in commissioning the frescoes. This essay will survey art historical commentary on the Brancacci Chapel to trace how this shift came about. The tradition of writing on the chapel illustrates how an excess of art historical verbiage can, and has, led to versions of postmodern academic despair. And yet, the latest spurt of research on the Brancacci Chapel illustrates less a crisis of art historical purpose than a vindication of the discipline's traditional scholarly methods. Serious archival research has uncovered new information, permitting a fresh reading of the chapel that highlights its surprising theological depths.

According to Elkins, the cumulative force of generations of Renaissance art history makes research in this area comparable to walking on Jupiter, where oppressive gravity makes each step laborious—as opposed, for example, to the contemporary art historian's graceful bounds on the moon.[12] One can sympathize, therefore, with another scholar's observation: "Is it ever possible to see the picture itself, or read the text, without needing or wanting to take account of the mass of accumulated earlier commentaries?"[13] But one advantage to examining past commentary, perhaps especially when considering a subject as studied as the Brancacci Chapel, is that we learn as much about art history as about the chapel itself. The "lush historiography"[14] of the Brancacci Chapel frescoes has itself been characterized as a work of art, "a picture that slowly grows under the hand of generations

[11] Alexander Nagel and Christopher S. Wood, *Anachronic Renaissance* (New York: Zone, 2010), 105. Wood and Nagel see icons as "comparable to the role played by the Greek texts in the development of Renaissance literature and scholarship . . ." (ibid.). But whereas this textual stimulus has been studied at length, the study of icons is only beginning.

[12] James Elkins and Robert Williams, "Hugging the Shore," in *Renaissance Theory*, ed. James Elkins and Robert Williams (New York: Routledge, 2008), 514.

[13] David Carrier, "Close Reading and Looking: Some Recent Books by James Elkins," *Art Journal* 59/2 (Summer 2000): 116.

[14] Elkins and Williams, "Hugging the Shore," 513. The phrase is Adrian Randolph's.

of art historians."[15] The painting of this picture, which will now be described, began shortly after the painting of the frescoes themselves.

Masaccio, the artist most associated with the chapel's innovations, died at the age of twenty-seven, only a few years after he completed them.[16] Soon thereafter, Florence began to reflect on his artistic accomplishments. Consequently, the reputation of Masaccio, who enjoyed little acclaim in his own lifetime, began to rise.[17] Nearly a decade after the artist's death, Leon Battista Alberti elevated Masaccio to high company, including him as the sole painter among Brunelleschi, Donatello, Ghiberti, and Luca della Robbia in the dedication to his *Della Pittura*. Each artist was hailed, "a genius for every laudable enterprise in no way inferior to the ancients."[18] But owing to the limited initial influence of Alberti's treatise, it was not until the late fifteenth century that Masaccio attained anything like the reputation he enjoys today.[19]

Some chroniclers, elaborating on Alberti, implied that Masaccio had been the chief catalyst for advances in Florentine painting.[20] "Close to our own age," wrote Rinuccini in 1472, "Masaccio in painting expressed the likeness of everything in nature so well that we seemed to see the things themselves with our eyes, and not images of the things."[21] Landino agreed, saying that Masaccio "was a first-rate imitator of nature . . . good in composing and simple without elaboration (*puro senza ornato*)."[22] Masaccio's role generally eclipsed Masolino's in these accounts. Leonardo also praised Masaccio for exemplifying those who submit to nature, the "mistress of the masters."[23] In the words of Antonio Manetti, another late-quattrocento chronicler, Masaccio was "an amazing man. . . . He painted in the Brancacci Chapel various scenes, the best of those there; it is painted by three masters, all good, but he is wonderful."[24]

These were the sources which Giorgio Vasari—the "father of art

---

[15] James Elkins, *Our Beautiful, Dry, and Distant Texts* (University Park: Pennsylvania State University Press), 220.

[16] Diane Cole Ahl, "Introduction," in *Cambridge Companion to Masaccio*, 1.

[17] Honor during Masaccio's life went instead to Gentile da Fabriano, who attained the most lucrative commissions (Francis Ames-Lewis, "Masaccio's Legacy," in *Cambridge Companion to Masaccio*, 202.

[18] Ibid., 205.

[19] Ibid., 204. Ames-Lewis also points out that Filarete mentions Masaccio briefly in his 1463–1464 *Treatise on Architecture*.

[20] Ames-Lewis, "Masaccio's Legacy," 204–205.

[21] Ibid., 205.

[22] Ibid.

[23] Ibid., 206.

[24] Ibid.

history"—drew upon when he penned his *Lives of the Artists* in the mid-sixteenth century.[25] Vasari's approach can be considered a sort of Whig art history, in which developments of the past are massaged into a progressive narrative that vindicates the present. Masaccio's work in the Brancacci Chapel, according to Vasari, "deserves unstinted praise, especially because of the way he formed in his painting the beautiful style of our own day."[26] To be sure, Vasari saw Michelangelo as the peak of artistic achievement, but Michelangelo had learned from Masaccio, whose "epitaph" recorded by Vasari reads, "Buonarroti taught, he learnt from me."[27] In need of a hinge figure, Vasari laid the artistic shifts of the early quattrocento squarely on Masaccio's shoulders: "[H]ungry for fame, Masaccio learnt so much from his endless studies that he can be numbered among the pioneers who almost entirely rid painting of its hardness, difficulties, and imperfections. . . . certainly everything done before him can be described as artificial, whereas he produced work that is living, realistic, and natural. . . . *he alone* brought painting to the excellence we know today."[28] The womb for this rebirth of painting, furthermore, was the Brancacci Chapel. Vasari continues, "Because of Masaccio's work, the Brancacci Chapel has been visited from that time to this by an endless stream of students and masters. . . . In short, all those who have endeavored to learn the art of painting have always gone for that purpose to the Brancacci Chapel to grasp the precepts and rules demonstrated by Masaccio for the correct representation of figures."[29] The Brancacci Chapel had become an art school, and a tumultuous one at that. Vasari tells how Torrigiano, envious of Michelangelo's draftsmanship as he copied Masaccio, struck Michelangelo on the nose, thereby producing that famously disfigured nose.[30]

Just as it had become an art school, the Brancacci Chapel also became a school of art history. As the discipline developed into a

---

[25] Ames-Lewis gives us two possibilities as to why Masaccio was not mentioned between the late fifteenth century and Vasari: "This may suggest, that by the High Renaissance, his reputation was so firmly established that it went without saying, or that later in the century, critical interest in Masaccio and his works had declined" (ibid., 206).

[26] Giorgio Vasari, *Lives of the Artists*, trans. George Bull (London: Penguin, 1965), 130.

[27] Ibid., 132.

[28] Ibid., 124–125, 129 (emphasis mine).

[29] Ibid., 130–131. Ames-Lewis suggests that art historical evidence does not support Vasari's assertion, as very few sketches that copy the frescoes survive ("Masaccio's Legacy," 209ff.). See, for example, Michelangelo's drawings of the chapel in Alexander Nagel, *Michelangelo and the Reform of Art* (Cambridge: Cambridge University Press, 2000), 3–4.

[30] Vasari, *Lives of the Artists*, 332.

modern academic pursuit, the question of which of the three artists—Masolino, Masaccio, or Lippi—worked on which of the frescoes became an irresistible art historical quandary, especially in
continental European art history. The dispute was nicknamed the
vexata quaestio, the ultimate art historical *Rätsel* (riddle), or the *ewi-
gen Streitfrage* (unending controversy).[31] The German scholar Carl
Friedrich von Rumohr (1785–1843), who was one of Hegel's chief
art historical sources, saw Masaccio's role as paramount, for the artist's realistic painting shows he was "ruled by a certain seriousness
and moral dignity."[32] The Italian art historian Gaëtano Milanesi
(1813–1895), who edited the definitive edition of Vasari's *Lives*,
went so far as to say that the controversy concerning the Brancacci
Chapel was "the most important question in the history of art."[33]
Masaccio's reputation was such that some suggested he painted
the entire chapel.[34] In 1876, the no-nonsense Austrian art historian
Moritz Thausing (1835–1884) suggested comparing the shape of
the halos to distinguish the artists.[35] In the 1890s, spurred by the
suggestion that Masolino "didn't paint a single stroke," the German
scholar August Schmarsow (1853–1936) attempted to prove otherwise, driven by the conviction that the Brancacci fresco attribu-
tions were "at the beginning of the question of style itself."[36] These
Germanic debates were the context in which the influential Vienna
School of art history would arise.[37] Some consider the debate to
have been finally settled with Roberto Longhi's (1890–1970) "Fatti
di Masolino e di Masaccio," published in 1940, which even includes
a fictional dialogue between Masolino and Masaccio. Longhi's attri-
butions were so thoroughly argued that the debate over who painted
what was effectively terminated.[38]

---

[31] Elkins, *Our Beautiful, Dry, and Distant Texts*, 199.

[32] C. F. von Rumohr, *Italienische Forschungen* [1827–1831], ed. Julius Schlosser (Frankfurt: Frankfurter, 1920), 378; quoted in Elkins, *Our Beautiful, Dry, and Distant Texts*, 205.

[33] Elkins, *Our Beautiful, Dry, and Distant Texts*, 205.

[34] Ibid., 202–203. By the mid-nineteenth century, Joseph Crowe and Giovanni Cavalcaselle, in their *New History of Painting in Italy* (1864), returned to the claim that Masaccio painted the entire chapel (Elkins, *Our Beautiful, Dry, and Distant Texts*, 206).

[35] Ibid., 213–214.

[36] August Schmarsow, *Masaccio oder Masolino?* vol. 4 of *Masaccio, der Begründer des Klassischen Stils der Italienischen Malerei* (Kassel, 1895–1900); quoted in Elkins, *Our Beautiful, Dry, and Distant Texts*, 199.

[37] See Christopher Wood, ed. and trans, *Vienna School Reader: Politics and Art Historical Method in the 1930s* (New York: Zone, 2003).

[38] Elkins summarizes Longhi's conclusions in *Our Beautiful, Dry, and Distant Texts*, 217ff. This is not to say that there have not been more studies, to be discussed below. Among them was Anthony Molho's argument that the Brancacci frescoes make claims about church-state relations and the issue of the new *catasto*,

Surveying the Brancacci question, James Elkins suggested that the history of writing about the chapel displays a combination of personal projections and serious historical research. Elkins sees the history of interpretation of the Brancacci Chapel as evidence of experiential encounter with the paintings which is then enhanced with facts to lend it historical credibility. Whereas for Rumohr, Masaccio exemplified ethical dignity, for Schmarsow he exemplified the modern artist. Writing in the mid-1990s, Elkins ends the book with his most extensive reflections on the Brancacci Chapel on a melancholic note: "The books we write—most emphatically including this one—are consigned to dust from the instant they appear. . . . To me art history is in a certain sense an arbitrary profession, since I tend to use it to explore my own thoughts and to learn about myself. . . . "[39] Having discerned projections of art historians' respective concerns in the history of Brancacci Chapel literature, Elkins seemed to project some fin de siècle disciplinary fatigue onto the frescoes as well.

But if the discipline of art history, and the humanities in general, experienced a general crisis of purpose in the wake of deconstruction, the situation has changed since, some of the change being facilitated by Elkins himself.[40] This shift parallels the return of religion as a subject of serious academic inquiry. "It was inevitable," writes William Johnsen, "that the shame associated with admitting religious belief in the secular world of the human sciences in midcentury would prepare the ground for the great *succès de scandale* of religious (re) turn at the end of the century."[41] Martin Jay speaks of how religion has generated "a tsunami of scholarly commentary in many different fields sweeping over the nascent twenty-first century in the way that reinvigorated religious practice promises to do as well."[42] This religious turn has especially affected art history, as evidenced by numerous recent texts aiming to correct the neglect of religion,[43] as well as

---

a tax issued in 1427 (Anthony Molho, "The Brancacci Chapel: Studies in Its Iconography and History," *Journal of the Warburg and Courtauld Institutes* 40 (1977).

[39] Elkins, *Our Beautiful, Dry, and Distant Texts*, 297.

[40] James Elkins and David Morgan, eds., *Re-Enchantment* (New York: Routledge, 2008). See also the openness to religion recorded in another Art Seminar publication edited by Elkins: James Elkins and Robert Maniura, eds., *Renaissance Theory* (New York: Routledge, 2008).

[41] William Johnsen, "The Religious Turn: René Girard," *English Language Notes* 44/1 (Summer 2006).

[42] Martin Jay, review of Charles Taylor, *A Secular Age*, in *History and Theory* 48 (February 2009): 76–84. Jay continues, "Making one's way through this thicket of new interpretation and appreciation, is not, however, easy, especially for those of us who remain religiously 'unmusical' . . ."

[43] See, for example, Jeffrey F. Hamburger, "The Place of Theology in Medieval Art History: Problems, Positions, Possibilities," in *The Mind's Eye: Art and Theological Argument in the Middle Ages*, ed. Jeffrey F. Hamburger and Anne-Marie Bouché (Princeton, NJ: Princeton University Press, 2005); Christian K.

organizations such as the Association of Scholars of Christianity in the History of Art (ASCHA).

This religious turn has perhaps been most acute in the now established focus on religion and religious images in the Renaissance.[44] Richard Trexler's famous declaration that "the pagan Renaissance is no more" was just the beginning.[45] "Historians of Renaissance art," explains Alexander Nagel, "no longer chronicle the progress of art away from religion. Instead they show, over and over again, . . . the various ways in which art was embedded in the elaborate structures that joined religious, social, and political life."[46] In order to counterbalance Vasari, Anthony Cutler explains that, "Everywhere Cennini and his contemporaries looked they saw the art that we call medieval . . ."[47] Robert Maniura asserts that the Renaissance "is characterized not so much by a rebirth of the antique as by a rejuvenation of established 'medieval' tradition. . . . the defining feature of the art of the period was its constructive transformation of the Christian pictorial tradition."[48] Fredrika Jacobs puts it this way: "Miraculous images, particularly those of the Virgin Mary, not only thrived during the Renaissance, they proliferated."[49] Hors Bredekamp has shown, contra Walter Benjamin's famous essay,[50] that mass production was not a modern phenomenon but was a technique long used to propagate the faith.[51] The result is a new focus on miraculous images within and

---

Kleinbub, *Vision and Visionary in Raphael* (University Park: Pennsylvania State University Press, 2011); Shelley Karen Perlove, *Rembrandt's Faith: Church and Temple in the Dutch Golden Age* (University Park: Pennsylvania State University Press, 2009); Nigel Aston, *Art and Religion in Eighteenth-century Europe* (London: Reaktion: 2009); Cordula Grewe, *Painting the Sacred in the Age of Romanticism* (Burlington, VT: Ashgate, 2009); Jefferson J. A. Gatrall and Douglas Greenfield, eds., *Alter Icons: The Russian Icon and Modernity* (University Park: Pennsylvania State University Press, 2011).

[44] There are, of course, exceptions, such as a book that Stephen Campbell calls "neo-Burckhardtian": Richard Goldthwaite, *Wealth and the Demand for Art in Italy 1300–1600* (Baltimore: Johns Hopkins University Press, 1993).

[45] Richard C. Trexler, "Florentine Religious Experience: The Sacred Image," *Studies in the Renaissance* 19 (1972): 7–14.

[46] Alexander Nagel, review of Jörg Traeger, *Renaissance und Religion: Die Kunst des Glaubens im Zeitalter Raphaels*, *The Art Bulletin* 82/4 (December 2000): 773.

[47] Anthony Cutler, "The Pathos of Distance: Byzantium in the Gaze of Renaissance Europe and Modern Scholarship," in *Reframing the Renaissance: Visual Culture in Europe and Latin America 1450–1650*, ed. Claire Farago (New Haven, CT: Yale University Press, 1995), 24.

[48] Robert Maniura, "The Icon Is Dead, Long Live the Icon: The Holy Image in the Renaissance," in *Icon and Word: The Power of Images in Byzantium. Studies Presented to Robin Cormack*, ed. Antony Eastmond and Liz James (Burlington, VT: Ashgate, 2003), 99.

[49] Fredrika Jacobs, "Rethinking the Divide: Images and the Cult of Images," in *Renaissance Theory*, 99.

[50] Walter Benjamin, "The Work of Art in the Age of Mechanical Reproduction," in *Illuminations: Essays and Reflections*, ed. Hannah Arendt, trans. Harry Zohn (New York: Schocken, 1969), 217ff.

[51] Hors Bredekamp, "The Simulated Benjamin: Medieval Remarks on Its Actuality," trans. Iain Boyd Whyte; first published as "Der simulierte Benjamin: Mittelalterliche Bemerkungen zu seiner Aktualität," in *Frankfurter Schule und Kunstgeschichte*, ed. Andreas Berndt (Berlin: Reimer, 1992).

through the Renaissance,[52] to the point that even the plastic dolls that so entranced Elkins, referenced at the beginning of this essay, have in fact been studied, right down to the ways in which they are dressed.[53]

To say that this disciplinary shift has affected scholarship on the Brancacci Chapel would be an understatement. While the personal element of art history indicated by Elkins need not be dismissed, recent research on the chapel has uncovered vital information to which previous generations did not have access. At the center of these concerns is Christian faith. The cleaning and restoration of the frescoes from 1984–1990 has led to a new spate of studies and of great technical detail, further prompted by the 600th anniversary of Masaccio's birth in the year 2000.[54] Art historians today have transcended the "obsession with attribution and dating, matters of less concern to [the Brancacci Chapel's] original audience."[55] In line with these developments came a 2005 volume on the chapel which focused especially on original religious context.[56] The chapel emerges in this volume not as an art school or a mirror for art historians but as sacred space embedded in a vibrant lay devotional culture. The Carmelite Order's need to compete with the Franciscans and Dominicans put them in a fierce contest of good works. Organized alms-giving spurred by lay devotion have everything to do with the rise of the chapel.[57] The Brancacci Chapel has become "a cultural site that cannot exist in isolation from the devotional experience of the entire city."[58]

This new focus has emphasized the *Madonna del Populo* icon in the Brancacci Chapel which—for most of the art historical tradition outlined above—was unjustifiably ignored. According to Erik Thunø, traditional Renaissance art history marginalized "art as an expression of religious devotion, especially if the devotees were from among the

---

[52] Erik Thunø and Gerhard Wolf, eds., *The Miraculous Image in the Late Middle Ages and Renaissance* (Rome: l'Erma di Bretschneider, 2004); Megan Holmes, "Miraculous Images in Renaissance Florence," *Art History* 34/3 (June 2011): 432–465; Megan Holmes, *The Miraculous Image in Renaissance Florence* (forthcoming).

[53] Richard Trexler, "Being and Non-being: Parameters of the Miraculous in the Traditional Religious Image," in *Miraculous Image in the Late Middle Ages and Renaissance*, 22ff. Trexler does, however, confess that "the ubiquity of these devotional images has not yet been appreciated by most religious or art historians" (27).

[54] For a bibliography since 1990, see Umberto Baldini and Ornella Casazza, *The Brancacci Chapel Frescoes* (London: Abrams, 1992), 365–373.

[55] Ahl, "Masaccio in the Brancacci Chapel," 139.

[56] Nicholas A. Eckstein, ed., *The Brancacci Chapel: Form, Function, and Setting* (Florence: Leo S. Olschki, 2005).

[57] Ibid., 17.

[58] Ibid., 9–10.

common people," choosing instead to focus on "the glorious secular achievements of the age."[59] But art historians now understand that it was *during* the Renaissance that earlier religious images "revealed themselves as miraculous, thereby becoming the focus of attention and artistic patronage."[60] The Brancacci Chapel is no exception. The *Madonna del Popolo* was moved into the Brancacci Chapel in the middle of the fifteenth century, just as Masaccio's reputation was on the rise.

The icon depicts a seated Mary surrounded by two angels pointing to her son. The Christ depicted above them, which was regretfully decapitated during a Baroque reframing, is itself a sign of the image's "lively and continuing veneration."[61] Christa Gardner von Teuffel has dated the icon to a Florentine workshop between 1260 and 1280.[62] This period of icon painting in Florence was under the spell of the Byzantine world, when devotional images burst upon Tuscany "with the violence of an explosion."[63] While Vasari's account gave us Byzantine stasis and Italian artistic freedom, the art historian Hans Belting has effectively reversed this dynamic. Western artists were impressed with the "living paintings" of the East, many of which arrived in the West due to the occupation of the Levant by the Crusaders. In the thirteenth century, images from the East had "an authority of their own because of their origin and age," which was copied by Western artists,[64] and may have influenced the workshop that created the *Madonna del Populo* in Florence, whose style would have testified to its supposed antiquity. Indeed, until only recently the image was believed to have originated in Byzantium or the Holy Land itself.[65]

The icon's reported antiquity had much to do with the Carmelite Order, which presided over the Brancacci Chapel. The Carmelites claimed an origin that even preceded Christianity, having Elijah as their founder, seven centuries before Christ.[66] The icon's ancient ori-

---

[59] Erik Thunø, "The Miraculous Image and the Centralized Church Santa Maria Della Consalozione in Todi," in *Miraculous Image in the Late Middle Ages and Renaissance*, 29.

[60] Ibid., 30.

[61] Christa Gardner von Teuffel, "The Significance of the Madonna del Popolo in the Brancacci Chapel: Re-Framing Assumptions," in *Brancacci Chapel: Form, Function, and Setting*, 48.

[62] Ibid., 38–39. The date is based on close comparative analysis with Coppo di Marcovaldo's *Virgin* at Siena (1261).

[63] Hans Belting, *Likeness and Presence: A History of the Image before the Era of Art*, trans. Edmund Jephcott (Chicago: University of Chicago Press, 1997), 349.

[64] Ibid., 351.

[65] Von Teuffel, "Significance of the Madonna del Popolo in the Brancacci Chapel," 43.

[66] Ibid., 43.

gins would have bolstered this identity, as did the Brancacci frescoes, which show tonsured Carmelite friars as contemporaries of Peter himself.[67] The realism of Masolino and Masaccio's frescoes "may have functioned in visual terms to reinforce the historical authenticity of the biblical narratives depicted,"[68] as well as that of the Carmelite founding. We need not project modern historical notions onto the Renaissance and consider such statements anachronistic or forgeries. Instead, as the "anachronic" paradigm of Wood and Nagel have asserted, such moves can be understood more as organic connections to the sacred past.[69]

The *Madonna del Popolo*'s original context, about which we can only speculate, would probably have had Gothic vaults, stained-glass, and Trecento frescoes.[70] It was perhaps on the Carmelites' Marian altar.[71] In 1440 it was placed above the door leading from the church into the cloister, and by 1460 it was placed in the Brancacci Chapel, where it remains today.[72] The fact that this move was made shows that the icon was at least as important as if not more important than the frescoes themselves.

The Brancacci Family would have concurred with the decision to move the icon into their chapel, as it would have increased the chapel's significance to the community.[73] Indeed, the Brancacci Chapel was even popularly referred to simply as "Madonna del Popolo" after the icon that—we can assume—mattered most.[74] The icon gained special notoriety when it was thanked for the Florentine triumph over Pisa in 1406.[75] Although the *Madonna Enthroned* in Florence's S. Maria Maggiore (1180–1200) technically predates it, the Carmelites

---

[67] Creighton Gilbert, "Some Special Images for Carmelites," in *Christianity and the Renaissance: Image and Religious Imagination in the Quattrocento*, ed. Timothy Verdon and John Henderson (Syracuse, NY: Syracuse University Press, 1990), 195.

[68] Megan Holmes, "The Carmelites of Santa Maria del Carmine and the Currency of Miracles," in *Brancacci Chapel: Form, Function, and Setting*, 165.

[69] Wood and Nagel explain, "To describe a work of art as an 'anachronism' is to say that the work is best grasped not as art, but rather as a witness to its times, or as an inalienable trace of history; it tries to tell us what the artwork *really is*. To describe the work of art as 'anachronic,' by contrast, is to say what the artwork *does*, qua art" (*Anachronic Renaissance*, 14). Historically speaking, the Order was established in the Frankish monastic settlements in Palestine in the early 1200s, just as, in truth, the icon was painted in that same century. While the *communion sanctorum* and the perspective of faith does respect history, it is not bound by its modern delineations.

[70] Ahl, "Masaccio in the Brancacci Chapel," 139.

[71] Von Teuffel, "Significance of the Madonna del Popolo in the Brancacci Chapel," 40.

[72] Ibid., 41. For a similar phenomenon with Guido's *Maestà*, see Nagel and Wood, *Anachronic Renaissance*, 81ff.

[73] Von Teuffel, "Significance of the Madonna del Popolo in the Brancacci Chapel," 46.

[74] Ibid., 47.

[75] Ibid., 44.

understood the *Madonna del Popolo* to be the oldest, and consequently the holiest, image in Florence.[76] Perhaps the move can also be explained by the growing anxiety stemming from overly sensuous religious imagery, as expressed, for example, by Savonarola.[77] According to Nagel, clearly Christocentric imagery such as the *Madonna del Popolo* icon "were forms of purification, means of restoring a clarity and doctrinal anchoring believed to have existed in the past, before the distractions and abuses introduced in later centuries."[78] By placing the icon in the midst of what was becoming an art school, perhaps the Carmelites were intentionally upbraiding what was slowly becoming an art culture independent of religion.

The *Madonna del Popolo* icon, furthermore, boasted stories at least as dramatic as Michelangelo's getting slugged. The dramatic importance of the icon in the life of the community is beautifully explained in the *Vita* (*Life*) of one of the Carmelites' great saints, Blessed Andre Corsini (1301–1374).[79] The *Vita* was composed after 1440,[80] just as the art historical tradition surrounding the Brancacci frescoes was emerging. Echoing a common biblical and hagiographic theme, the *Vita* tells of Nicolò Corsini and Pellegrina Stracciabende, struggling to have a child. They petitioned the *Madonna del Popolo*, which would then have stood in its earlier setting.[81] They had good reason to go to this icon, as it had earned its "Madonna of the people" designation for curing infertility before. The petition worked, and the couple had a child, whom they named Andrea.

The *Vita* then tells of the happy mother's horrible dream: "It seemed as if a wolf appeared to her in her sleep, and she sorrowed greatly at this in her vision and complained with much lamenting to the Virgin Mary: Grieving thus, she saw the wolf enter the church and at once turn into a white lamb."[82] As her son Andrea began to live a

---

[76] Ibid., 48.
[77] See Marcia B. Hall, "Savonarola's Preaching and the Patronage of Art," in *Christianity and the Renaissance*. This retroactive sensibility has been called the "archaism of the year 1500." For bibliography, see Nagel, *Michelangelo and the Reform of Art*, 239, note 12.
[78] Nagel, *Michelangelo and the Reform of Art*, 86.
[79] Nicholas A. Eckstein, "The Brancacci, the Chapel, and the Mythic History of San Frediano," in *Brancacci Chapel: Form, Function, and Setting*, 20.
[80] Ibid., 21.
[81] Ibid., 22.
[82] "[. . .] in somnis videbaur sibi lupum parere, de quo in vision nimium tristabatur, & de Maria Virgine lamentabiliter conquerebatur, & sic dolendo videbat lupum ecclesiam intrare, quod statim agnus candidus efficiebatur" (ibid., 22).

reckless, licentious life, Pellegrina came to understand that the wolf was her son. Repeatedly afflicted by his appalling behavior, she finally betrayed the secret: "Truly, truly, Andrea my son, you are the wolf of which I dreamed." She then related to her puzzled offspring the story of his conception: "And so, my son, you are not ours, except in so far as we brought you into being; you are the son of the Virgin Mary. It is for this reason that I ask you never to disdain her service."[83] The words struck him like arrows, and Andrea found himself before the *Madonna del Popolo* icon that had resulted in his birth: "[T]hroughout the whole night he never withdrew his gaze from the Virgin, saying 'in so far as I am yours, O Mary the Virgin, I will serve you with all my heart, both day and night.'"[84] The wolf had indeed become a lamb, leading a life of heroic and frequently miraculous charity to the poor in service to the Virgin.[85] He washed the feet of plague-ridden victims with putrid sores, curing the illness with his tears of compassion.[86] His miracles continued even after his death, as he cured a woman who had visited his tomb in the Carmine. Far from having an otherworldly tone, the miracles are verified in a coda to the *Vita* by local notaries, just as they would verify the sale of a house.[87]

To relate this story is not to neglect the Brancacci frescoes in favor of the icon, but to shed new light on the frescoes as well. Nicholas Eckstein has shown how "the frescoes evince a cognate relationship to the miraculous cures described in the *Vita*."[88] Saint Andrea served the poor with heroic vigor, inspiring the Carmelites to do the same in the immediate neighborhood. Eckstein makes a direct connection between Saint Andrea and Saint Peter in the frescoes as well, and suggests that the naturalistic beggars depicted in the Brancacci frescoes are patterned after the concern for the real living poor just outside the church.[89] Indeed, Masaccio and Masolino's depictions of the poor "are the most specific, human and vivid of their time."[90] The realism of the

---

[83] "Itaque, fili mi, tu non es noster, nisi quantum ad generationem, tu es Virginis Mariae; ideo te rogo, vt tante Virgini seruire no dedigneris" (ibid., 23).
[84] "Que verba fuerunt Dei sagittal cor eius vulnerans, & per totam noctem illam ad Virginem oculos direxit, dicens: Ex quo tuus sum, Virgo Maria, animo magno tibi die noctuque seruiam" (ibid., 23–24).
[85] Ibid., 25–28.
[86] Ibid., 25.
[87] Ibid., 27.
[88] Ibid., 28.
[89] Eckstein expands upon this point considerably (ibid., 34–36).
[90] Dale Kent, "The Branacacci Chapel Viewed in the Context of Florence's Culture of Artistic Patronage," in *Brancacci Chapel: Form, Function, and Setting*, 63.

figures in Masaccio's frescoes become less a triumph of artistic technique than a way to inspire Christian service, and guilt from the lack of it as well. It is possible that the depiction of Ananias and Sapphira withholding their gift is connected to Felice Brancacci's remorse from having embezzled funds—a visual confession.[91] The focus on Peter paralleled Felice who, like Peter, had failed but was here pledging to resume an upright life.[92]

In addition, the frescoes have been connected to Florence's liturgical and rhetorical tradition. While the frescoes were being painted, the Dominican archbishop of Florence, Fra Antonino Pierozzi, showed there to be less reason to juxtapose the "realistic" frescoes to "religious" icons. Instead, *all* images were meant to hasten the imagination to move beyond representation to the divine.[93] Preachers and painters worked together to achieve this pedagogical aim.[94] The frescoes were birthed from the "womb of memory" of Scripture and the stories of saints."[95] When these liturgical patterns are studied, the frescoes emerge as "visual counterpart of the didactic formation of the spoken word, holding permanently before the Carmelite devotee the lessons heard during the sanctoral cycle of the liturgical years."[96] The cycle was created from a complex interweaving of this devotional ethos, the needs of the Order, and a patron's desires, all orbiting around the miraculous icon, *Madonna del Popolo*.

What accounts for this alarming surge of theologically sensitive scholarship from art historians who may or may not have religious commitments themselves? Much of it is a reaction to the way in which Renaissance perspective has been used to vindicate an ostensibly secular point of view. Part of the reason that the Brancacci question was so pressing is that Masaccio was seen to have been the inventor of perspective,[97] making the Brancacci Chapel—in a sense—our first view of the modern world. For Jacob Burckhardt (1818–1897),

---

[91] Ibid., 64.

[92] Ibid., 66.

[93] Peter Howard, "The Womb of Memory: Carmelite Liturgy and the Frescoes of the Brancacci Chapel," in *Brancacci Chapel: Form, Function, and Setting*, 180. See also Peter Howard, *Beyond the Written Word: Preaching and Theology in the Florence of Archbishop Antoninus, 1427–1459* (Florence: L. S. Olschki, 1995).

[94] Peter Howard, "The Womb of Memory: Carmelite Liturgy and the Frescoes of the Brancacci Chapel," in *Brancacci Chapel: Form, Function, and Setting*, 181.

[95] Ibid., 184.

[96] Ibid., 197.

[97] For a careful examination of this claim, see J. V. Field, "Masaccio and Perspective in Italy in the Fifteenth Century," in *Cambridge Companion to Masaccio*.

the Renaissance was the beginning of the "general disintegration of belief," and was therefore the "mother of our modern age."[98] Though expanded and modified, this view unconsciously influenced later art historians such as Erwin Panofsky,[99] for whom the perspective exemplified by Masaccio offered a vision of the universe which was essentially "detheologized."[100] Twentieth-century introductory art historical textbooks repeatedly show how this influential view was disseminated. Speaking of Masaccio's *Trinity*, H. W. Janson went so far as to say, "In a universe ruled by reason, not even the Lord was exempt from the laws of perspective."[101]

Considering the success of this secular narrative, it is inevitable that scholars would seek to highlight hitherto ignored Christian dimensions, attempting—however imperfectly—to see as others saw.[102] Timothy Verdon, for example, aims to "'put on the mind' of the Christian age we want to study if we wish to understand its cultural products."[103] In a text that is regretfully absent from nearly all art historical discourse on perspective through the twenty-first century, the Russian priest and art historian Pavel Florensky thoroughly criticized Panofsky's Kantian outlook and anticipated the best advances in the discipline. Suppressed for nearly a century, Florensky's landmark essay has only recently been translated.[104] Such advances have resulted in

---

[98] Jacob Burckhardt, *The Civilization of the Renaissance in Italy*, trans. S. G. C. Middlemore, rev. and ed. Irene Gordon (New York: New American Library, 1960), 356–383; quoted in *Christianity and the Renaissance*, 1.

[99] Eugenio Marino, "Art Criticism and Icon-Theology," in *Christianity and the Renaissance*, 582. Obviously Warburg and Panofsky would have been aware of theology and faith, but it strikes me as fair for Marino to suggest these were serious *methodological* concerns. Marino continues, "If the critic who looks at such works does not approach them in terms of icon-theology, it means he has not entered into the intuition from which they arose—probably because he lacks the 'familiarity' (Vertrautheit) and the 'equipment' (*Ausrüstung*) which, as Panofsky himself taught, are the methodological prerequisites for art criticism" (583).

[100] Erwin Panofsky, *Perspective as Symbolic Form*, trans. Christopher Wood (New York: Zone, 1997), 66. Originally published as "Die Perspektive als 'symolishche Forme,'" in the *Vortrage der Bibliothek Warburg* (1924–1925) (Leipzig and Berlin, 1927), 258–330. Panofsky celebrated Masaccio, especially in his *Trinity*, as one for whom perspective is "exactly and uniformly constructed" (62).

[101] H. W. Janson, *History of Art* (Englewood Cliffs, NJ: Prentice-Hall, 1962), 323. For an alternate perspective on Masaccio, see Timothy Verdon, "Masaccio's Trinity: Theological, Social, and Civic Meanings," in *Cambridge Companion to Masaccio*.

[102] Examples would include Robert Nelson, ed., *Visuality before and beyond the Renaissance: Seeing as Others Saw* (Cambridge: Cambridge University Press, 2000); or Alister Chapman, John Coffey, and Brad Gregory, eds., *Seeing Things Their Way: Intellectual History and the Return of Religion* (South Bend, IN: University of Notre Dame Press, 2009).

[103] Timothy Verdon, "Christianity, the Renaissance, and the Study of History: Environments of Experience and Imagination," in *Christianity and the Renaissance*, 8.

[104] Pavel Florensky, "Reverse Perspective," in *Beyond Vision: Essays on the Perception of Art*, trans. Wendy Salmond, ed. Nicoletta Misler (London: Reaktion, 2002). The lectures, delivered in 1920, preceded Panofsky's *Perspective as Symbolic Form* (1924–1925) but did not appear in print in the Soviet Union until 1967. Florensky's criticism of perspective anticipates James Elkins's critique of Panofsky in *The Poetics of*

one of the broadest perspectives on the Brancacci Chapel in centuries, requiring us to reimagine the space based on the latest round of research. The naturalistic paintings of Masaccio and Masolino may have ultimately resulted in a "de-theologized" vision, but their realism may also have been intended to spur Christian service to the actual poor. Masaccio's reputation might have been elevated to bolster an emerging art history, but so was the famous *Madonna del Popolo* icon, which found its way to the most distinguished place among Masaccio's frescoes. Perspective, for Panosfky, "seals off religious art from the realm of the magical, . . . [and] the miraculous finds its last refuge in the soul of the human being represented in the work of art."[105] But this contrasts quite dramatically with the notarized miracles recorded in association with the *Madonna del Populo*.[106] As Vasari and other artists were copying Masaccio's sketches and creating what would become art history, powerful all-female lay confraternities named themselves after the icon. As artists copied Masaccio's frescoes, the faithful (which can include artists as well) implored a miraculous icon and engaged in richly beautiful liturgical rites. The *Madonna del Populo*, furthermore, might have impressed Michelangelo equally as did the frescoes. He too had deep anxieties about the direction of art, and hoped to restore "the figural focus and simplicity of traditional icons and cult statues."[107] In short, the Brancacci Chapel now appears as a reassertion and intensification of religious vision rather than its eclipse. Andre Corsini, we have already seen, turned from a wolf into a lamb before the *Madonna del Popolo* icon. Might art history, by continuing along this path of religiously enriched scholarship, change from a secular wolf into something more like a lamb as well?

It will come as no surprise to those who know John Walford and his scholarship that he anticipated these developments in Renaissance

---

Perspective (1996) and may have inspired the Lacanian ideas that inform Hubert Damisch in *Origine de la Perspective* (1987). See Joseph Masheck, "The Florenskian Icon 'in' Lacan?" *Word and Image* 26/1 (January–March 2010): 52–58. In addition, Florensky's view of Michelangelo as a man of the Middle Ages anticipates Nagel's in *Michelangelo and the Reform of Art*. See also Nicoletta Misler, "Pavel Florensky as Art Historian," in *Beyond Vision*, 29ff. For an excellent biographical essay that accents his religious vision, see John McGuckin, "Florensky and Iconic Dreaming," in *Alter Icons*. For a full biography, see Avril Pyman, *Pavel Florensky: A Quiet Genius* (New York: Continuum, 2010). For an important discussion of Florensky that puts him in conversation with other Russian thinkers, see Clemena Antonova, *Space, Time, and Presence in the Icon: Seeing the World with the Eyes of God* (Burlington, VT: Ashgate, 2010),
[105] Panofsky, *Perspective as Symbolic Form*, 72.
[106] Eckstein, "Brancacci, the Chapel, and the Mythic History of San Frediano," 27.
[107] Nagel, *Michelangelo and the Reform of Art*, 106.

scholarship. An unpublished paper, which accurately exudes the dynamism of Walford's lectures in the area of Italian Renaissance art, conveys his openness to theology—albeit a distinctly "visual theology."[108] "Only when restricted by the most narrow blinkers of humanistic scholarship," announced Walford, "could one afford to ignore the theology and practice of the Renaissance church as a pertinent factor in the dynamic interchange between patron, artist, and Renaissance spectator."[109] Walford sees in the best Renaissance art "a visual rhetoric . . . one that harmonizes with, and reinforces the verbal rhetoric of the preacher."[110] For Walford, Renaissance art was less a "harbinger of the Enlightenment" than it was a "supernatural naturalism" that bolstered Christian faith.[111] Fortunately, the field of art history is finally catching up.

---

[108] E. John Walford, *Humanist Readings of Incarnational Theology and Its Impact on Renaissance Visual Culture* (unpublished paper, March 1996).
[109] Ibid., 2.
[110] Ibid., 22.
[111] Ibid., 3 and 15.

Joachim Patinir, *Landscape with Saint Jerome*. C. 1520. Oil on panel, 30" x 54". Musée du Louvre, Paris.
Photo: Réunion des Musées Nationaux, Paris/Art Resource, NY.

5

THE SHAPE OF PLACE
Joachim Patinir's
Landscape with Saint Jerome

HENRY LUTTIKHUIZEN

Landscapes are never neutral places. In his book *Jacob van Ruisdael and the Perception of Landscape*, John Walford suggested, "a painted landscape, however realistic, and from whatever period or place of origin, is never a pure copy of nature and therefore can never be rendered value free."[1] There is no unbiased view. Cultural expectations and personal convictions shape the way nature is seen. Artists make visual choices; they select the places that deserve a second look. In addition, they suggest how these places should be viewed.

Landscape paintings are fundamentally about the significance of particular locations, both real and imagined. Yet there is almost always more to these places than meets the eye, for the localities represented in landscape paintings usually point to something beyond themselves. Within the history of Christianity, nature has frequently been described as a book written by the finger of God. Like Scripture, the visual world is believed to be capable of revealing the presence of the divine.[2] Artists producing landscapes for a Christian audience have readily recognized this understanding of the world. This essay focuses our attention on a landscape painting revealing this religious response, a work made by the sixteenth-century Flemish artist Joachim Patinir (c. 1480–1524). The novice to art history may not recognize his name. Nonetheless, he is probably the first European artist to specialize in landscape painting.

Yet it is important to remember that he did not invent the genre.

---

[1] E. John Walford, *Jacob van Ruisdael and the Perception of Landscape* (New Haven, CT: Yale University Press, 1991), 1.
[2] Cf. Peter Harrison, *The Bible, Protestantism, and the Rise of Natural Science* (Cambridge: Cambridge University Press, 2001).

The earliest known landscape is a fresco, completed over three-and-a-half thousand years ago on the Aegean island of Thera (present-day Santorini). The fresco shows the undulating contours of the terrain, crowned with brightly colored blossoming flora. Slightly above the vegetation, swallows mate as they gently flutter through the sky. However, the painting does not simply indicate the appearance of springtime. The decoration strongly elicits notions of regeneration and growth. Not only does the fresco present the natural surroundings that exist beyond the painted wall; it was likely produced in the hope that this world would flourish with abundance.[3]

In ancient Greece and Rome, theatrical backdrops were occasionally painted with landscape scenery. Although these scenes may have been designed to show natural appearances, their primary function was to complement the drama performed on stage. Within this setting, the naturalistic representation was closely tied to the power of the imagination. As David Summers has suggested, landscapes were appreciated for their painterly brilliance and *phantasia* (fantasy), a term originally associated with bringing things into the light.[4] Consequently, there is more to landscape painting than what meets the eye. The imagination also comes into play. The word *landscape* itself points beyond the mirror of nature. After all, to scape is literally to shape a view.[5] Consequently, landscape painting is no less subjective than other kinds of visual presentation. Even though its apparent naturalism can dupe naïve beholders into believing that they are witnessing a direct transcription of nature, the pictorial arrangement and style of the rendering of landscapes are rooted in the interpretive vision of the artist and her or his cultural context. Furthermore, the reception of landscapes, as with all images, is also subjective. Although viewers need the biotic capacity of sight to see a painting, they cannot do so in a manner that escapes cultural expectations. In other words, what someone sees is guided by what one desires to see, and that is something shaped by culture. Landscapes may look

---

[3]Christos Doumas, *The Wall Paintings of Thera*, 2nd ed., trans. Alex Doumas (Athens: Thera Foundation, 1999).

[4]David Summers, *Real Spaces: World Art History and the Rise of Western Modernism* (London: Phaidon, 2003), 29.

[5]The Dutch word *landschap* makes the connection between place, shape, and view even more explicit than it is in English. Furthermore, application of the Dutch term to painting likely served as the source for modern English usage.

naturalistic, but that does not mean that they are natural phenomena or that they can be perceived naturally. Otherwise, they would not have a history.

When ancient Roman painters represented a garden scene on the walls of the house of Livia, the wife of Caesar Augustus, they were not simply rendering her backyard. On the contrary, they were, like stage designers, presenting an idyllic scene, one for the most part absent within an urban setting. Although numerous landscapes were produced in ancient and medieval Europe, landscape did not become a distinctive genre or type of painting in the West until the early sixteenth century.[6]

The genre of landscape painting did not develop in isolation. It occurred around the same time that artists began specializing in other subjects, such as tavern and market scenes. As E. H. Gombrich has noted, this transformation likely developed out of the division of labor within particular workshops, between artists who painted the figures and those who painted the landscapes for specific images.[7] Of all the new genres introduced, landscape was the most revolutionary. Its introduction, however, cannot be explained solely in terms of personal expression. Artists produced landscapes because there was a demand for them. For some reason or another, people wanted to see and purchase these kinds of pictures. Without such a desire, the genre of landscape would never have been established.

Landscapes, unlike portraits and liturgical images, were seldom commissioned. They were sold in the marketplace. To sell their paintings, artists had to recognize the expectations of potential buyers. Economic success was often tied to the repetition of appreciated artistic motifs and the ability to promote product identity noted for its fine quality. Artists made use of prevailing artistic formulae, but they also developed their own personal brand or style in hopes of obtaining a marketing edge over their competitors.[8]

---

[6] China developed the genre of landscape painting numerous centuries before it was established in the West. Already during the Song dynasty (960–1279), Chinese artists regularly made landscape paintings to illuminate the presence of *qi*, the rhythmic breath or spirit running through the cosmos.

[7] E. H. Gombrich, "The Renaissance Theory of Art and the Rise of Landscape," in *Norm and Form*, vol. 1 of *Gombrich on the Renaissance*, 4 vols. (London: Phaidon, 1966), 109.

[8] Dan Ewing, "Multiple Advantages, Moderate Production: Thoughts on Patinir and Marketing," in *Patinir: Estudios y catalogo critico/Studies and Critical Catalogue*, ed. Alejandro Vergara (Madrid: Museo del Prado, 2007), 81–95; Larry Silver, *Peasant Scenes and Landscapes: The Rise of Pictorial Genres in the Antwerp Art Market* (Philadelphia: University of Pennsylvania Press, 2006), 26–52.

As a genre, landscapes first appeared in early sixteenth-century Antwerp. Built on the Scheldt River, Antwerp replaced the city of Bruges as the financial center of Europe, after the Zwijn harbor silted up. In fact, the port of Antwerp was far busier than that of Venice. More commercial traffic took place in Antwerp in a month than went through Venice in an entire year. Not surprisingly, Antwerp was an incredibly prosperous city, and it attracted merchants and painters in droves. Within its bourse, or stock exchange, lucrative commodities, imported from places around the world, were traded. Spanish, French, English, Portuguese, and Italian businessmen all had offices in Antwerp. Landscape painting flourished within this cosmopolitan and wealthy city.

Innovations in cartography, growing interest in the exotic, and greater ease in travel may all have contributed to the development of the genre. Nonetheless, as we shall see, contemporary religious sentiments continued to play an important role in the depiction of nature. In the earliest examples of this new genre, such as Patinir's *Landscape with Saint Jerome* (c. 1516–1518), it is often difficult to determine whether one is viewing a landscape with religious figures or a devotional painting with a landscape.

Very little is known about the painter of this image. The exact details concerning his year of birth and his birthplace remain unknown, though he was likely born sometime between 1480 and 1485 in either Dinant or Bouvignes, neighboring villages on the river Meuse (Maas). In 1515, Patinir's name appears in the records of the Antwerp painters' guild, but it seems likely that he was trained elsewhere.[9] However, he was well known by contemporary artists. Patinir collaborated with local artists, such as Quentin Massys and Joos van Cleve. In addition, the German artist Albrecht Dürer not only attended the Flemish artist's second wedding in August of 1521; he also referred to Patinir in his diaries as "the good landscape painter (*der gut landschafft Mahler*)."[10]

Joachim Patinir died in 1524. Nonetheless, members of the next generation of Antwerp painters, such as the Master of the Female Half-Lengths, Lucas Gassel, and Herri met de Bles, continued to pay trib-

---

[9] Vergara, *Patinir*, 326–333.
[10] Hans Rupprich, *Dürer: Schriftlicher Nachlass*, 3 vols. (Berlin, 1956–1969), 1:169, line 60.

ute to Patinir by closely emulating the style and content of his imagery. Patinir's art was also lauded throughout the sixteenth century. In 1556, Felipe de Guevara claimed Patinir had produced a seascape while on board a ship in the midst of a tempest between Ireland and England. According to the Spanish humanist and diplomat, Patinir's ship was the only one of seventy to survive the storm. Unfortunately, there is no evidence that the Flemish painter took such a journey.[11] Nonetheless, Guevara's remarks reinforce the notion that Patinir was closely attuned with the forces of nature.

In this particular image, one of Patinir's earliest works, the life of Saint Jerome is revealed within a panoramic landscape. The rich diversity of the terrain extends below the painting's high horizon. Patinir's panel contains mountains, rivers, and meadows, rendered in meticulous detail. Rather than indicate a particular locality, it appears to show snippets of places across the globe. The early-twentieth-century art historian Ludwig von Baldass described paintings such as this one as *Weltlandschaften*, or "world-landscapes," for they seem to embody the desire to depict the contours of the earth in their entirety.[12]

Although the panel's jutting peaks resemble rock formations found near Dinant, they are not directly copied after the Flemish topography. On the contrary, they are shaped by the artist's memory and imagination. In addition, Patinir seems to have tapped into the prevailing taste for Boschian imagery. However, it is doubtful that his fantastic landscapes derive from careful study of works made by 's-Hertogenbosch's most famous artist. More likely, they are based on Patinir's knowledge of images produced by Hieronymus Bosch's popular Flemish followers, Pieter Huys and Jan Mandijn.

In the center of the painting, Saint Jerome (c. 340–420) kneels on the dirt floor of his makeshift hut. His eyes are fixed on the crucifix before him. The large book located near the entrance of the crude shack is likely a copy of the Vulgate, Jerome's Latin translation of the

---

[11] Cited in Vergara, *Patinir*, 19–20.
[12] Ludwig von Baldass, "Die niederländische Landschaftsmalerei von Patinir bis Bruegel," *Jahrbuch der Kunsthistorischen Sammlungen in Wien* 34 (1918): 111–157. Cf. Walter Gibson, *The Mirror of the Earth* (Princeton, NJ: Princeton University Press, 1989). The two canonical studies of Joachim Patinir remain Robert Koch, *Joachim Patinir* (Princeton, NJ: Princeton University Press, 1968); and Reindert Falkenburg, *Joachim Patinir: Landscape as an Image of the Pilgrimage of Life*, trans. Michael Hoyle (Amsterdam and Philadelphia: J. Benjamins, 1988).

Bible. Although the text served as the standard version of the Bible throughout the Middle Ages, its primary role in the painting is as a pictorial attribute helping to identify the saint. After all, little attention is given to the saint's intellectual prowess.

Rather than focus on Jerome as an erudite translator or as an eminent theologian, Patinir represents him as a hermit, someone who strives to be in the world but not of it. His isolation in the wilderness is modeled after Christ's. Jerome lives alone in hopes of conforming to the life of his Lord. Like Jesus, he aims to overcome sinful temptations. A switch of twigs is placed on the floor of the saint's dilapidated shack. In his right hand, Jerome holds a rock. He is preparing to strike himself with the stone repeatedly on the chest. Through this activity, the penitent saint means to renounce the flesh and to discipline the spirit. Jerome's pain is closely associated with the suffering of Christ. By beating himself, the hermit saint aspires to become, like his Savior, more compassionate. His intense gaze at the crucifix reinforces his desire to purify his soul, to imitate Christ more closely in his thoughts and deeds.

Just beyond the saint's humble hut, the bright red robes and hat of a cardinal are draped across the dead branch of a nearby broken tree stump. However, Jerome never served the church as a cardinal. The ecclesiastical title did not exist until three centuries after the saint's death. Nonetheless, the scarlet attire frequently appears in representations of Jerome to mark his status as one of the four Latin Fathers of the church (the others being Saints Ambrose, Augustine, and Gregory). In this painting Jerome, dressed in a tattered blue gown, has removed his clerical vestments, a gesture that simultaneously unveils his ecclesiastical authority and utmost humility. The placement of the robe over a lifeless branch suggests the transience of nature, as it reveals the church's role in the triumph over death.[13] On the other side of Jerome's hut there is a long, slender tree. The arbor might symbolize the saint himself. In a thirteenth-century letter, Jerome is described as a tall tree reaching to the heavens.[14] Unlike the dead stump, the lightly

---

[13] Falkenburg, *Joachim Patinir*, 83. As Falkenburg notes, this motif was also used by Albrecht Dürer to indicate the suppression of carnal lust. However, it is difficult to say whether this is the case in Patinir's painting.
[14] Ibid., 84.

leafed tree thrusts upwards, suggesting vitality and perhaps the desire to unite with God.

The rugged terrain behind Jerome seems inhospitable and harsh, unsuitable for human life. Yet this wilderness serves as the hermit saint's temporary home. Jerome appears to reside somewhere between mountains and the desert. Although Jerome is said to have lived alone in the desert, his hut is located at the foot of jagged peaks. Mountains, like the desert, often signified places where one might overcome temptation and find union with God. Late medieval mystics such as Jean Gerson and Gerard Zerbolt van Zutphen actively promoted spiritual ascension up the contemplative mountain.[15] Their writings did not advocate lofty pride but lowly self-denial as a means to move closer to God. The kneeling figure of Jerome in quiet meditation appears to follow this ideal. Humbly crouching on a desert-like floor, he empties himself of selfish desire.

Jerome may be a hermit saint, but he is not alone. Above and to the left of his humble shack, the half-length figure of a man can be seen walking up a narrow path as he approaches a shelter, accessible only by ladder. The stranger may be interpreted as an imitator of the hermit saint. His secluded retreat is built into the untamed hillside, removed from the hamlet and countryside down below.

In the rocks to the right of the saint's hut, there is an opening. Inside the cavity, a merchant with a donkey and three camels can be seen. The traveler fearfully lifts his arm as a ferocious lion leaps into view. This small detail derives from a tale in *The Golden Legend*, a popular anthology of lives of the saints compiled by Jacobus de Voragine, a thirteenth-century Dominican monk. In 1505, an Antwerp publisher translated the book into Flemish.[16]

The *Golden Legend* offers a vivid account of the life of Saint Jerome.[17] After spending four years in the wilderness, the penitent hermit joined a monastery in Bethlehem, vowing to live as a domesticated animal at the foot of Christ's crib. One day, while Jerome was listening to the reading of the Bible, a wounded lion entered the monastery.

[15] Jean Gerson, "The Mountain of Contemplation," in *Jean Gerson*, trans. Brian P. McGuire (New York, 1998), 75–127; and Gerard Zerbolt van Zutphen, "The Spiritual Ascents," in *Devotio Moderna*, trans. John van Engen (New York: Paulist, 1988), 243–315.

[16] Vergara, *Patinir*, 326.

[17] Jacobus de Voragine, *The Golden Legend*, trans. William Granger Ryan, vol. 2 (Princeton, NJ: Princeton University Press, 1993), 211–216.

The monks fled, with the exception of Jerome, who, reminiscent of Androcles in Aesop's famous fable, fearlessly pulled a thorn from an injured lion's paw. In gratitude for his recovery, the lion turned away from its life as a wild beast and became the loyal companion of his healer.

At the monastery, the domesticated lion was given the duty of protecting the monks' donkey. One day, the lion fell asleep on the job, and a group of merchants, seeing that the donkey was unguarded, stole the creature, adding it to their caravan. Upon noticing the disappearance of the donkey, the monks believed the animal had fallen victim to the lion's appetite. As punishment, the monks ordered the lion to carry firewood, the task previously given to the donkey.[18]

Although neither the removal of the thorn nor the theft of the donkey appears in the Louvre panel, the next episode in this tale, namely, the lion's discovery and rescue of the donkey, is shown. According to the narrative, the roaring lion chased the thieves back to the monastery. In the upper right of the painting, the contrite merchants, having reached Bethlehem, kneel before the lion, vowing to change their ways in hopes of receiving undeserved mercy. Unfortunately, as Alejandro Vergara has noted, this area of the panel has been damaged. Jerome is often shown pardoning the penitent thieves, but he does not appear in this vignette.[19] Nonetheless, the gift of mercy is revealed.

The penitent may receive forgiveness, but that does not erase the dangers of sin. Iconographical details within Patinir's landscape call attention to the presence of worldly temptation. In the rocks directly above Jerome's shack, a lone white goat can be seen. The figure may relate to Aesop's fables. In one of his tales, a fox trapped in a well coaxes a thirsty goat to jump into the cool waters. Once the goat enters the well, the fox climbs over the foolish creature's horns and makes his escape, leaving the unthinking goat behind. The moral of the story is, look before you leap. In this panel, there is no fox or well. The goat is upright and has not fallen. Yet contemporary viewers familiar with Aesop's fable would have likely associated the animal with folly and with those easily led into temptation. A similar goat appears in the

---

[18]This episode as well as the pulling out of the thorn can be seen in another version of Patinir's painting, now housed in the Prado.
[19]Vergara, *Patinir*, 326.

background of Albrecht Dürer's 1504 engraving depicting the fall of Adam and Eve. The Bible also makes numerous references to goats, most of which have negative connotations. In Patinir's panel, the pale-skinned saint and the goat are located on the same vertical axis. However, they face in different directions. The learned hermit meditates on the life of Christ, while the goat seems to be preparing to make a potentially perilous leap over a crevice in the rocks. Yet Jerome and the goat are not alone. Two birds share their central placement.

Cleverly disguised by the darkness of a mountainous cleft, an owl stares out toward the viewer. Although the little bird looks somewhat harmless and cute, it is deceptively dangerous. Unlike in Greek culture, where the owl is associated with wisdom, in Netherlandish culture it is linked with evil and misfortune. Averse to light, the owl waits for nightfall, the moment it can prey on the weak and the vulnerable.

Meanwhile, a yellow parrot is perched on the roof of Jerome's hut. Unlike owls, this exotic bird was often associated with paradise. Due to their ability to mimic human speech, parrots were also praised as birds of the Word. In addition, they were linked to Christian hospitality, for parrots were believed capable of greeting strangers with the appropriate call "ave," a double entendre on the Latin term which means both birds and "Hail," as in the opening word of the greeting "Ave Maria."[20]

In the left foreground, salamanders scurry up the banks of a nearby stream. These slimy creatures were not only associated with deception; they were also thought to be poisonous. The ancient Greek philosopher Aristotle claimed that these amphibians were impervious to heat. Due to their legendary power to withstand fire, salamanders were considered to be devilish. Salamanders appear to be crawling in the general direction of the hermit saint's shack. One of them seems only inches away. Nonetheless, they will not likely be able to enter. The intensity of Jerome's devotion appears capable of warding them off or, at least, of keeping them at bay.

Rabbits can also be seen near the saint's home. Although they may look innocent, rabbits often connote carnal desire, due to their ability to multiple rapidly, and this seems to be the case in Patinir's painting. According to the *Golden Legend*, Jerome repeatedly beat himself to combat the fires of lust that burned within his flesh. The presence of

---

[20] Carol Purtle, *The Marian Paintings of Jan van Eyck* (Princeton, NJ: Princeton University Press, 1982), 92.

the rabbits in the Louvre panel reveals the temptations of the flesh as well as Jerome's power of resistance.

Although much of the flora in Patinir's painting is not easily identifiable, the thistles and thorns that appear in the lower left and on the right side of the hermit's hut allude to the hardships of life. Not only do the thorns remind the viewer of the wounded lion in Jerome's hagiography; they also suggest the painful presence of sin that pricks the flesh of humanity, while simultaneously advocating penance as a means for its removal.[21]

Patinir's landscapes demand an active attention to details. His paintings do not unfold in a continuous fashion. Rather than employ linear perspective, which is typically constructed from a stationary and singular point of view, Patinir arranges his composition as a series of disjointed vignettes, thus encouraging beholders to shift their eyes from one site to another. In the Louvre panel, viewers are invited to make mental journeys and discover paths they can call their own. As imaginative travelers, observers are not only presented with opportunities to see distant places, they are also given chances to look within themselves, to see which road they are following in the pilgrimage of life.

As Reindert Falkenburg has suggested, Patinir's landscapes frequently present two potential paths for the viewer to take on their spiritual journey. They are shown an easy route and a difficult one. Like the wide and narrow ways described in Matthew 7, one road leads to perdition, whereas the other offers a path toward spiritual perfection. Patinir's panel also alludes to Saint Augustine's *City of God*. On the left (sinister) side of the painting, figures can be seen traveling by horseback, by ship, and by foot. In the middle ground, a shepherd tends his flock in green pastures, while a farmer plows his fields. Meanwhile, a man escorts his donkey, laden with grain, to a nearby windmill. Everything seems to be running smoothly in this pleasant countryside and quiet hamlet. Yet life here is not as innocent as it appears. In the middle of the village, a man and a woman speak with one another over the threshold of an inn. Although their conversation may seem harmless, the architecture indicates otherwise. The building includes a large dovecote, surrounded by numerous flying birds. Most likely, the inn

---

[21] Falkenburg, *Joachim Patinir*, 94. Cf. Reindert Falkenburg, "The Devil Is in the Detail: Ways of Seeing Joachim Patinir's 'World Landscapes,'" in Vergara, *Patinir*, 61–79.

is a house of ill repute. The Greco-Roman goddess of fertility is often depicted with doves. Consequently, contemporary viewers would have readily associated the birds with lust. Furthermore, in Dutch slang, the verb *vogelen*, literally "to bird," was often used in reference to sexual relations. By extension, aviaries and birdhouses were common euphemisms for brothels. The apparent purity of the scene is deceptive, for it is a place of lustful temptation. Most of the figures on this side of the painting seem to move easily from one place to another. Yet they fail to recognize that they are on a spiritual journey. For them, life is merely a mundane affair. In the distance, a larger community can be seen, offering a destination akin to the *civitas terrena* or earthly city described by Augustine.

By contrast, on the right (dexter) side of the painting, a solitary traveler walks toward the Bethlehem monastery, which resembles a Romanesque pilgrimage church. Like Augustine's *civitas Dei*, it offers a place where the converted can unite with God. The traveler in Patinir's panel is approaching a large wayside cross, a resting place where visitors are encouraged to meditate on the life of Christ. Soon the pilgrim will encounter a monk guiding his recently rescued donkey, laden with goods, down the pathway. Unlike their counterparts on the left, these righteous travelers demonstrate concern for their souls, for they recognize that life is a spiritual journey.

Patinir's landscape is not merely a naturalistic description of the world, nor is it simply a passive illustration of a text or sermon. On the contrary, it served as devotional image, actively promoting opportunities to meditate on the pilgrimage of life. From an elevated viewpoint, beholders are invited to consider two paths of life: an easy one descending into a fertile valley, and an arduous one through mountainous terrain leading to a monastic church. Although the idyllic dale appears to be a more enticing destination, Patinir's painting encourages viewers to imitate Saint Jerome by taking the more difficult trail, for it is the route directed toward greater proximity with the divine. Choosing the alternate path may be less laborious and lead to earthly prosperity, but it will bring the sojourner no closer to God or eternal life.

Although Patinir's painting seems to warn against worldly desires, there is no reason to believe that it was made primarily for monks. *Contemptus mundi*, condemnation of the world, was not merely a monastic concern. Contemporary humanists and merchants also strove to be in the world but not of it. We may not know who purchased Patinir's panel on the open market. Nonetheless, contemporary viewers would have found pleasure in poring over the visual details of the painting, as they sought the proper walk of life. Consequently, Patinir's landscape should not be interpreted as a telltale sign of modern secularization, whereby concern for this world takes priority over the next. Although the scale of the saintly figure is diminished in relation to the landscape, this need not imply that the sacred is of lesser significance. In fact, Patinir's painting complemented and reinforced contemporary religious commitments and practices by encouraging viewers to see the presence of the spiritual within the material world. The desire to find traces of the divine in nature did not end with Patinir, either. As John Walford and others have effectively shown, seventeenth-century Dutch and Flemish artists continued to promote religious interpretations of terrain.[22] For instance, Jacob van Ruisdael did not merely describe Haarlem's famous bleaching fields and cityscape in his Zurich canvas (which is reproduced on this book's cover and discussed in the introduction). On the contrary, he subtly rearranged the topography and exaggerated the scale of the Grote Kerk, otherwise known as Saint Bavo. Although his landscape is not mountainous and is more naturalistic than Patinir's panel, it reveals spiritual concerns associated with the pilgrimage of life. Not only does the low horizon reveal the depth of the land and the height of the sky; it also shows the blessings that God has extended to this city. Throughout the painting, local residents live in peaceful harmony with their tranquil surroundings. Signs of divine providence seem to permeate the place. The enlarged church, the delicate luminosity, the pervasive sense of order, and the abundance of pristine linen indicate the presence of a gracious God.[23] Like Patinir's landscape, this seventeenth-century painting delights beholders as it promotes religious contemplation by revealing the shape of a place in relationship to the divine.

---

[22]Walford, *Jacob van Ruisdael*, 15–28. Cf. Josua Bruyn, "Towards a Scriptural Reading of Seventeenth-century Dutch Landscape Paintings," in *Masters of Seventeenth-century Dutch Landscape Painting*, ed. Peter Sutton (Boston: Museum of Fine Arts, 1987), 84–103.
[23]Walford, *Jacob van Ruisdael*, 153–154.

Hans Holbein, *The French Ambassadors*. 1533. Oil on panel, 81 1/8" x 82 1/4". National Gallery, London.
© National Gallery, London/Art Resource, NY.

6

THE PERCEPTION OF SPIRITUALITY
Hans Holbein's
The French Ambassadors

WILLIAM DYRNESS

A central focus of John Walford's scholarship has been to expand the human issues reflected in art history to include spirituality—an emphasis that, incredibly, has often been missing from many art history texts. Of the themes that Walford addresses in his popular art history text *Great Themes in Art*, he places spirituality first before the self, nature, and the city. Under this first theme he wanted to inquire,

> How do artists express spiritual aspirations, religious beliefs and concerns about humanity's place in the universe? How have artistic responses to this powerful dimension of human life changed over time?[1]

In subsequent discussions of artists and periods in his text he begins by posing these questions and placing his discussion of their subject matter squarely in this spiritual context. This essay examines how the viewer perceives such spiritual content. In his book *Jacob van Ruisdael and the Perception of Landscape*, Walford develops a meaning-directed method.[2] Interpretation involves an ordered process of exploring themes, iconography, and context to bring to light the possible spiritual meaning. This involves, Walford proposes, not only specific religious beliefs but also concerns about humanity's role and purpose in the world.

When Walford discusses *The French Ambassadors* (1533) by Hans

---

[1] E. John Walford, *Great Themes in Art* (Upper Saddle River, NJ: Prentice-Hall, 2002), 14.
[2] E. John Walford, *Jacob van Ruisdael and the Perception of Landscape* (New Haven, CT: Yale University Press, 1991).

Holbein (c. 1497–1543), for example, he acknowledges the rich display of objects reflecting the multiple interests of the two subjects.[3] This magnificence would have been typical of Renaissance portraits. But as Walford suggests, there is another story being told in this painting. Below, hovering over the floor, there is a distorted skull, and barely visible in the upper left corner, a crucifix. He notes, "These two objects . . . place human accomplishments, literally and figuratively, in a different 'perspective'." Though these two persons represented the height of humanist culture, Holbein has invested their portrait with a realism that subverts much of the self-confidence often celebrated in Renaissance portraiture.

Following Walford's model, this essay follows further that other story that Holbein is telling in this portrait. What does this show us about the spiritual and religious struggles of this time? And how did Holbein expect this other story to be perceived? Most importantly, are we able to perceive this today in the way Holbein intended?

Holbein (1497–1543) lived during some of the most turbulent years of the Reformation. Though we know much about this period, Holbein himself remains something of a mystery to scholars; unlike Dürer, he did not keep notebooks or diaries. Though we may not know in detail what he thought about these developments, the two images that we explore, primarily *The Ambassadors* but also *The Body of the Dead Christ in the Tomb* (1521), display depths of spiritual meaning that illumine both the artist and his time.

Hans Holbein, designated "the younger" to differentiate him from his artist father, was born in Augsburg.[4] By 1515, he had moved with his brother Ambrosius to Basel, where he excelled at fine portraits and drawings—including illustrations (at age 17 or 18) for *In Praise of Folly* by Erasmus, who was to become a close friend. Holbein studied with the humanist scholar Beatus Rhenanus, who taught him Latin and the classics, an unusual pursuit for a painter. In addition to his portraits, during his time in Basel he likely painted religious subjects, some of which, it is believed, were destroyed during subsequent episodes of iconoclasm. By 1522, Basel had become a Lutheran city and

---

[3] Walford, *Great Themes in Art*, 260–261. The quote that follows is from 261.
[4] A good introduction to his life is Derek Wilson, *Hans Holbein: Portrait of an Unknown Man* (London: Weidenfeld & Nicolson, 1996).

was under the influence of the Reformer Johannes Oecolampadius. Holbein surely sat under his preaching, and he provided illustrations for Luther's German translation of the New Testament when it was published in Basel in 1522.[5]

From 1526 to 1529 Holbein lived in London, where he was warmly received by the humanists there, including Sir Thomas More, whose portrait he painted. He may have been motivated to leave Basel by the iconoclastic episodes that were increasing, assuming, rightly as it turned out, that there would be no market for his religious painting there. In England, More was influential in obtaining commissions for Holbein, whose portraits were admired in the royal court. From 1529 to 1532, he lived again in Basel, where Oecolampadius was desperately seeking to manage radical elements intent on throwing down images in city churches. Holbein formally sided with the Reformation during this time and quietly worked on portraits and murals. Though no records remain of his movements during this period, it is widely believed he visited Italy, or at least was exposed to Italian work during his travels in France. By 1532 he was back in London, and early in 1533 Jean of Dinteville, the French ambassador to the Court of Henry VIII, contacted him to do a portrait of himself and a visiting friend, Bishop Georges de Selve. *The Ambassadors* was finished by mid-year, in time for Dinteville to take it back with him when he returned in November to his home in Polisy, in the south of France.

What is to be made of this magnificent portrait? More to the point, what does it show about the religious longings of the time when Holbein painted it? How did Holbein capture spiritual meaning? Many of the details, even the identity of the subjects, were lost to art historians until 1900, when Mary Hervey published a scrupulously researched study of the painting and of the two figures.[6] She brought to light many details of the portrait. Jean de Dinteville, to the left, was the 29-year-old ambassador of Francis I to the court of Henry VIII. His friend Bishop Georges de Selve, age 25, was serving as an ambassador to Emperor Charles V. De Selve was in England visiting Dinteville, whom he had known for years. The two friends no doubt shared their

---

[5] Wilson, *Hans Holbein*, 90. Erasmus complained in 1524 that "Oecolampadius is reigning here," and left the city soon afterward (96).
[6] Mary F. S. Hervey. *Holbein's 'Ambassadors': The Picture and the Men* (London: George Bell & Sons, 1900).

concerns over the religious divisions in Europe and the violence that threatened, turmoil that de Selve had occasion to witness firsthand.

Dinteville had his own reasons to be worried. A liberal Catholic, he had had significant interaction with Reformers in France. In fact earlier, Francis I had placed his youngest son, Prince Charles, under Dinteville's immediate care. And Francis, no doubt influenced by Dinteville, called on the famous Reformer Lefèvre d'Etaples to educate his son.[7] Up to this point, Dinteville had been able to keep himself above the battles that were brewing. At the time of this portrait, however, this was becoming increasingly difficult.

Dinteville had returned to France in February 1533 for his second assignment as ambassador. By all accounts, he had proven himself a highly successful diplomat. But now in early 1533 things were not going well between Francis and Henry, and Dinteville struggled to smooth things over, or at least delay a breach.[8] In fact, on the night he returned, February 4, Henry welcomed him with a great banquet. Henry, who had secretly married Anne Boleyn in January, was anxiously awaiting news about his proposed divorce from Katherine of Aragon that he expected Dinteville had brought. It was around this time that Dinteville approached Holbein to paint a portrait of himself and his friend, Georges de Selve.

So what does the painter intend to represent, beyond a simple reminder of a friendship and a visit to England? The display of rich drapery and robes typically located the sitter in their social and economic situation and gives some indication of their interests and vocation. The floor patterning (copied from the floor of Westminster Abbey) picked up a central Renaissance trope symbolizing humanity as a microcosm in the macrocosm. The two men lean on a sideboard, or what-not, with an upper level containing objects for exploring the heavens, the lower with references to life on the earth.[9] Of particular interest on the lower shelf, along with a book of mathematics, are a lute with one broken string and a German Lutheran hymnbook. While the hymnbook may have been familiar to Holbein from Basel, since both of his subjects

---

[7] Ibid., 40–43. Hervey comments, "At no time, perhaps, were the prospects of the Reformation brighter at the court of France than in these years" (45).

[8] Ibid., 96. See the account of Dinteville's arrival, 70–77.

[9] A good description of the objects and their meaning is found in Susan Foister, Ashok Roy, and Martin Wyld, *Holbein's Ambassadors*, Making and Meaning (Washington and New Haven: National Gallery and Yale University Press, 1997), 30–43.

were Catholics, it is not likely that he would have included this without their consent—probably that of Bishop de Selve in particular, since the book is at his side. Perhaps the hymn "Veni Sanctus Spiritus" ("Come, Holy Spirit," from the eleventh century), which is clearly visible, is meant as an appeal to the whole of Christendom to pray for the unity that the bishop sought, but which only the Spirit can bring.

From this richly furnished space these two figures stare out dispassionately at the viewer, Dinteville dressed in ermine and wearing the Order of Saint Michael, de Selve dressed in a clerical fur-lined robe and collar. All this is characteristic of Renaissance portraits of this time. But as Erika Michael says, Holbein was known for his "augmentation of the formal and pictorial language of the Renaissance."[10] That is, Holbein is taking that language further than any previous painter had been able to do. Indeed, it is to the interrogatory presence and gaze that the viewer is drawn when looking at the picture. No doubt the objects display a world and time out of joint, but the figures stand out sharply from this background story. They look back at our looking. There is evidence of Italian influence on this work, and the attention to detail recalls the Netherlandish painters. But as one scholar points out, "It is difficult to decide whether Holbein was following Netherlandish or German models, or if he drew rather on Italian patterns."[11] The fact is, he was able to draw on all these influences to forge an illusion of individual presence that has captivated viewers and artists ever since. How did he accomplish this?

Keith Moxey argues that Holbein is able to do this because he stands at the seam of a cataclysm over representation that was taking place at this time.[12] Though the elements were chosen jointly by the patron and the artist, according to the usual custom, there is little doubt that the overall feel of the picture is the result of Holbein's skill. In fact Erika Michael goes so far as to say the image represents the "self-fashioning of Holbein."[13]

These portraits radiate a presence, Moxey believes, because

---

[10] Erika Michael, "The Legacy of Holbein's *Gedankenreichtum*," in *Hans Holbein: Paintings, Prints and Reception*, ed. Mark Roskill and John Oliver Hand (Washington and New Haven: National Gallery of Art and Yale University Press, 2001), 227.
[11] Oscar Bätschmann and Pascal Griener (London: Reaktion, 1997), 102. Though they are speaking of his paintings of the Virgin, this comment applies as well to this portrait.
[12] Keith Moxey, "Mimesis and Iconoclasm," *Art History* 32/1 (2009): 59–73.
[13] Michael, "Legacy of Holbein's *Gedankenreichtum*," 228.

Holbein "exploit[s] verisimilitude for anthropological purposes that are much older and deeper, and which are associated with the kind of power attributed to images in [medieval] spiritual practice."[14] The struggles reflected in the portrait were not only religious and political, but also deeply metaphysical, and this struggle is reflected, Moxey believes, in Holbein's images.

To understand Moxey's point it is necessary to remind ourselves of the context of this painting. The religious longings of the time had issued in what might be called a crisis of representation. How does one represent an invisible God? More importantly, how might divine power be mediated? At the end of the medieval period for a variety of reasons there occurred what Carlos Eire called the "externalization of piety."[15] The commissioning of religious paintings in Zurich, for example, increased a hundredfold between 1500 and 1520, and religious observance focused almost entirely on the external practices of pilgrimage and feast days. But the increase of altars in churches and religious imagery, which paralleled in many ways the exponential growth of learning, did nothing to still the religious anxieties—as the experience of Luther and also of Erasmus amply demonstrate.

In the medieval period the eye had long been privileged. The exchange that took place between what one sees and the eye that sees, was understood to be an actual physical exchange. For this reason, while images told stories of the saints and biblical personages, they did more than this. In 1492, barely a generation before Holbein, a Dominican preacher, Fra Michele da Carcano, described the levels on which medieval images were understood to work. Images were important, he said, for three reasons:

> First, on account of the ignorance of simple people, so that those who are not able to read the scriptures can yet learn by seeing the sacraments of our salvation and faith in pictures. . . . Second, images were introduced on account of our emotional sluggishness; so that men who are not aroused to devotion when they hear about the histories of the Saints may at last be moved when they see them, *as if actually present*, in pictures. Third they were introduced on account of our

---

[14] Moxey, "Mimesis and Iconoclasm," 59.
[15] Carlos M. N. Eire, *War against Idols* (Cambridge: Cambridge University Press, 1986), 13. On this see also William Dyrness, *Reformed Theology and Visual Culture: The Protestant Imagination from Calvin to Edwards* (Cambridge: Cambridge University Press, 2004), 40–48, and the literature cited there.

unreliable memory . . . because many people cannot retain in their memories what they hear, but they do remember if they see images.[16]

Much is interesting in this explanation, not least the assumption that the eye was more effective than the ear for holding something in the mind—memory being such an important component of what Mary Carruthers calls the medieval craft of thought.[17]

But with the preaching of the Reformers these longstanding assumptions were being called into question. John Calvin, for example, writing sometime after Holbein's portraits were painted, insisted that, "In the preaching of the word, the external minister holds forth the vocal word and it is received by the ears. The internal minister, the Holy Spirit, truly communicates the thing proclaimed . . . so that it is not necessary that Christ, or for that matter his word be received through the organs of the body, but the Holy Spirit effects this union by his secret virtue."[18] But of course it *is* necessary for this to be communicated through a physical organ, and here, in contrast to the medieval pattern, the ear has been privileged over the eye. Now the ear rather than the eye has become a vehicle of divine presence. Images no longer serve to recall biblical persons and events, and, in particular, they no longer move viewers by making figures "actually present."

To clarify this power one needs only to look at an artist working on the other side of the seam introduced by the Reformation, Lucas Cranach the Elder. While he earlier painted allegorical scenes common in the Renaissance, during the 1520s Cranach became friendly with Martin Luther and his associate Philip Melanchthon. Luther had no problem with images, recognizing their importance in illustrating biblical texts. For example, *The Crucifixion (Allegory of Redemption)*, an altarpiece done for Saints Peter and Paul in Weimar in 1555, illustrates the role of images that Luther encouraged. The picture itself is really an extension of the preaching ministry of the Reformer—the blood streaming from the side of Christ falls into a chalice. This is,

---

[16] Quoted in Michael Baxandall, *Painting and Experience in Fifteenth-century Italy*, 2nd ed. (Oxford: Oxford University Press, 1988), 41 (emphasis mine). Baxandall describes these as "readily accessible stimuli to meditation on the Bible and lives of Saints."

[17] Mary Carruthers. *The Craft of Thought 400–1200* (Cambridge: Cambridge University Press, 1998).

[18] John Calvin, *Theological Treatises*, ed. J. K. S. Reid (London: SCM Press, 1954), 173.

Neil MacGregor says, "the word made paint . . . art as argument."[19] The image of Christ on the cross is present in the worship space, but it has nothing to do with that space, other than underlining what is being preached from the pulpit.

For Cranach, a version of the first of Carcano's prescriptions about images is allowed, but neither of the other two—especially not the emotional force of these figures being actually present, actually looking back at the viewer. Joseph Koerner calls these images "confessional portraits"[20] and contrasts them with the visceral sense of presence of Holbein's portraits. Cranach's project, he argues, is a mirror of disenchantment—explaining why perhaps so many commentators see Cranach's work as almost modern in its impact. This is Koerner's summary: "Lucas Cranach represents persons in order to demand what persons ought to do. They give orders and establish order, positioning bodies in a field of force."[21] Meanwhile, behind Holbein's portraits, Koerner says, "supported only by substances whose earthy names have been revived, stand presences singular, local and real."[22]

Koerner's observations resonate with Keith Moxey's argument. The portrait at this period, Moxey argues, is "still haunted by its role in religious practice."[23] Holbein draws on this role; Cranach rejects it. Moxey sees a further clue to this struggle in the anamorphotic skull that appears in the lower center of the picture. The skull as a vanitas symbol of death and mortality was a common medieval trope. Interestingly, however, the majority of Holbein's portraits seem uninterested in mortality.[24] And this image is not immediately recognizable—only when the viewer bends down and looks at the image from the right is it clearly seen as a skull. What does Holbein intend by this intrusion? The fact that the shadow of this image falls in the opposite direction to others in the picture suggests that Holbein intends more than a subtle reference to mortality. While it may underline Dinteville's

---

[19] Neil MacGregor with Erika Langmuir, *Seeing Salvation: Images of Christ in Art* (London: National Gallery, 2000), 202. See on this point the excellent article by Dieter Koepplin, "Cranach's Paintings of Charity in the Theological and Humanist Spirit of Luther and Melanchthon," in *Cranach*, ed. Bodo Brinkmann (London: Royal Academy of Arts, 2008), 63–79.
[20] Joseph Leo Koerner, "Confessional Portraits," in *Hans Holbein: Paintings, Prints, and Reception*, 126. Cranach's altarpieces, Koerner writes, are the "visual equivalent of confessional texts." In fact, says Koerner, in Cranach's work one sees in part the emergence of the confessional church (130).
[21] Ibid., 126.
[22] Ibid., 135.
[23] Moxey, "Mimesis and Iconoclasm," 61.
[24] Foister, *Holbein's Ambassador*, 46.

melancholy at his fruitless diplomacy and de Selve's despair over the religious conflicts, it surely does more than this. Moxey believes the fact that the skull tears at the fabric of the picture surface suggests Holbein intends it as a metaphor for the iconoclasm of the period—it is a trace of the cataclysm that challenged the medieval representation of reality. Meanwhile its power is parasitic on the medieval views of images. Cranach's work stands on the other side of the clash. His images have no life of their own; they do not, in themselves, invite prayer or move the viewer to praise.[25]

Most Protestant readers would find the images of Cranach unproblematic; in fact we see them as clear and convincing. We have come to accept that paintings should not have an aura of spirituality. We are comfortable with the fact that pictures are inert. But in the last generation important voices have been raised to dispute the notion that images can ever be completely without power. Let me cite two examples. David Freedberg has argued that the whole attempt to suppress images is futile. Indeed he suggests that aniconism is a myth. Since Plato, he argues, people have tended to invest images with divine quality, "as if that were the only way to grasp it."[26] According to Freedberg, we cannot divorce ourselves from this history entirely. More recently W. J. T. Mitchell has argued that "there is no way of getting beyond pictures. . . . [they] are our way of gaining access to whatever . . . things are."[27] Rather than images losing their aura, as Walter Benjamin predicted, they have increasingly come alive. Mitchell suggests that an epithet for our times is "not the modernist slogan: 'things fall apart,' but an even more ominous slogan: 'things come alive'." He proposes that we understand images as "'go-betweens' in social transactions, as a repertoire of screen images or templates that structure our encounters with other human beings." We cannot eliminate either their ubiquity or their power.

But something has to do with the expectation that viewers bring to images. When we suppose images merely illustrate, that is what they do. But what if we imagined that they do more? What if, when we

---

[25] Moxey, "Mimesis and Iconoclasm," 67, 73.
[26] David Freedberg, *The Power of Images: Studies in the History and Theory of Response* (Chicago: University of Chicago Press, 1989), 54–77 (the quote is from 66).
[27] *What Do Pictures Want? The Lives and Loves of Images* (Chicago: University of Chicago Press, 2005), xiv; subsequent quotes are from 335 and 351.

were not noticing, they *did* do more? What if we stood before them as though they did? Freedberg notes that it is only when stared at, when prayed before, that figures come alive.[28]

Something of the power of Holbein's images is illustrated by the experience of viewers of an earlier work, *The Body of the Dead Christ in the Tomb*. The long, horizontal image of a decaying body has powerfully affected many viewers, but none more deeply than the writer Dostoyevsky.[29] Perhaps it was his Orthodox practice of praying before an icon that motivated Dostoyevsky in 1876 to stand transfixed before this image, while visiting Basel in 1876. His wife described the experience:

> [Dostoyevsky] stood for twenty minutes before the picture without moving. On his face there was the frightened expression I have often noticed during the first moments of his epileptic fits. He had no fit at the time, but he could never forget the sensation he had experienced . . . : the figure of Christ taken down from the cross, his body already showing signs of decomposition, haunted him like a horrible nightmare.[30]

For Dostoyevsky the image told the story of Christ taken down from the cross, ready for burial, but it did more: it moved him to devotion by showing the body *as if it were actually present there*—the long thin legs, swollen feet, and spindly fingers reaching out beyond the picture plane, the gaping mouth of a man who is God, capture a power that can only be described as spiritual in its impact. In the words that Swiss writer Jules Baillods put in Holbein's mouth, "I, Hans Holbein, do not lie! There is your God. He is dead. You cannot doubt it, can you? Look at him . . . behold those eyes of a cadaver—are you weeping?—the eyes turned up, turned toward somewhere else in limitless desperation, in total defeat, absolute surrender. Look at your God."[31] Baillods here captures something not only of the energy of this image but also of the habits of seeing that allow that power to be seen and felt.

---

[28] Freedberg, *Power of Images*, 320.

[29] The story has been told by Anna, his wife, in her *Reminiscences*. See Michael, "Legacy of Holbein's *Gedankenreichtum*," 202.

[30] From the preface to *The Idiot*; quoted in John de Gruchy, *Christianity, Art, and Transformation* (Cambridge: Cambridge University Press, 2001), 99. This experience almost certainly influenced Dostoyevsky's portrayal of Prince Myshkin in that novel.

[31] From Baillods's essay "Le Christ Mort," 1942; quoted in Michael, "Legacy of Holbein's *Gedankenreichtum*," 231–232.

But despite the increasing impact of the visual on our culture, casual habits of viewing steeped in the long-term influence of icono-clastic impulses tend to reduce images to the information they convey. We have lost a great deal of the power of images as likeness and not as illustration. Protestants, the heirs of Cranach and not of Holbein, in many places are rediscovering images and employing art in their places of worship. But can long-term habits be broken so that images can stand on their own to awaken sluggish emotions as well as prod lagging memories?

A recent and admirable reference to Holbein may be taken as an example of this challenge. Missiologist David Smith, in a fine discus-sion of current mission prospects, makes use of Holbein's *Ambassadors* in his chapter on secularization.[32] Smith sees in Holbein's image an allusion to the challenges associated with the process of seculariza-tion—a process that was surely begun, he argues, by the spirit repre-sented in the painting. On the one hand Holbein celebrates the new learning of the Renaissance—the compass, terrestrial and celestial globes, and sundial. Yet, according to Smith, the picture displays an unease with all this: the men stare unblinking at the viewer, the lute has a broken string, and most significantly the cross is almost hid-den while the skull intrudes into our space. Smith concludes, "The ability to plot the motion of the stars will not help a man find direc-tion in his own life, nor will the sweet sound of the lute soothe his nerves once the whiff of a corpse has penetrated his nostrils."[33] With faith pushed to the margins, he wonders, how will these men escape the chaos of the wars of religion? Of course much of this was in the future, but Smith argues that the subsequent history, especially the bloody twentieth century, more than justified the concerns that Holbein puts on display.

The reference to Holbein in this discussion is to be commended; it surely adds nuance to Smith's reference to the problems of secular-ization, and is both effective and unusual. It is a helpful illustration of the argument of this chapter. But it does not attempt to say why the images have the strange ability to stick with viewers, to move them in ways that are unexpected. It does not acknowledge that this image

---

[32] David Smith, *Mission after Christendom* (London: Darton, Longman, & Todd, 2003), 13–14.
[33] Ibid., 14.

wants to do more than convey information; it wants a response from the viewer.

This, then, is part of the other story that John Walford sees this picture telling. It is a window into a religious struggle, to be sure, to an uncertain time in which the rapid advancement of culture was offering more than it could deliver. But beyond this it was actually participating in that struggle and, if we have eyes to see, it calls us to do the same.

Pieter Bruegel the Elder, *Hunters in the Snow*. 1565. Oil and tempera on panel, 3'10" x 5'4". Kunsthistorisches Museum, Vienna. Photo: Erich Lessing/Art Resource, NY.

7

A LOCALIZED PROVIDENCE
Pieter Bruegel the Elder's
Hunters in the Snow

RACHEL-ANNE JOHNSON

Pieter Bruegel the Elder's *Hunters in the Snow* is an imaginative and thought-provoking image of a winter's day. It is a bleak day as the hunters return to the village. The dogs are weary, though the hunters' catch is meager. Outside an inn, peasant women stoke a large fire, as a man brings a wooden table outside, both activities in preparation for the singeing of a fattened pig whose meat will be stored for the long winter months. In the town below, a woman hauls firewood across a snow-laden bridge while across the pond a cart, fully loaded with wood and kindling, makes its way through the village. In contrast to these labors that must be completed to survive the season, the majority of the villagers are making the most of the day on frozen ponds at the foot of the hill, skating, curling, and playing hockey. Beyond them, in the distance, jagged cliffs cut through the frozen flats, shielding a riverside town from the onslaught of snow that presses in from the right. On the edge of this town, the river is frozen over and figures venture on foot and with carts from its banks.

Hunters in the Snow (1565) was painted as part of a series of landscapes by Bruegel that depict the seasons of the year, often referred to as the *Months*, which also includes *The Gloomy Day* (Kunsthistoriches Museum, Vienna), *Haymaking* (Lobkowicz Palace, Prague Castle, Prague), *The Harvesters* (The Metropolitan Museum of Art, New York), and *Return of the Herd* (Kunsthistoriches Museum, Vienna). On one level, *Hunters in the Snow* depicts the traditional labors for the months of December and January.[1] In medieval prayer books, calendar illumina-

---

[1] For a detailed discussion of the debate about which months seem to be represented in Bruegel's panels compared with medieval precedents, see Iain Buchanan, "The Collection of Niclaes Jongelinck II: The 'Months' by Pieter Bruegel the Elder," *The Burlington Magazine* (August 1990): 541–550.

tions depicted the labors and activities appropriate to certain times of year. December was characterized by singeing the pig and January by hunting motifs,[2] conventions that were well-established by the sixteenth century and present in almost every illuminated manuscript from the Bruges workshop of Simon Bening, the most likely precedent for seasonal imagery with which Bruegel would have been familiar.[3] Bruegel includes various aspects of hunting in the image by depicting the group of hunters and dogs in the foreground, the inn's sign to their left that references Saint Hubert, the patron saint of hunters, and a bird-trap in the left middleground.[4] The slaughter of a pig is a conventional motif for December, while singeing the pig is typical for January.[5] Though no pig is present in Bruegel's winter landscape, this progression of activity is suggested by the large fire on the left and the man carrying the table outside, which could represent the next stage—quartering the animal.

On another level, however, there is much more going on in Bruegel's image than these traditional activities, and the composition raises a number of questions regarding how contemporary viewers would have understood *Hunters in the Snow*. Why at this time does Bruegel monumentalize a typically small-format genre? *Hunters in the Snow* measures forty-six by sixty-four inches, compared with a calendar illumination that rarely would have been larger than six by five inches.[6] Why do so many figures and motifs diverge from the conventions of previous calendar illustrations? The traditional labors are subtle and peripheral in relation to the entire image. Why the elaborate detail and unconventional motifs within images that were traditionally formulaic in subject matter? And, ultimately, how were these elements meant to be understood at the time, in their original context?

In an attempt to explain Bruegel's elaborations and monumental scale, many scholars have situated Bruegel's series of the *Months* firmly within the realm of world-landscapes. In this artistic tradition, land-

---

[2] Ibid., 544, 546.

[3] For the history of seasonal and months imagery, see Charles Boutell, "Symbols of the Seasons and Months Represented in Early Art," *The Art Journal* n.s. 3 (1877): 233–236; and James Fowler, "On Medieval Representations of the Months and Seasons," *Archaeologia* 46 (1873): 137–224.

[4] Buchanan, "Collection of Niclaes Jongolinek II," 544.

[5] Ibid. In E. John Walford, *Great Themes in Art* (Upper Saddle River, NJ: Prentice-Hall, 2002), 264, the author mentions that the motif of the pig is slightly anachronistic in the series, as it references the traditional labors from November. Late autumn was, in fact, the traditional time for fattening the pig that would be slaughtered later, in the winter months. The appendix in Buchanan's article clarifies these distinctions.

[6] 6.75 x 5 inches are the dimensions for the calendar illuminations of the months in Simon Bening's *Da Costa Hours* (Bruges, Belgium, ca. 1515; reprint New York: Morgan Library, 1972), MS. 399).

scapes were constructed to embody a cosmic significance, connecting the seasons and their activities to a higher order of religious providence and celestial harmony. The labors of the seasons reflect an order to the world that is both cyclical and divinely ordained. Another branch of scholarship takes the world-landscape characteristics of Bruegel's *Months* and attaches to them the conventional devotional practices of the medieval calendar tradition and the use of religious symbols that one sees in the work of the Flemish landscape painter Joachim Patinir.[7]

To these interpretations, discussed further below, this essay argues for another crucial element in understanding the original context of *Hunters in the Snow*, which is that the image, and its fellow panels from Bruegel's series of the *Months*, are descriptive of Antwerp's suburbs specifically, rather than merely monumentalized calendar illustrations of seasonal activity based on the prescribed models of medieval sources. It is, like many other images from Bruegel's oeuvre, a localized genre painting—a scene from everyday life that derives its meaning from the perception of familiar objects or activity within it. Bruegel's personal experience of Antwerp's countryside has been noted as a possible factor in the creation of landscapes like *Hunters in the Snow*, but only in general terms, and without regard to the experience of the panel's original audience.[8] The artist's inclusion of local and historical elements, common to all five of Bruegel's *Months*, contributes to the images' function as visual chorographical narratives, or descriptions offering an embodied perspective of a region (*choros*), stressing local details and characteristics. This perspective is uniquely experiential in its depiction of local agricultural activity, the connection of landscape elements, travel, local economic interests, and idiosyncratic details of life in and around 1560s Antwerp.[9] This interpretive framework takes into account the original suburban location of *Hunters in the Snow* and an ensemble of motifs that would have been recognized by its original owner, Niclaes Jonghelinck, as referring to Antwerp itself and his own role in the city's social fabric.

---

[7]R. L. Falkenburg, "Antithetical Iconography in Early Netherlandish Landscape Painting," in *Bruegel and Netherlandish Landscape Painting from the National Gallery Prague* (Tokyo: The Asahi Shimbun, 1990), 25–36.

[8]Walter S. Gibson, "In Detail: Pieter Bruegel's *The Harvesters*," *Portfolio* 3 (May/June 1981): 40–45.

[9]The description of local details in Bruegel's series of the *Months* informs the core argument of the author's forthcoming dissertation, "Suburban Bruegel: Chorography and Rhetoric in Pieter Bruegel the Elder's Series of the Month" (PhD Diss., University of California, Santa Barbara, 2012).

The goal of this essay, then, is the reconciliation of the secular and spiritual understandings of *Hunters in the Snow*, and the entire series of the *Months* by extension, demonstrating that its contemporary audience would have extrapolated meaning from the image by drawing on both local knowledge and experience of Antwerp's countryside, and a spiritual understanding of the motifs Bruegel includes based on the artistic traditions from which they derive. The precedents of medieval calendars and the world-landscape tradition provide a spiritual context for Bruegel's landscapes, while the localized details within them provide the means by which their original viewers inferred significance from them. It is through the recognition of the familiar and the knowledge of artistic precedents that meaning emerges. Ultimately, these elements work together to reveal the perception of a landscape of providence—both the divine providence of God and nature, and the local providence of the region of Antwerp as it went about its seasonal labors.

Although scholars have acknowledged that Bruegel's series of the *Months* can be seen as "faithful transcription[s] of the countryside,"[10] and thus an appropriate comparison to a chorographic view of the region around Antwerp, there has been a tendency to pass over chorographical considerations in favor of placing the landscapes within the larger geographical context of world-landscapes. It seems that because the series has traditionally been called *Months*, and cycles of seasonal motifs were meant to be nearly universal in their application, one is immediately inclined to think of these images in the same context. Svetlana Alpers, in *The Art of Describing*, uses the categories of cartography, or map-making, to place Bruegel's work within the confines of the world-landscape genre:

> We might also want to use mapping terms to distinguish the larger *geographical* ambitions of Bruegel's *Season* landscapes from the specific *chorographic* concerns of his drawings of the Ripa Grande or the painting of the Bay of Naples. . . . By combining the traditional themes of the seasons with an extensive mapped view of the earth, Bruegel gives the yearly cycle a world rather than a local dimension . . .[11]

Alpers differentiates images like *Hunters in the Snow* from works like *Naval Battle in the Bay of Naples* (1558–1562), arguing that we

---

[10] Gibson, "In Detail," 40.
[11] Svetlana Alpers, The Art of Describing: Dutch Art in the Seventeenth Century (Chicago: University of Chicago Press, 1983), 142–144.

do not have a specific topographical location to connect with the former as we do the latter. Furthermore, because Bruegel composed *Hunters in the Snow* using a bird's-eye perspective of the winter scene, the viewer is set apart from the image, asked to contemplate it with a particular detachment from an impossible vantage point. This view, as Walter Gibson has described it, is "truly cosmic in scope, showing the great forces of nature playing over immense portions of the earth's surface"[12] as they "subordinat[e] the world of the peasant to the much vaster world of nature."[13] The implications of the world-landscape context, thus, also apply to the human activity within *Hunters in the Snow*, suggesting that the overarching view of reality presented in this image is that nature and cosmic forces determine the activities of the everyday. Furthermore, Gibson connects Bruegel's view of nature, and the peasants' subordinate position within it, to Virgil's *Georgics*, a classical poem that moves from the "mundane details of farming and cattle-breeding to rhapsodic descriptions of the celestial constellations and the great meteorological forces affecting the world."[14] In these interpretations, then, Bruegel is presenting a view of reality that is shaped by the cosmos—a world that is not lived in, but looked upon.

One way in which a viewer might look upon such a world is with an eye for spiritual perception. Medieval books of hours, where the conventional labors of the months were first codified and presented within a devotional context, depicted the activities of each season under the divinely ordained cycles of both the cosmos and the church. These books directed their readers through devotions that were to be done at certain times of the day and on particular holy days throughout the year, complementing each devotional text with illustrations of the agricultural and leisure activities that marked such times. The illustrations were most often juxtaposed with zodiac imagery or celestial maps, emphasizing the cosmic structure that dictated the labors shown beneath them.

The labors are further contextualized by the inclusion of details pertinent to the patron or owner of a particular book of hours. In the case of the *Très Riches Heures* of Jean, the Duke of Berry, the activities

---

[12] Walter S. Gibson, "Pieter Bruegel the Elder and the Flemish World Landscape of the Sixteenth Century," in *Bruegel and Netherlandish Landscape Painting*, 21.

[13] Gibson, "In Detail," 44.

[14] Walter S. Gibson, *Bruegel* (New York and Toronto: Oxford University Press, 1977), 156.

in the calendar illustrations take place not only beneath the zodiac signs and a star map, but also in the shadow of the duke's palaces, depicted as accurate portraits in the background of many of the illuminations.[15] In this way, the spiritual meaning of seasonal labor within a divine and cosmic cycle is focused for the book's reader through the association with recognizable places. Similarly, in *Hunters in the Snow*, the labors and activities presented are subordinate to the broad landscape that suggests the region of Antwerp. Though the celestial and zodiac imagery are no longer present in the *Months*, Bruegel retains the idea of attaching familiar places to the activities depicted. Jongelinck's world, like the duke's in the *Très Riches Heures*, looms over and around the seasons that Bruegel depicts.

The way in which this spiritual mode of perception may have functioned in regard to *Hunters in the Snow* is argued by Reindert Falkenburg, who discusses the series, not only in terms of its composition and vantage point, but in terms of small, religious motifs that connect Bruegel's work with that of Patinir and others, who used large-scale landscapes to frame biblical scenes. Similar to the way in which the world-landscape tradition encourages a detached evaluation from the viewer, Falkenburg suggests that Bruegel's series encouraged devotional contemplation, much closer in function to the medieval calendar illustrations of the seasons described above. The engagement of the viewer, who is put in the position of exploring the paintings to find the small vignettes, is the key to understanding how sight leads to insight in these images.[16] In this interpretation, we move from an elevated meditation on the cosmos, to a more interactive relationship with the image itself.

Within *Hunters in the Snow*, Falkenburg points to various details that implicate both the figures in the image and the viewer of the image on a spiritual level. He begins by considering the sign above the inn depicted in the left foreground of the panel, which reads, "Dit is inden Hert" ("This is in the Stag").[17] The sign also displays a rough image of Saint Hubert dropping to his knees in front of a large stag. Saint Hubert was the patron saint of hunters because he converted to Christianity after

---

[15] *Les Très Riches Heures* (Chantilly, Musée Condé, MS 65).
[16] Reindert L. Falkenburg, "Pieter Bruegel's *Series of the Seasons*: On the Perception of Divine Order," in *Liber Amicorum Raphael de Smedt*, ed. Joost van der Auwera (Leuven: Peeters, 2001), 261–262.
[17] Ibid., 268.

being shown a vision of the cross in the antlers of a stag. Falkenburg connects this sign and the reference to Saint Hubert to the fact that it appears that the only catch the hunters return with is a single fox and, thus, any appeal the hunters may have made to the patron saint was not terribly effective.[18] He then suggests that this is Bruegel's way of showing that the meager catch is a result of the hunters not having Saint Hubert properly in their hearts, and that the figures of the hunters, looking down at their feet as they pass by the inn, function as negative examples for the viewer. They go about their labors without regard to the sign at the inn or that which it represents; they are spiritually blind to their patron saint and, by extension, oblivious to the revelation of Christ indicated in the sign's portrayal of Saint Hubert's vision of the cross.[19] The viewer of the image, if focused on exploring the painted terrain while ignoring the spiritual signs (and the inn's actual sign), is implicated alongside the distracted hunters and their consequent meager spoils. Consequently, the viewer's spiritual mode of perception reads these motifs as reminders to acknowledge the role of divine providence in the labors of the seasons.

Based on this scholarship that places Bruegel's work with the world-landscape tradition and a devotional context, a religious interpretation of *Hunters in the Snow* is certainly tempting. There is little doubt that these influences contributed on at least some level to Bruegel's construction of the image. Nevertheless, neither interpretation discussed above takes into account the image's physical location in a suburban home or the interests of its original owner, a wealthy merchant. Rather than remain detached from the image in cosmic contemplation, or engaged only on a level of devotional searching, the panel's contemporary audience viewed the painting in terms of the inhabitable world outside the walls on which it hung. Just as Bruegel's large-scale panels of *The Peasant Wedding Feast* (1567) and *The Peasant Dance* (1567), or his compendiums of folk culture such as *Netherlandish Proverbs* (1559) and *Children's Games* (1559–1560), are generally accepted as displaying the artist's interest in documenting local customs,[20] the series of the *Months* also attends to daily life

---

[18] Ibid.

[19] Ibid., 269.

[20] Gibson, *Bruegel*; Ethan Matt Kavaler, *Pieter Bruegel: Parable of Order and Enterprise* (New York and Cambridge: Cambridge University Press, 1999); Mark Meadow, *Pieter Bruegel the Elder's Netherlandish Proverbs*

in Antwerp's countryside. Bruegel was first and foremost a storyteller. His worlds were populated by peasants and parties, their activities defined by the artist's use of proverbs and local flavor. Considering *Hunters in the Snow* within this more comprehensive context allows for interpretations of the image based on a regional understanding of a particular suburban locale.

Unlike many other landscapes and peasant scenes by Bruegel, the original location of the *Months* is known, and this fact sheds further light on how to contextualize our questions regarding *Hunters in the Snow*. In the mid-1550s, the prosperous Antwerp merchant Niclaes Jongelinck purchased a house just outside the city walls in a newly developed suburban area called Ter Beke. The neighborhood was a plot of land in the agricultural region surrounding Antwerp, located a short distance to the southeast of the Saint Jorispoort, the main gate of the city.[21] The land was sold in 1547 to the property developer Gilbert van Schoonbeke, who used the property to build a series of suburban residences for some of Antwerp's wealthiest burghers and nobility with the specific intention that they would be idyllic "pleasure gardens" where the city's elite could retreat from urban life.[22]

It was here where Thomas Jongelinck acquired the residence that he later sold to his brother Niclaes in 1554.[23] By 1565 this villa was home to one of Antwerp's most impressive art collections, most prominently including Bruegel's *Months*, a number of other Bruegel paintings, and two large-scale series by the artist Frans Floris. Jongelinck owned a house in the Kipdorp neighborhood within the city walls, but the *Months* were listed in an inventory of Jongelinck's Ter Beke villa the same year that the panels are dated, suggesting that they may have been specifically commissioned for this suburban residence, or at least purchased with its decoration in mind.[24]

Their presence in Jongelinck's country home may be demonstrative of the prescriptions for villa decoration found in the writing of

and the Practice of Rhetoric (Zwolle, Netherlands: Waanders, 2002); Edward Snow, *Inside Bruegel: The Play of Images in Children's Games* (New York: North Point, 1997).

[21] Francine de Nave, "De Vrijheid van Antwerpen," in *De Stad Antwerpen van de Romeinse Tijd tot de 17de EEUW* (Gemeentekrediet van België, 1978), 76.

[22] Ibid.

[23] Buchanan, "Collection of Niclaes Jongelinck II," 547.

[24] Antwerp Stadsarchief, Tresorij 1711, no. 1551, February 12, 1565.

Renaissance art theorists like Sebastiano Serlio, who based their work on the writings of the classical author Vitruvius.[25] Jongelinck himself was highly educated and interested in the humanist scholarship of the early-modern period, and it has been proposed that it was Jongelinck himself who may have introduced Bruegel to the writings of Virgil.[26] It has also been argued that Bruegel's *Months* would have been displayed in Jongelinck's dining room, their subject matter of agricultural labor and food appropriate to such a setting.[27] It is here where *Hunters in the Snow* hung, along with the rest of the series, forming an impressive assembly of monumental seasons.

Within this context, our questions about the composition and subject matter of *Hunters in the Snow* must be further focused. Though the agricultural and seasonal activities discussed may derive from conventional models, they take on more specific meanings in Bruegel's monumentalized panels hanging in a merchant's suburban villa. How would Jongelinck have understood the painting? Which details and motifs would have spoken to him and the guests he invited to his country home? Just as the details of Saint Hubert and the distracted hunters would speak to the devotionally minded, there are regional details within the image that would have resonated with an Antwerp citizen like Jongelinck.

First of all, Bruegel creates a landscape that is localized rather than generic. Compositionally, Bruegel connects the activities of the foreground and middleground with a riverside town in the background—a motif that, in the mind of the viewer, would undoubtedly be associated with the city of Antwerp on the river Schelde. Starting at the elevated position on the hill with the hunters, the curves of the land move down to the central village and frozen ponds. A network of roads and frozen canals moves through the flat middleground, indicating a network of water transport that would have been available in the warmer months of the year and possibly referencing the canals, used for market trans-

---

[25] Sebastiano Serlio, *The Five Books of Architecture: An Unabridged Reprint of the English Edition of 1611* (New York: Dover, 1982); Vitruvius, *Ten Books on Architecture*, trans. Ingrid D. Rowland (Cambridge and New York: Cambridge University Press, 1999).
[26] Gibson, *Bruegel*, 157.
[27] Claudia Goldstein, "Artifacts of Domestic Life: Bruegel's Paintings in the Flemish Home," *Nederlands Kunsthistorisch Jaarboek* 51 (2000): 173; for a broader contextualization of paintings as domestic objects and their locations with Flemish households, see also Claudia Goldstein, "Keeping Up Appearances: The Social Significance of Domestic Decoration in Antwerp, 1508–1600" (PhD Diss., Columbia University, 2003).

port, that traversed Antwerp's suburbs during the period.[28] As in many of Bruegel's landscapes, tree lines also help the viewer navigate the image. The diminishing diagonal of snow-covered branches leads from the inn at the left toward the church steeple in the village in the center of the image, while the top branches of the last tree draw the viewer's eye left to the riverside town. The viewer is taken on a journey through this landscape, not simply to delight or instruct devotionally, but to point out elements of the scene that are recognizable and important to both the artist and the viewer. In relation to Jongelinck himself, this landscape was one through which he traveled regularly, moving from the riverside city of Antwerp, through the suburban areas and peasant villages, to his own country estate in Ter Beke.

This understanding of a recognizable landscape also explains the decidedly foreign elements that Bruegel includes in *Hunters in the Snow*, and other paintings in the series, most prominent of which are the rocky outcroppings and snow-capped peaks of mountains. These rise dramatically behind the much lower hill of the immediate foreground and the relatively flat middleground, complicating any reading of the panels as topographically accurate chorographies of Antwerp's suburbs, an area with very little variation in its elevation. These inclusions certainly increase the dramatic viewing experience of the landscapes, and situate the activity of the image within a diverse and visually interesting setting, again connecting Bruegel's image with the world-landscape tradition. Beyond decoration within the landscapes, however, these elements suggest further that the image is tailored to a particular viewer. The incorporation of rocky peaks most immediately references the artist's drawings of the Alps made during his travels to Italy in the early 1550s. The combination of dramatic mountainscapes with agricultural land of much lower elevation is similar, especially, to his *Saint Jerome in the Wilderness*, drawn around 1555–1560. While Jongelinck would certainly have recognized the rocky mountains as foreign to the region around Antwerp, he also would have remembered Bruegel's travels across the Alps and recognized *Hunters in the Snow*'s connection to other images by the artist.

Within this local, yet composite, landscape, the individual figures and activities encountered on Jongelinck's virtual journey would

---

[28] For maps and diagrams of Antwerp's suburbs in the period, see de Nave, "De Vrijheid van Antwerpen."

speak to the merchant's everyday experience. Jongelinck may have used these panels to contemplate the divine providence of the seasons and be reminded of the need to acknowledge the patron saints of various activities, but the means by which he would achieve any such meditation were the details that referenced his own life and livelihood. While escaping the city at his country villa, for instance, Jongelinck certainly would have gone on hunts; even as it was a necessary endeavor for peasants to obtain supplemental food in the winter months, hunting was also a common recreational activity among the wealthy.

As mentioned above, there is also a small detail of a woman hauling firewood across a bridge at the bottom of the foreground slope, and a cart with more firewood making its way along a snowy road toward the center village. Though commonplace enough, the presence of such figures within Bruegel's winter landscape represents a much-needed winter product which the city of Antwerp relied on its suburban area to provide.[29] As someone with not one but two homes to keep warm throughout the year, Jongelinck would have been familiar with the need to procure vast amounts of firewood as part of his own seasonal activity. The particularities of the background town also reference winter activities relevant to Jongelinck's livelihood as a merchant. The freezing over of the river Schelde alongside the city of Antwerp would have had serious implications for the business activities of the commercial town, and seeing a cityscape in the distance of *Hunters in the Snow*, with its beached ships and frozen banks, would be particularly meaningful to him.

Although the focus of this essay is the *Hunters in the Snow*, and indeed, each panel in the *Months* series can be discussed for its own composition and subject matter, it is a disservice to each if they are not considered as part of a complete whole. The panels were hung together in one room, providing Jongelinck with a visual repository of the life that occurred outside the windows of his suburban villa over the course of each year, and thus the panels did not originally stand alone. The bleak winter of *Hunters in the Snow* has no real context without the *Return of the Herd* that comes before it and *The*

---

[29] Michael Limberger, *Sixteenth-century Antwerp and Its Rural Surroundings: Social and Economic Changes in the Hinterland of a Commercial Metropolis (ca. 1450–ca. 1570)* (Turnhout, Belgium: Brepols, 2008), 24, 39.

Gloomy Day that comes after. The frozen river in *Hunters in the Snow* flows into the turbulent spring waters of *The Gloomy Day*. In this next image, shipwrecks litter the river's edge, another reminder of the cycles of nature that affect a merchant's business. Those same waters bear large, sea-faring vessels in the rivers of *Haymaking*, *The Harvesters*, and *Return of the Herd*. The storm clouds moving to the right in *Return of the Herd* are followed by a rainbow, possibly refer-encing Noah and the flood in Genesis, but certainly indicating that divine providence will at least keep the cycles of weather in motion. The plentiful fruits and vegetables in the verdant *Haymaking* and the massive wheat harvest in *The Harvesters* promise that the bleakness of winter and the meager haul of the hunters will soon be replaced with the abundance of good harvests.

These details, within Bruegel's elaborations on and deviations from previous seasonal imagery, serve to characterize highly particular aspects of the region where Antwerp's food production occurred and where Jongelinck and his friends enjoyed time away from the city in suburban villas. Antwerp is both pictorially and contextually the back-ground of Bruegel's seasonal landscapes, and the artist's inclusion of localized motifs in the *Months*, a cycle that by its nature attempts to characterize a repetitive experience of time and place, would have been read by Jongelinck and his contemporaries as a visual chorography of Antwerp. These are landscapes of experience, specifically Jongelinck's, and it is the sight of such familiar spaces and places that allows for his insight into the series. Regardless of the actual weather conditions or activity outside his doors, Jongelinck is able to view his entire world within the confines of his dining room as it transforms from season to season, through changes in weather, agricultural production, and busi-ness interests. The function of the images, therefore, is not primarily to elicit detached contemplation of the cosmos or devotional medi-tation on religious motifs, but to present a world that is inhabitable and familiar, accessible to Jongelinck and his contemporaries. This interpretive framework allows the meaning of Bruegel's winterscape to emerge as it did for its original audience. *Hunters in the Snow* presents a view of the world where providence is contextualized not only as cos-mic and divine but also as local and personal. This perception is based on a certain pride for Antwerp and its region that informs Bruegel's production of the image and Jongelinck's reception of it.[30]

Within *Hunters in the Snow*, Bruegel's view of reality and his knowledge of the artistic styles informing his work are presented to a viewer who filters the image through his experience of the world around him. The work blurs the boundaries between conventional image types— medieval calendars, world-landscapes, and genre scenes—and allows for multivalent interpretations. In *Great Themes in Art*, John Walford uses the themes of spirituality, the self, the city, and nature to categorize the levels of meaning that were drawn out of images in a given period of history.[31] Though he discusses *Hunters in the Snow* as presenting a particular view of nature,[32] it is evident here that just as Bruegel's work defies categorization as an image type, it also blurs the lines between these levels of meaning. Bruegel's perception of nature and divine providence, presented in quite specific relation to the city and its suburbs during the period, provides the foundation for Jongelinck's conception of himself and his position within the socioeconomic fabric of Antwerp.

---

[30] The idea of praising the region of Antwerp for its provisions for the city, and the rhetorical reception of Bruegel's images in Jongelinck's home, are argued further in the author's forthcoming dissertation. See note 9.

[31] Walford, *Great Themes in Art*, preface.

[32] Ibid., 264–265.

Pieter Saenredam, *Interior of Saint Odulphus Church, Assendelft*. 1649. Oil on panel, 19 1/2" x 30". Rijksmuseum, Amsterdam.

8

SPACE, SYMBOL, AND SPIRIT
Pieter Saenredam's *Interior of the Church of Saint Odulphus at Assendelft*

JAN LAURENS SIESLING

Among art history survey textbooks, only John Walford's *Great Themes in Art* opens its chapter on seventeenth-century Dutch art with a painting by Pieter Jansz. Saenredam (1597–1665).[1] This choice of *Interior of the Church of Saint Odulphus at Assendelft* (1649) is judicious and another proof of the thorough composition of Walford's book. Walford was right to suggest that, to understand seventeenth-century Netherlandish art, one must start with a visit to a Dutch church.

The seventeenth-century Dutch were, indeed, a religious people; if for no other reason, Saenredam's *Saint Odulphus* may be called truly Netherlandish. However, Saenredam's painting evidences many traits that the Dutch regard as characteristic of themselves and their art. *Saint Odulphus* combines sobriety and solemnity, isolation and self-containment, artfulness without adornment, rationality rather than reasonableness, listening without obeying, self-consciousness and sin-consciousness, and, in all modesty, an abiding belief in being the providentially chosen people of God.

In suggesting that *Saint Odulphus* exemplifies seventeenth-century Dutch Calvinist values, it should be clarified that it was not Calvinism that forged the Dutch character; it was the Dutch who found in Calvinism an appropriate religion. Nevertheless, in examining Saenredam's *Saint Odulphus*, both against the historical background

---

[1] Written for John Walford, this essay is dedicated to our mutual friend and colleague at the Vrije Universiteit, Erik Bloemen, who left us after long years of intense struggle against disease.

151

of Calvinism in the seventeenth-century Netherlands and as a visual manifestation of Calvinist values, it is possible to develop an in-depth interpretation of Saenredam's painting. This essay both contextualizes the historical, religious, and nationalist motivations behind the making of this image and explores what may be described as more personal axes of influence predetermining the artist's making of this image and the fascination it still exerts on viewers.[2]

Twentieth-century scholars have shown much appreciation for this seventeenth-century painter of churches. Critics, supposing that an empty church is no subject at all, have suggested that Saenredam's goals apparently foreshadowed Modernist ones: subject-free compositions the impact of which are defined by the successful interplay of line and color. Modernist, i.e., formalist critics have proposed that the painter's churches have more to do with perspective than with religion. But that is nonsense. It is like stating that reading a poem has more to do with sitting in a chair than with poetry. It is a mistake to separate form from content. Saenredam's single and singular subject seemed to reveal an artistic ascetic, who had done away with narrative or symbols to reach out for pure description or composition, whose daring iconoclasm, while rooted in seventeenth-century values, has fascinated modern taste.

Saenredam's *Saint Odulphus*, however, is far from empty. For the artist, as for his contemporary public, the subject matter of his paintings was not merely a pretext for complex but meaningless geometry. Saenredam's patrons valued the faithful portrait of this church in their city, a monument to their pride, while the painter was avid to give sense to an art based on perfectly rendered reality. Saenredam was a Calvinist; he was a well-to-do burgher, connected to well-known families and influential personalities; and he was a respected member of the artists' guild, assuming heavy administrative functions. Although Saenredam didn't invent the genre of church-interior paintings, he gave it its *lettres de noblesse*. He had immediate and numerous followers. A leading artist and a learned man, his art was well received in his city and beyond. Saenredam's visual method may be described as objective observation and silent glorification. Saenredam represents his country

---

[2] The best text on the painter and his work is Gary Schwartz and Marten Jan Bok, *Pieter Saendredam* (New York: Abbeville, 1990). Their sensitive and profound assumptions only invite further exploration.

and defends its values, not surprisingly, since he was a son of an epoch-making war of independence.

In *Interior of the Church of Saint Odulphus at Assendelft*, Saenredam opens his childhood church before the viewer, who is present, but not participating, during a *gereformeerde* service, presumably on a Sunday morning, during the sermon.[3] Though, regretfully, the church of Saint Odulphus is no longer extant, it is still possible, four centuries later, to catch the very atmosphere of Saenredam's scene in many Protestant churches in the Netherlands. In the sparse and strictly circumscribed universe of this church, we discover numerous interconnected details, like planets in the solar system. For example, at the image's lower-right edge is a Latin epitaph, written upside down; this marks the graves of the painter's father, uncle, and nephew. Further into the church, there is the massive tomb in gray Ardennes stone of the Lords of Assendelft, an austere parallelepiped inscribed in Gothic Dutch. Against the wall opposite the tomb, on this side of the transept, there is the pew, empty on this particular day, reserved for the living lords. Although this bench of honor is simple in material and form, it is a significant reminder of the ancestral possessions of the powerful family. The painter uses this pew as a support for writing, in Dutch, the name of the place, the date, and his own signature. Thus Saenredam takes his place among his ancestors.

In this highly personal painting of his family church, Saenredam demonstrates the two skills that underlie his artistic method: detailed realism, to show the visible; and geometrically organized space, to evoke the invisible. Saenredam's detailed depiction of the pew, the tomb, and the gravestone means to convince the viewer that these looked the way they appear here and were actually sitting on the spots in the choir where the painter placed them. These details fit so well into the perspective construction that the viewer may presume that the painter arranged and staged them for the benefit of his composition.[4] Saenredam, on many verifiable occasions, demonstrated that painting, even at its most

---

[3] The central axis of the Saint Odulphus church from entrance to apse was west-east and, indeed, the light in the painting falls in on the left through the vast, though invisible, window in the south end wall of the transept, where it hits the ground. All the windows are generous light sources on this fresh and windy spring or summer day, midmorning, a typical hour for a service lasting two to three hours. I propose here that the date of the signature is not the imaginary day of this idealized scene.

[4] The gravestone of Jan Saenredam has been recovered from the destruction of the old church in the nineteenth century. It features the text as in the painting, though not quite exactly lettered and laid out the same (see Schwartz and Bok, *Pieter Saendredam*, 95, fig. 104).

realistic, is not the hostage of reality. An artist must obey the laws of his art; he must adapt reality, whenever necessary, according to his conception. Belonging to a higher reality than sight, painting is a reality with its own internal logic. In discussing the art of the seventeenth-century landscape painter Jacob van Ruisdael, John Walford observed, "The more closely an image approximates to natural appearances, the more easily one can overlook the modes of perception that inevitably influence the transformation of [observed reality] into art."[5]

While Saenredam's painting seems to capture a single specific moment, in fact, there is a fifteen-year distance between known preparatory drawings, from at least 1634, and when Saenredam finished *Saint Odulphus* in 1649.[6] In that span of time the artist designed a very consciously conceived composition, in which the initial reality is only a faint memory and the picture a perfectly executed illusion.[7] After so much time, plastered walls and plain windows, stone floor and wooden vault, architecture, decoration, narration, the tiniest detail becomes, consciously or unconsciously, loaded with significance.

The painting is the painter's perception. Saenredam both possesses and inhabits this church at the moment he paints it; that gives him the license, the authority, to write his name on the church pew. What in reality may be an accident, such as the angle of the pew or the position of a figure, is in the painting a deliberate decision. The *real* gravestone, for example, with its family inscription, becomes in Saenredam's painting a *symbol*, a presence, that pervades the whole painting with its meaning. It sets the tone at the moment the eye enters the composition. Set in the symbolic position, at the right hand of the viewer, it becomes the viewer's introduction to the work. The painting's apparently objective atmosphere suddenly vibrates, like organ music, with undertones of meaning.

While the details of Saenredam's realism ground the viewer and convince him or her of reality before them, a viewer distracted by this realism might miss the structuring of these details within the scope of

---

[5]E. John Walford, *Jacob van Ruisdael and the Perception of Landscape* (New Haven, CT: Yale University Press, 1991), 15.
[6]A pen and chalk drawing from 1634 and a very precise life-size construction drawing from 1643 are known (see Schwartz and Bok, *Pieter Saenredam*, 94, figs. 101, 102).
[7]Saenredam made another painting of the interior of the church, a view into the north transept, based on a drawing from 1633. The signed but undated panel of 46 x 64 cm. belongs to the Galleria Sabauda in Turin (Italy). Schwartz and Bok (ibid., 93, fig. 100) want to see here an impossible viewer's position; more compelling seems to me the variant in iconography with the choir view.

Saenredam's wide-angle vision. The most obvious role these pictorial elements serve is the painting's method of perspective. This is sustained by the dominating lines formed by the stone floor tiles that rush the observer's eye toward the center of attention—the nave and its congregation, facing the pulpit with its occupant. The key to Saenredam's *métier* and fame, the rule of his outspoken conviction, is scientific perspective. The principle of perspective is laid out here in its most fundamental and mysterious expression, the central vanishing point: it is the means by which a sacred presence is visibly manifested. Every appearance in Saenredam's painting depends on the choice of a single creative mind. Saenredam's rigorous, logical, and organized character escapes from the ordeal of this freedom by imitating visual reality with the best tools and science of perspective. The effect is one of transforming the church into a *real* fiction where everything has, the viewer believes, its predestined place. The relentless rigor of Saenredam's perspective means eliminating even the shadow of accident. The scientific or objective appearance of Saenredam's art may disguise its constructed and suggestive character.

Walford, in his discussion of Ruisdael, called this process "selective naturalism," by which an artist "may thus embody a religious and contemplative attitude towards observed reality."[8] He added, "This intertwining of material and spiritual levels of reality is typical in Dutch seventeenth-century thought and in contemporary artistic practice."[9] Walford argued that a fundamental assumption of seventeenth-century Dutch art, including genre, still-life, and landscape painting, was a belief that "aesthetic delight in the visible world conveyed inherent spiritual significance."[10] In fact, there is a potential connection between this conception of contemplative realism and the Dutch church. Walford notes, "Exhortation to delight in the visible world was instilled by the influential Confession of Faith and Catechism of the Netherlands Reformed Churches. They were the subjects of weekly evening sermons."[11] Perhaps this contemplative mode of seeing was preached from the very pulpit that is pictured in Saenredam's *Saint Odulphus*.

Walford notes that in Saenredam's art, "selective naturalness is

---

[8] Walford, *Jacob van Ruisdael*, 18.
[9] Ibid., 18.
[10] Ibid., 21.
[11] Ibid., 20.

driven by his Calvinist, purist aesthetic, and he chooses his subject, his composition, and his palette accordingly—pure geometry, and pure color as an associative symbol of the purity of the Reformed church, and of the God it worshiped, a God of order and reason, not of emotion, passion and feeling, as evoked through medieval color, decoration, and profusion of images, sounds, smells, incense, etc. In *Interior of the Church of Saint Odulphus at Assendelft*, the rational laws of perspective and mathematics make visible the rationality of God, as perceived through Reformed eyes."[12]

Saenredam's depiction of *Saint Odulphus* runs from east to west, from apse to tower door; this is significant. The flow of a traditional Roman Catholic church would be in the opposite direction, from occident to orient, with the strong symbolic overtones of darkness and light, or death and life. The liturgy had been adapted to this orientation in the Middle Ages, when the altar found its definitive place in the eastern choir and could be approached only from the west. The architecture of the Catholic church building was literally the pathway to salvation as the faithful moved in a symbolic walk eastward to the altar.

The modern viewer, even one inclined to recognize the relationship between architecture, art, theology, and liturgy, may still not fully imagine Saint Odulphus as a pre-Reformation era church, as it would have been before Calvinist iconoclasm. John Walford writes, "It would have had wall and ceiling frescoes, as nearly all pre-Reformation churches had, it would have had an altar, with candlesticks, a painted or sculpted altarpiece, other paintings and sculptures all around, painted armorial escutcheons all around, a screen separating the area for the laity and the clergy, and so on. All that has been stripped away, and what is now given center stage is the pulpit, used for the verbal proclamation of the Scripture."[13] This awareness of the inherent liturgical significance of the church architecture as well as the significance of those changes brought upon Saint Odulphus would not have been lost on Saenredam's contemporary viewers. Indeed, this connection between past, present, and future motivated, at least in part, Saenredam's selection and treatment of his motifs. Jeroen Giltaij notes that, "with only the odd exception, Saenredam painted medieval churches almost

---

[12]John Walford, e-mail message to James Romaine, August 1, 2011. Used with permission.
[13]Ibid.

exclusively."[14] Saenredam was himself a Calvinist; nevertheless, he was not isolated from the Catholic community or their views on religious art and architecture. Lyckle de Vries writes, "Although Saenredam was brought up in strictly Calvinist surroundings, his first teacher [Frans de Grebber] was a Catholic, as were also, most probably, a fair number of his early patrons."[15]

The Reformation was only one century old in Saenredam's time, and the conversion of the Dutch population to Protestant denominations was slow and far from complete. The "conversion" of the church buildings was equally a slow and painful process—one that was never exempt from psychological and/or physical violence. Some of the most visible violence had been practiced against the sacred images and objects of the church. In the English language this is called "iconoclasm," but the Dutch use a stronger and more plastic term, "beeldenstorm." Literally translated, this means "picture storm." One of the most devastating storms occurred in 1566, at the outbreak of the Eighty Years' War that would change the destiny of the Netherlands. This war, and the questions of how to contend with its immediate consequences, continued to dominate the Dutch experience during most of Saenredam's life.

The Reformation in the Netherlands had done away with the idea of the symbol. Visual symbols particularly were suspected as superstition and idolatry.[16] The church building had been stripped of any claims of its own sacred meaning. Its new purpose was to be a roof over the assembly. In Assendelft, the church's main altar had been removed, destroyed presumably, along with its altarpiece. Images were regarded as idols, representations of God contrary to the second commandment, and were therefore destroyed. The leaders of the iconoclasm were motivated by conviction, not ignorance. They understood that the profusion of images and objects that had pervaded churches for centuries had nothing to do with decoration. These images and objects were the visual means for a profoundly spiritual, sacramental, experience. In the eyes of both Catholics and Protestants, these

---

[14] Jeroen Giltaij, book review of *Pieter Saenredam: The Painter and His Time, Simiolus: Netherlands Quarterly for the History of Art* 20/1 (1990–1991): 88.

[15] Lyckle de Vries, book review of *Pieter Saenredam: The Painter and His Time, The Burlington Magazine* (July 1991): 457.

[16] In the Calvinist interpretation, even the sacraments of the Lord's Supper and baptism were explained without recurrence to the idea of the symbol, replacing it with faith.

images had everything to do with the salvation of the soul, their own and that of their country. For the Catholics, this was the reason to preserve images in the church; for the Protestants, this was cause to forbid them.

The iconoclasm raised many critical and urgent spiritual issues, both for the church and for art. Did the purging of churches work to the advantage of art? Or was art condemned to be nothing more than skillful decoration for burgher mansions? The critical question posed by Saenredam's *Saint Odulphus* is, how spiritual could an artwork be in the hands of a painter whose conscience forbade religious images, symbols, superstition, and idolatry? This was a question not only for a painter of churches, throughout the seventeenth-century in the Netherlands; the question was posed to artists working in the areas of genre, still life, and, in the case of Ruisdael, landscape.

In Saenredam's art, churches, which had recently been the site of controversy and violence concerning art, are here depicted in art as realms of spiritual serenity with a sense of order and well-being, as signs of God's providence. Saenredam restored belief in the visibility of the invisible. He places the viewer on the spot where the main altar once stood.[17] The viewer becomes, as it were, the officiating priest, if not Saint Odulphus himself, and looks upon the faithful crowd in the nave. Saenredam's choice of this viewpoint is anything but arbitrary; the viewer stands just to the right of the recently removed tabernacle, containing the sacramental host, probably crowned by a crucifix or an image of the Madonna. The altar table was more than a mute rectangular monolith; it was the symbolic grave of the founding saint of the local Christian community, Adolf of Utrecht, named the Apostle of the Frisians. In the foundations of this altar were placed one or more of his relics, probably bones, to commemorate the canonized Benedictine missionary. These relics had sanctified the ground for some seven hundred years. More than a protection against bad weather, the church was in the eyes of its Carolingian founders a uniquely holy place and space. Saenredam may have conceived his interior as the view through a camera obscura, setting his eye on the very spot of the main altar. The viewer cannot escape from the solemnity of this position. Saenredam

---

[17] In fact, one of Saenredam's drawings of Saint Odulphus, of 1634, looks toward this apse stripped of its altar and altarpiece.

replaces the destroyed altar painting; and the painting is a perfect mirror, a speculum immaculate.[18]

What did Saenredam see in the impeccable looking glass[19] he had put on the spot of the former speculum immaculate that was the virginal image of the holy church of Saint Odulphus? The choir, where the viewer's eye floats just above altar height, seems high and spacious, the distant nave narrow and low. The transept in between is almost lost in the perspective foreshortening. For the more insistent observer, however, it plays its role in the light distribution. It separates with thin rays the foreground from the central scene. This foreground is dark and empty, like the earth in the first verse of Genesis. What was the most holy part of the church one life span ago is now occupied by the dead—family, patrons, the past. The medieval practice of privileged burial places in the holy ground around the altar saint, awaiting the resurrection, had never been abandoned. An inscribed gravestone, a mausoleum, and mortuary tablets on the walls (plus an empty pew)—these are all rudimentary vestiges of art in a sphere where its exile was most blatant. In Saenredam's *Saint Odulphus*, the church itself becomes a memento mori, one of the thematic constants in Dutch painting. The church, with its graves, is no less a vanitas image than a still life and landscape. Here lies in passing an unchanged, spiritual sense of art, not as a servant of religion but as a visible reminder of the body long after this body has turned to dust.

However, Saenredam's vision, and that of viewer, is not bound to the grave. Our perspective rises; the obsessive omnipresent parallel lines carry our eyes away and transport them to the light, milk-colored by the morning hour. They bump into a warm caramel or honey-hued wooden wall. It encases what resembles a small but veritable fortress (or, as Martin Luther would say, *Ein Feste Burg*). Inside these highly protective walls are the people of God, the elected holy flock. Towering above them, as if descending from the vault of heaven via the dome of the pulpit and the mouth of the minister, is the Word. The Protestant minister's credo is, "He who has ears to hear, let him hear." This listening-to-the-word-oriented worship is definitely not the same as looking

---

[18]Saenredam's ambivalent position between Catholic past and Protestant present is a constant in his earlier works, often outspoken. Here, in my opinion, it is unwilled, but the more significant, Assendelft being not only the place of his birth but a documented place of resistance to the conquest of Calvinism.
[19]"For *now we see* in a *mirror*, dimly" (1 Corinthians 12:13).

at paintings and sculptures. The physical experience of walking through the church, kneeling in front of a painting, touching a sculpture, kissing a relic has been replaced by the more spiritual experience of silently sitting motionless for hours. In the Protestant mystique, elegant but solid pews replace the altars and altarpieces.[20] In Saint Odulphus they bathe in an almost heavenly light.[21] That terrible discipline of sitting still is the requirement of election.

The painter's quickening brushstrokes bring some life into a forbidding monument. Saenredam needs the figures to give a sense of scale, proportion, time, life, communication, drama, and death.[22] Most notably, in this painting, are two figures, a mother and her child.[23] She sits, apart from the rest of the congregation, on the floor, in the manner of the poor or the backward or the sinners (whereas the older woman at the other end has at least taken her own chair with her). Her son lies on his stomach, turning his back, if not his ears, to the preacher. He is reading his own book, a book no doubt of images, childish, leading astray.[24] Does this little couple form an alternative Madonna and child? Some Calvinists, like Saenredam's uncles and cousins of the De Jonge family, objected to the use of Mary as a spiritual model. Images of the Madonna were regarded as a papist error, whose theological foundation was not to be found in the Holy Writ.

Calvinists of the seventeenth-century Netherlands proposed to read the Bible afresh, in the vernacular Dutch, as if they were the first Hebrews. They insisted on the individual relation with God, founded on an individual reading of the texts taken literally. In this context, works of art were perceived to stand between God and the individual, separating rather than connecting God and his people. And yet, as demonstrated in the profusion of art, including paintings of churches, in the seventeenth-century Netherlands, visual representation is integral to the very nature of human communication and the human condition. The image is the fundamental means of this communication, as basic as language. The image becomes art when it attains a spiritual

---

[20] In the other Saint Odulphus (see note 7), the faithful gather in the medieval, pre-Protestant way, disorderly sitting on the floor in the dark of the north (!) transept arm.
[21] Note also the brass chandeliers in this part of the church—human light sources not lit, evidently, during this hour of divine enlightenment.
[22] It is noteworthy that Saenredam drawings rarely include figures. These are included in the paintings to give a sense of scale and life to the architecture.
[23] Experts attribute these figures to Adriaen van Ostade.
[24] The same little couple appears in Rembrandt's *Honderd Gulden Prent*.

dimension, and that is why it must be made beautiful. Saenredam was the first to recognize the proper beauty of the relatively simple Dutch churches. These spaces might have seemed empty and even awkward at first glance, especially if compared to their grandiloquent Italian, French, or Spanish counterparts. They were made even more awkward now that their artworks were destroyed, their frescoes bleached, and their windows broken, to be replaced by cheap greenish and yellowish glass. These churches were as naked as Adam and Eve in the garden of Eden. Saenredam, in a stroke of genius, shows these churches as an apparition of the terrestrial paradise. Inside, the presence of the unseen sun is made visible by the light; this is the presence of the Lord. The dark Catholic past has given way to the bright Calvinist future.

Calling Saenredam's *Saint Odulphus* a "Calvinist altarpiece" would be a diabolic contradiction in terms, but doing so may help the viewer realize how this new, so-called secular art was founded, in form and spirit, on the very spot of the old, so-called religious art. However novel Saenredam's depiction of them might be, church interiors were fairly common sights in the art of the Low Countries (and of other countries). Most artists did not depict the churches as empty as he did. As a first impression, Saenredam's churches would seem to provide no more than the stage for a story. However, our understanding of their significance soon grows beyond that of a pious space construction. If we define the spirit as the invisible dimension of visible things, Saenredam's *Saint Odulphus* (like much Dutch art of the seventeenth century) possesses a colossal spiritual potential. Its purpose is to bring objective visual reality to what was loaded with religious significance. But it is religious significance that stands outside of religious institutions. Saenredam's *Saint Odulphus* will never hang in a church. It will hang in the house of the prominent Calvinist family, probably at Assendelft, who commissioned it.[25]

Saenredam finished this painting of his childhood church a year after the Dutch War of Independence.[26] Outside the walls of Saint Odulphus, the Netherlands was a free country, a political realization

---

[25] Schwartz and Bok suggest the painting was a commission of the family De Jonge and a memorial to Johannes Junius, prominent Calvinist preacher in Assendelft from 1612–1634, this last year being the date of Saenredam's drawing.

[26] The Eighty Years' War ended in 1648; it had started as one of the consequences of the iconoclastic fury of 1566.

unseen until then. Its freedom was commented upon as a miracle, after eighty years of battles and prayers, against the most powerful king of the century and his tyrannical religion. David's psalms were sung in the churches, where only Moses' Ten Commandments embellished the walls. Dutch Calvinists, as they read the Old Testament daily, inevitably drew parallels between themselves and the Hebrews. The free Netherlands was, after a long sojourn in the desert of war, the new Promised Land. The Netherlands was freed by the Lord, and the sword, from false gods and superstitions, including altars and idols. The Holy Land was Holland and all its soil; its martyr, William of Orange, was venerated like a Protestant saint.[27]

Although its very conception was iconoclastic, the Protestant Netherlands, however, still required a visual element. This urgency pushed Dutch artists, including Saenredam, to develop forms of spiritual patriotism reflective of the age, and the visual arts played a determining role in communicating this sentiment. This art was spiritual, even Christian, but it was not for inside the church. This holy land was the spiritual soil ready to welcome Saenredam's paintings. His essential discovery of reality as beauty, of architectural space as art, employing an idiom of simplicity rather than of opulence, and light rather than of idolatry, parallels Dutch self-perception about the righteousness of their divinely chosen nation and deserved prosperity.[28] In Saenredam's *Saint Odulphus*, utmost realism is the symbolic language par excellence. Its exacting realism and strict perspective evoke a sacred presence; the work has a sense of spiritual expectation, fulfilled in this moment of the viewer's arrival.

---

[27] William's tomb in the New Church in Delft was a feature of the greatest number of painted church interiors.

[28] Such a biblical patriotic reading of Saenredam's work may partly, and subconsciously, explain the choice of one of his paintings in the Dutch Gift to King Charles II of England in 1660.

Antoine Watteau, *The Dance* (*Les Fêtes Vénitiennes*). C. 1717–1718. Oil on canvas, 21 1/2" x 17 3/4".
National Gallery of Scotland, Edinburgh.

9

CATEGORIES FOR ART HISTORICAL METHODOLOGY
Antoine Watteau's *The Dance* (*Les Fetes Venitiennes*)

CALVIN SEERVELD

Great Themes in Art, by John Walford, is a magisterial introduction to Western art. The meticulous description of painterly, sculptural, and architectural work is deft, funneling a connoisseur's firsthand knowledge of the pieces observed to concise paragraphs intelligible to students. The choices of artworks for analysis, interpretation, and evaluation are consistently significant. The illustrations in color are produced with museum quality. And Walford's precise exposition in comparing different artistic expressions gives a vibrant intelligence to the book.

Employing the categories of spirituality, the self, nature, and the city to structure a narrative of *great themes*, Walford carefully shapes his story of Western art under these rubrics "so the reader can follow and compare artists' responses to humanity's enduring concerns from one historical period to the next."[1] This essay attempts to ground these categories philosophically and to test how they could be developed to give a different slant to Walford's treatment of Rococo artistry, with special attention to *The Dance (Les Fetes Venitiennes)* (c. 1718–1719), by Antoine Watteau (1684–1721).

Walford's four recurrent categories, which systematically govern his book, are subtly informed by his Christian sensibility, but they are presented in an unapologetic fashion that seems reasonable to most readers who do not have an ideological ax to grind.

---

[1] E. John Walford, *Great Themes in Art* (Upper Saddle River, NJ: Prentice-Hall, 2002), 9.

Walford states clearly certain formal features one needs to read in observing art—"line, shape, mass, light, color, texture, and space"[2]—but would find formalistic art histories going back to Heinrich Wölfflin and Alois Riegl to be narrow-minded, specialist attempts. Walford does not agree with the corrective Marxian focus of Arnold Hauser and Frederick Antal, which reads artworks to be in dialectical tension with their economic means of production. Despite their illuminating close reading of the times and places of the art being examined by us later critics, Walford finds that such expositions over-read the art and swallow up aesthetic appreciation into class-conscious societal problems.

Walford's thematic approach, and his appreciation for iconographic/iconological matters, is more in line with the approach of Erwin Panofsky and of Walford's mentor, Hans Rookmaaker: discern the cultural setting and the artist's stance on what his or her art products symbolically purport to be important for human life. *Great Themes* evokes a Jacob Burckhardtian aura of large cultural context, which a recent art critic like Clement Greenberg would consider too expansive, idealistic, and specious, yet Walford hones in empirically on the given artworks, to help beginners perceive what is actually being offered to us as latter-day viewers.

A philosophical orientation which accepts the biblical witness to honor the sovereign God revealed in Jesus Christ, whose kingdom is coming in world history, thanks to the ongoing work of the Holy Spirit, will posit that that scripturally revealed reality of the triune God operative in history has to be faced somehow by humans whose nature seems bent on recognizing the finality of things. Walford's category of "spirituality" gives somewhat a voice to this fact, yet leaves open what it might be that artists do assume is or is not finally transcendent in the universe. But every man or woman does make that pivotal decision, and what one decides on as final affects one's judgment on the nature of humanity. James Elkins's hovering around Sufism and Zen, while pretending to dispense with transcendence, is a good example of an inconclusive, zetetic stance that still does not escape adopting a negative kind of "religion."[3]

---

[2] Ibid., 15.
[3] Cf. James Elkins, *On the Strange Place of Religion in Contemporary Art* (New York: Routledge, 2004), 90–94.

The theme of "nature" simply recognizes the inhabited cosmos and gives a countenance to the nonhuman creatures humanists tend to ignore or disparage. That the mountain-plant-animal world habitat of creatures needs to be ranked as important for actual daily lives as well as for understanding the scope of artistry is a matter "other-worldly" believers and mystics have often missed.

The "self" category sprawls a bit but seems to encompass the inescapable necessity that artists, like all humans, have to decide what to live (or die) for. What does a person, with a particular identity, hold to as the meaning of what is going on? One's answer to this key problem results in the "values" a person holds dear and could be instrumental in shaping one's vision of the world to which one, consciously or not, is committed, as one's subterraneanly formed operational framework. "The self" designates the priorities anyone assumes as normal.

Walford's fourth coordinate to plot his account of Western art is "city." To situate artists with the task of city design allows architecture, a good index to lifestyle, to be given an important consideration along with painting and sculpture. The category of "city" makes society and also societal leadership integral to the mix of panoramic concerns artists, like other humans, face, even though this reality be discounted by individualists.

Great Themes's systematic categorical framework, reinterpreted as just done here, fits well with a perception of reality impinging upon humans responding to artistry in God's world throughout the ages. Fully human artists act imaginatively in their societal circumstances upon the myriad nuanced realities extant, and forge artifacts defined by an allusive quality, from out of a spirited vision to which they are more or less committed. The creational ordinance for artistry to be checked against is the injunction to disclose whatever meaning is being embodied in a metaphorical, symbolical, suggestion-rich way.[4]

The artwork or artistic event can be weakly or strongly formed, thin or deep in significance, and has many other-than-aesthetic dimensions, but its primary artistic task, and responses by other humans to its artistry, must be first of all imaginative. Whatever vision and dynamic spirit breathes through an artwork can usually be approximated

---

[4]I discuss these themes in *A Christian Critique of Art and Literature* (1972; 3rd ed. with illustrations, Dordt College Press, 1995), 42–47; and *Rainbows for the Fallen World* (Toronto: Tuppence, 1980/2005), 125–135.

through a careful reading. The exact import of given artworks remains elliptical; so every judgment about the historical contribution of an artist's oeuvre for its time and place and for posterity is always moot. Nevertheless, the art critic and art historian are called upon to give a wise prolegomenon to the art in question, for the sake of other would-be responders.

A full-orbed conception of artistry will explicate its stance regarding final allegiance ("spirituality"), definitely focused/slanted meaning ("the self"), cosmic setting ("nature"), and societal horizons ("city"). It should also be said that a given artist or art critic and art historian may default on or go beyond the limitations imposed by one's assumed categories.

To avoid settling for an anthology of atomic monographs, a genuine history of art needs categories that collocate artworks into groups while noticing important differences among them, and allow a historian to track significant changes of before and after and within and between given artists' oeuvres. "Centuries" ("Eighteenth-century art") is too colorless and merely chronological a term to give cultural unity.[5] "Nationality" ("Dutch art") gives a specific locus but isolates such work from contemporary cross-national neighbors.

Perhaps art historians do best to recognize the synchronic category of cultural periods as unrepeatable historical events that breathe a kind of communal spirit that informs enough cultural leaders somewhere at a given time for so long that their embracing of its power wields a generational dominance.[6]

For example, no matter how one precisely loads the term, there existed at least three generations of Renaissance culture in Europe which, trailing clouds of classical learning, embodied a this-worldly and mathematical fascination with earthly phenomena, driven by Pico della Mirandola's notion of *sacra ambitio*—discover nature's secrets so that humans, by their own *virtù*, can strive for and achieve *humaniora*. Inventor artist Leonardo da Vinci, politician Machiavelli, philosophers

---

[5] The scholarly "American Society for Eighteenth-century Studies" struggled with this matter in its founding charter, and stated that its field of cultural investigation officially stretched from the late 1600s until the early 1800s.

[6] For a developed argument on the existence and nature of "cultural periods" as historical realities and their complications, cf. my "Towards a Cartographic Methodology for Art Historiography," *The Journal of Aesthetics and Art Criticism* 39/2 (Winter 1980): 143–154; and "The Influence of Periodisation upon Art Historiography of the Enlightenment," *Studies on Voltaire and Eighteenth-century Studies* 190 (1981): 183–189.

Giordano Bruno and Campanella, the mature Michelangelo, Medici bankers, painterly artists Botticelli and Titian, explorer Columbus—all were buoyed by this exciting dynamic to relish new worldly abundance—it is even apt to talk about "Renaissance popes" (Borgia Alexander VI, Medici Julius II, Leo X, and Clemens VII), who spent prodigious wealth on adventuresome art.

So too, one can document that there has been a relatively brief but deeply formative Rococo Enlightenment period for a couple of generations in Europe, and exported abroad. This could be called a spirit of sunny-side-up ludic rationalism. John Locke's *Letter on Toleration* (1690) and the articles in the French *Encyclopédie* spearheaded by Diderot and d'Alembert, as well as Addison and Steele's *Tattler* and *Spectator Papers* (1709–1712), or Benjamin Franklin's *Poor Richard's Almanack* (1732–1757), all have an infectious, popularizing feel to their reflection, not at all like the rigorous, sustained philosophical systems proposed by earlier thinkers like Leibniz and Spinoza. Rococo paintings by high society fashion portraitist Jean-Marc Nattier and François Boucher's *Madame de Pompadour* (and Boucher's more banal, girlish pin-up nudes affecting to be nymphs) intimate leisure, luxury, coquetry, a world of chaste décolleté and aristocratic gallantry. The predominant decorative character of Johann Balthasar Neumann's *Vierzehnheiligen* church and the *Residenz Kaisersaal* in Wurzburg, by their intricate variety, "lead the eye a wanton kind of chace," as William Hogarth's *Analysis of Beauty* (1753)—the key philosophical treatise on Rococo aesthetics—puts it, and gives one visually and practically a delightful place and floor for dancing a decorous minuet under banks of flickering candles.[7]

If one compares Thomas Gainsborough's *Mary Countess Howe* (1765) with Philippe de Champaigne's *Cardinal Richelieu* (c. 1760), one sees acutely the difference between *la grande manière* of Louis XIV with his spacious, grandiose Versailles gardens and the miniatured elegance of Rococo-spirited art. Champaigne's stern, stately robed *Richelieu* figure bespeaks the aura of the *ancien régime*, whereas *Mary Countess Howe*'s pinched-toe shoes, rose-colored dress, and chinoiserie hat carry the mien of the Louis XV era with the expensive, fragile delicacy of the

---

[7]For extended analysis, cf. my "God's Ordinance for Artistry and Hogarth's 'Wanton Chace,'" in *Marginal Resistance, Essays in Honour of John Vander Stellt* (Sioux Center, IA: Dordt Press, 2001), 322–330.

Rococo Enlightenment milieu. To my eye, Gainsborough's painting of *Mr. and Mrs. Andrews* (c. 1749), though they be English gentry with a stiff upper lip, relaxing on farmland, has a blue and white primness and pretty gaiety (although more restrained than Gainsborough's *The Painter's Daughters Chasing a Butterfly*) that telltales a light Rococo playfulness. (Mr. Andrews's crossed legs with long stockings reminds me of the turned legs in Rigaud's Rococo portrait of Louis XIV.) Gainsborough's *Mr. and Mrs. Andrews* presents figures as precious in a picturesque landscape not unlike that of Jean-Honoré Fragonard's *The Swing*, although "swinging," with light touching and flying skirts, is probably a bit more risqué than British gentry would appreciate for their portraiture. Gainsborough's light touch carries a different verve, it seems to me, than Joshua Reynolds's brown and muted-colored, more reserved Neoclassical full-length portraits.

Lancelot "Capability" Brown's art of landscaped gardens at Blenheim Place, with serpentine lines and pleasantly surprising vistas, maybe with a hired hermit on an artificial island in the garden lake, is a British version of Madame Pompadour's retiring with her ladies-in-waiting to go play rustic cottagers in huts constructed for the nonce. Even Hessian military tactics were dominated by this Rococo Enlightenment spirit: they marched in step in rows of red-and-white uniforms and polished black boots, like marionettes, to fire at enemies in rhythmic salvos, as gentlemen should—which seemed absurd to American revolutionary woodsmen with muskets crouching hidden behind rocks and trees.

That there be a unifying cultural dynamic which historians with hindsight can see and name a "Rococo Enlightenment" period that, again for example, drives philosophers to write belles-lettres essays "On Taste" (David Hume) and tell stories like "Candide" (Voltaire) rather than pen argued "Discourses" (Descartes) or a *Leviathan* tome (Hobbes), helps people recognize the depth of communion cultural leaders like philosophers, artists—and military strategists—show is held in common by the style of a period. Cultural periods evidence, I believe, the unseen principalities (*archai*) and powers (*exousiai*) the Bible says take hold of humans and their cultivating actions.[8]

---

[8] Ephesians 6:12; cf. Walter Wink, *Naming the Powers: The Language of Power in the New Testament* (Philadelphia: Fortress, 1984).

It is important to note, however, that there are different period dynamics overlapping a given time frame; no one *Zeitgeist* blankets a given century. And even within Rococo Enlightenment–spirited art there are several different casts which frame artworks, thanks to the different fundamental visions of reality held by given artists. Boucher, for example, and Fragonard revel in the sensuous richness of the erotic, as if hedonic activity be the *summum bonum* of life, while others like Jean-Baptiste Greuze, Hogarth, Henry Fielding, John Gay (*The Beggars' Opera*), and Pietro Longhi take a fundamentally picaresque view of reality, glorifying the pitiful or underdogs in society. Francesco Lazzaro Guardi, like a miniaturizing Canaletto (Giovanni Antonio Canal), presents a scenic landscape of a world inhabited by tiny humans, while Giovanni Battista Tiepolo champions large heroic figures struggling to do great deeds, albeit rosy tinted with washed-out pastel colors. Jean-Baptiste-Siméon Chardin and Alexander Pope have a paradigmatic order to their universe of discourse, but their art—*nature morte* and "Rape of the Lock" in heroic couplets—still brushes ordered, ordinary sights and doings with a gentle Rococo touch.

So there are different "brands," so to speak, of Rococo Enlightenment artistry, dependent on how the artist conceives and takes a stance on possible relational priorities in the panorama of creatural glories. But the framing world-and-life vision one adopts is distinct from, though interwoven with, the (period) spirited dynamic which drives the artist on. The different world-and-life formats which structure the artist's imaginative take on whatever nuanced realities he or she treats seem to have repeatable attraction for artists in different epochs of history.

The vision that the cosmos is caught up in an ongoing heroic struggle seems to stamp the perspective of Michelangelo Buonarroti, Peter Paul Rubens, Jacques Louis David, Eugène Delacroix, Max Beckmann, and Jackson Pollock, despite the utterly different period dynamics pulsing through their artistry. A hedonic focus toward reality orients the artworks of Titian (Tiziano Vecellio), Bronzino (Agnolo di Cosimo), Lucas Cranach the Elder, Jean Auguste Dominique Ingres, Pierre-Auguste Renoir, William-Adolphe Bouguereau, Paul Gauguin, and Gustav Klimt, where not heroic struggle so much as being bathed in pleasure seems to be the fundamental coordinate of meaning.

Awareness of such similar perspectival formats, almost like spectral artistic traditions, which may have no empirical historical connections but do recur in history (perchronic—enduring through time) does help students recognize the similar parameters of given artists' oeuvres. These several framing outlooks are "typiconic idioms."[9]

Therefore, it would help clarify art historical judgments if one kept in mind the joint designation of both dynamic period spirit and typiconic perspectival frame, so one would be able to designate roughly heroic-Rococo, picaresque-Rococo, hedonic-Rococo artistry (see table 9.1). Then one would not judge Chardin and Hogarth art as offering "a striking contrast to the lyrical escapism of Rococo art,"[10] because both Chardin and Hogarth are prime representatives of the ludic rationalist Rococo Enlightenment spirit. But one can, without denying the common Rococo temper to their art, not only point out that Chardin "recalls the themes of Dutch genre painters such as [Johannes] Vermeer,"[11] but posit that the typiconic paradigmatic idiom of Vermeer resurfaces in Rococo Chardin, and that William Hogarth's painting is "in the tradition of Dutch genre painters such as Jan Steen,"[12] but does so with a deeply committed, whimsical Rococo Enlightenment flourish.[13]

Table 9.1 Typiconic Idioms in Historical Periods

	Renaissance	Reformation	Enlightenment	Neoclassical	Romantic
Heroic	Michelangelo	Dürer	Tiepolo	David	Delacroix
Picaresque		Steen	Hogarth		
Scenic					Stubbs
Idyllic	Botticelli	Goyen		Reynolds	Wright
Paradigmatic	Raphael	Vermeer	Chardin	Mengs	
Hedonic	Titian	Cranach	Boucher	Ingres	Prud'hon

If one were to reorganize the chapter of *Great Themes* entitled "English Baroque and Eighteenth-century European and American

---

[9]Several typiconic idioms (there are more) include: Heroic (*Michelangelo* Buonarroti, Albrecht *Dürer*, Giovanni Battista Tiepolo, *Jacques*-Louis David, Eugène *Delacroix*); Picaresque (Jan Steen, William *Hogarth*); Scenic (George *Stubbs*); Idyllic (Sandro *Botticelli*, Jan van Goyen, Sir *Joshua Reynolds*, *Joseph Wright*); Paradigmatic (Raphael, Johannes Vermeer, Jean-Baptiste-Siméon *Chardin*, Anton Raphael *Mengs*); and Hedonic (Titian, Lucas *Cranach* the Elder, François *Boucher*, Jean Auguste Dominique *Ingres*, Pierre-Paul *Prud'hon*).

[10]Walford, *Great Themes in Art*, 348.

[11]Ibid., 349.

[12]Ibid.

[13]There is no logical or dialectical connection to succeeding period dynamics. Their coming and going is as unpredictable as the rising and wearing out of idolatries, so far as I can determine.

Art" around cartographic terms with dynamic cultural periods and typiconic idioms clearly denoted, then one could recognize the sharp antagonisms between deft Rococo Enlightenment–spirited art and its Neoclassical Academy opponents buoyed underneath by a straitlaced, atavistic Winckelmann mania, rather than relegate the matter of "spirituality" to the difference between Roman Catholic and Protestant church architecture,[14] and one would not catalog Neoclassical artists like "Reynolds, Kauffmann and J.-L. David" as "enlightened."[15] Furthermore, one would point up the sweet familial kinship of spirit in Neumann, Gainsborough, Fragonard, Boucher, Chardin, and Hogarth—a Rococo communion of committed, seriously playful artists pursuing and promoting a beguiling happiness. Finally, and most importantly, one should recognize the Rococo Enlightenment cultural period as having singularly important, historical weight, with its own cohering independent period identity that significantly altered the direction and character of art, philosophy, and human cultural leadership. Rococo Enlightenment artistry is not the frazzling degeneration of Baroque period culture, in my judgment, but is a vigorous, deeply secularizing, yet progressively stimulating force in European (and world) culture in response to which the Neoclassical and Romantic periods were reactionary, backward, and esoteric movements.[16]

Fashionable Parisian society during the reign of Louis XV (1715–1774), where his mistress Madame Pompadour set the style for royal pastimes and the courtly entourages of nobles and ladies, was indeed a kind of earthly paradise of operetta-like amusement, as if there were no sin in the world. A spirit of ludic rationalism governed these circles of rich aristocratic socialites who were insulated against earning a living. They spent their lifetime in salons, attending soirées and masked balls, polishing up their light conversation with witty repartee, promenading in the parks to show off their refined taste in clothes, etiquette, and hairdos. Women with their boudoirs encouraged gallant intrigues, a *négligé* yen for amorous dalliance and rendezvous near fountains in secluded gardens.

---

[14] Walford, *Great Themes in Art*, 341–344.
[15] Ibid., 359.
[16] Cf. my "The Moment of Truth and Evidence of Sterility in Aesthetic Theory and Art of the Later Enlightenment," in *Transactions of the Sixth International Congress on the Enlightenment* (Oxford: The Voltaire Foundation, 1983), 149–151; and "Idealistic Philosophy in Checkmate: Neoclassical and Romantic Artistic Policy," *Studies on Voltaire and Eighteenth-century Studies* 263 (1989): 467–472.

Into this unreal milieu of unthreatened prosperity, leisure, and civilized frolic came the penniless Jean-Antoine Watteau (1684–1721) in 1702. Apprenticed to the artist Claude Gillot, who also ran a marionette theatre, to copy paintings for clients, Watteau was introduced to the Mannerist style of Primaticcio and the fastidious school of Fontainebleau which had defined culture at the court of Francis I (1515–1547) (to whom Jean Calvin dedicated the *Institutio Christianae Religionis*). The elegance celebrated by Francis I, including the troubadour courtly love ethic, was codified by Louis XIII (reigned 1610–1643, before Louis XIV, 1643–1715). So Watteau was trained early not in *la grande manière* of Louis XIV, but in the silk-color tones, the bright soft atmosphere, fairy-tale and dress-up world of archaic clothes of the days of Louis XIII.

By 1707, Watteau had worked his way up to collaborate with Claude III Audran, curator of the Luxembourg Palace, which held the magnificent Rubens paintings of the Marie de Medici cycle, and who was one of the best-placed decorators of the day. Watteau was engaged in drawing, designing, and painting arabesques to fill the panels of salons in hotels and chateaux of high society with gallant figures and scenes of *commedia dell'arte* in demand by engravers. Watteau's delicate artworks of these years introduced the folk pastime of the swing into the stilted vocabulary of *fêtes champêtres* in fashionable society; he also dubbed into the scenes of fountains and gardens a Bacchus and satyr or two, also bagpipes, a folk emblem for genitalia. That is, by 1710 Watteau was deftly mixing diluted mythical figures with bumptious *commedia dell'arte* notes into settings of Arcadian dreamscapes of love.

In fact, the age-old *topos* (metaphoric framework) of *locus amoenus* (an enchanted place), which is the model for Elysium in Virgil's *Aeneid*, "the isle . . . full of sweet airs" in Shakespeare's *Tempest*, and the garden of Eden in Milton's *Paradise Lost*, is the fundamental framework for Watteau's whole oeuvre of art. And Watteau joins to the "enchanted garden" *topos*, the *gradus amoris* (steps of love-making) tradition which *Le Roman de la Rose* follows and which Rubens's *The Garden of Love* painting depicts, where the same couple is pictured moving from hesitant encounter through arousal of passion on to fulfillment of bodily love. Such a joined setup to structure one's imaginative artistic production constitutes the "Idyllic" typiconic idiom. This idiom of a treasured unreachable ideal is situated in an acutely observable natural setting—such is the makeup of the world for Idyllic artists in which humans are to find meaning (for example, the reflective Renaissance artist Giorgione).

To become a member of *l'Académie royale de peinture et de sculpture* (begun in 1648)—otherwise an artist was nobody—the artist had to submit a painting within one of several categories—history painting, portraiture, still life—to be accepted by officers of the *Académie*, and then that was the category of paintings henceforth the artist was allowed to produce. Watteau was given the exceptional liberty to submit his *morceau de réception* in any category, *à sa volonté*. His *Pilgrimage à Cythara* (Pilgrims en route to the Isle of Love-making) was accepted in 1717 but did not fit any of the categories; and the Academy minutes rewrote the accepted painting as *une feste galante* (a festival of gallant escorts in love-making). Watteau's innovation became a popular new category of painting in the Rococo Enlightenment period, as the *fêtes galantes* paintings of Nicolas Lancret, Jean-Baptiste Pater, and many others attest. These paintings present the world as a park on a late autumn afternoon where women and men play out their amorous roles of flirtation, subtle waiting games for a prospective lover, in fine clothes with music-making, dancing, tender serenades, aching for the fragile pleasures of fulfilled love.

But Watteau goes deeper than the run-of-the-mill Rococo-idyllic *fêtes gallante* calls to twilight assignations and intimacy world without end, because Watteau is critical of this societal circuit of untrammeled trysts for erotic advances. In many paintings Watteau adds a black-caped stranger to the scene of courting young ladies and overeager lovers; the unengaged gentleman acts like a disturbing intruder into this make-believe world of *courtesia*. The statues in Watteau's paintings offer critique of the coquettish charades encouraging gallants in their "progress" in the stages of *amour* aiming at consummation.[17] The statues of nude women Watteau presents in his paintings are not background garden statuary, as they are in the artwork of Lancret and

---

[17] Calvin Seerveld, "Telltale Statues in Watteau's Painting," *Eighteenth-century Studies* 14/2 (Winter 1980–1981): 151–180. Watteau probably knew Rubens's *Garden of Love* painting, and adroitly reverses the "progressive" stages of love-making in his two versions of the *Cythara Isle* masterpieces, so that the paintings are better read as "Pilgrims departing the Isle of love-making," as shown by their *post amorem* stages as they leave the statue behind (cf. *ibid.*, 162, 167, 169).

Pater, but are vivid naked female presences that expose the reality of the disguised and suppressed sensuality that the *fêtes galantes* art alludes to but denies.

A good example of Watteau's critique is his *The Dance (Les Fêtes Venitiennes)*; elsewhere, I have described this work as,

> a brilliant kaleidoscope of pied colors and outrageous hues, all vying for attention but still melted together into a luxurious masterpiece and centering on the white prima donna. Her slight, doll's body is tensed for the opening step of the dance, and her eyes betray some apprehension as to what might happen to her, opposite this imposing, paunchy fellow got up in a costume of oriental pomposity. Already at her right elbow, on the side lines, a "faux pas" attack is being disdainfully repulsed. On her left is a peasant in short pants playing his genital bagpipes, as if in collusion with her partner. Directly over the woman in white, high up on a vase in the shadows, as in the early arabesques, is a horned ram's head. And behind her is our critic, fitted with a blue cloak for the occasion, explaining the scene to a rather shocked companion. His left-handed gesture toward the statue, if not intentionally obscene, is at least heavily sarcastic: "Here, my good woman, you have an honest mirror of what you see before you. The primping, strutting pair stage-center are really a couple of gamecocks in an arousal scene before mating. The truth of the matter, behind the facade of sweetness and light, ravishing modesty, endless fantasy and schooled elegance, is our full-breasted, reclining beauty here, odalisque-hipped, arm raised above her head in an age-old artistic sign of seduction, about to sink out of sight on the back of a dolphin. That is the true reality, which, in our society, of course, is only statuary."[18]

The statue is not a reclining marble memento or tribute to a mythical Venus, but is a very alive, robustly naked woman exposing ironically what is the shameless prostituting gut of the falsifying Louis XV and Pompadour societal lifestyle.

The fact that Watteau's artworks are critical of what he portrays from within and out of his Rococo-idyllic standpoint explains why there is always a deeper sense of bittersweet tristesse in Watteau's artistry, which note is lacking in most other Rococo-idyllic Enlightenment artists. Like the blue-caped figure in *Les Fêtes Venitiennes* and like Jacques in Shakespeare's *As You Like It*, Watteau is a candle-holder outsider

---

[18] Ibid., 174, 177.

looking in at the goings on of a sophisticated circle of courtiers caught up in the precarious game of awakening erotic consciences as women and men try to maneuver through the narrowing selection that leads to a coupled man and woman's happiness. Woefully undeep about Watteau's delicate painterly art is the tentativeness to love-commitment as he presents it—there is no place for (baroque Rubens's) marriage-bonds; Watteau's perception is confined largely to the caresses of daydreaming wistfulness and the world of opera comique. But it is not so, in my judgment, that "Watteau's painting . . . is also an early example of art that does not try to express morally uplifting themes, but whose emotional and aesthetic satisfactions are enjoyed as ends in themselves."[19] While that moral judgment may be correct for much Rococo Enlightenment artistry, it is not so for Watteau's oeuvre (nor for Hogarth's artwork), both of whom in their art were highly critical of the hypocrisy and moral laxity of their age. Watteau's chagrined critique of his current culture was missed by his *fêtes galantes* imitators, by his collectors, and by most subsequent art critics and art historians. Yet neither Watteau nor Hogarth moralized about wrongdoing.

Rococo art does not deserve to be neglected by art historians. Watteau's significant diachronic contribution to the art historical record is that his Rococo artwork trusted painterly elements to carry his artistic meaning. Though caught in the radical secularizing trend of European culture which the Enlightenment dynamic exacerbated, one should credit Rococo artistry—especially Watteau—with excising the fixed literary coefficients encrusting graphic art, so entrenched, for example, in Nicolas Poussin's painterly art. Rococo art was thoroughly integrated with (its decadent) societal milieu, and did free painting to be just artistic painting, so that its references to meanings were made through thoroughly graphic symbolic analogues, not by literary devices. This professional refinement of artistic representation helped painterly art and sculpture deepen its peculiarly pre-lingual imaginative reach, so that color, compositional design, foreground and background, scale, tension, recurrent figures, and images themselves needed to be imaginatively read for detecting irony and meaning that had formerly been carried by classical humanist iconography or Scholastic Christian emblems and allegorical doublespeak. Although

---

secularized artistry easily turned superficial without the former literate connections and iconological dimensions, that does not mean painterly artistry necessarily became weaker in form. On the contrary, painterly art assumed the responsibility to evoke appreciation and understanding of art by its own painterly elements. And that was a sound artistic development.

John Walford's careful exposition of artworks in *Great Themes* offers trenchant and cross-referenced readings of many artworks. Having to sum up Watteau's cultural contribution to the history of art in two short paragraphs was an impossible assignment. For those with eyes to see, the shimmering rich colors of *Les Fêtes Vénitiennes*, the juxtaposed peacock bravado of the strutting dancers and the lively coarseness of the "statue," along with the cool unmasking gesture by the gentleman voyeur within the scene, while strongly critical of deceptive sophisticated pretense in affairs of the heart—because so much is at stake—does backhandedly catch the need for quiet elation and the presence of rue in genuine human love, and hints that erotic desire deserves leisure and a gentling imaginative dimension if it would be fully human.

Caspar David Friedrich, *Tetschen Altar* (*Cross in the Mountains*). 1808. Oil on canvas, 45 1/5" x 43 3/10" (without frame). Gemaldegalerie, Dresden. Photo: akg-images.

10

DEPARTING LIGHT
Caspar David Friedrich's *Tetschen Altar* (*Cross in the Mountains*)

KAIA MAGNUSEN

A masterpiece of nineteenth-century German Romanticism and the first oil painting by Caspar David Friedrich (1774–1840) to receive significant acclaim,[1] the *Tetschen Altar* (1808), also known as *Cross in the Mountains*, caused quite a stir when Friedrich exhibited the work, including its custom-made frame.[2] At that time, it was his "largest and most ambitious [work] to date."[3] The painting depicts a mountainous landscape scene. A dark, shadowy, triangular mountaintop rises from the bottom of the canvas. Shadowy green fir trees dot the mountain peak and rise up vertically toward the sky. Nestled in a rock cleft positioned slightly to the right of center and echoing the verticality of the trees that flank it stands a wooden cross with a gilded metal image of Christ. This type of crucifix, known as a *Gipfelkreuz*, was and still is a fairly common sight on mountaintops in Germany.[4] A slender vine of delicate ivy climbs around the base of the cross, which is positioned in a three-quarter turn away from the viewer. The crucifix appears to be addressing the sun setting behind the mountain. The disk of the sun can no longer be seen but its presence is indicated by the pale yellowish-white rays of light that resemble searchlights emanating from behind the mountain. One of these sunbeams casts its light on the metal figure of Christ, which produces a faint glimmer on the surface of his body as the light reflects from it. In the sky, horizontal bands of

---

[1] Timothy F. Mitchell, "From Vedute to Vision: The Importance of Popular Imagery in Friedrich's Development of Romantic Landscape Painting," *The Art Bulletin* 64/3 (September 1982): 414.
[2] Norbert Wolf, *Caspar David Friedrich 1774–1840: The Painter of Stillness* (Cologne, Germany: Taschen, 2003), 26.
[3] Joseph Leo Koerner, *Caspar David Friedrich and the Subject of Landscape* (New Haven, CT: Yale University Press, 1990), 47.
[4] Ibid.

vibrant pink and dusky grayish-purple clouds line the twilight sky. The reddish-pink clouds closest to the cross give the impression of parting in deference to the cross so that the figure of Christ is silhouetted against the dim purple sky.

Friedrich enclosed the painting within a gilded frame that he designed himself and which was executed by a friend and sculptor named Gottlieb Christian Kühn.[5] Below the canvas, in the middle of a mossy green horizontal panel lies a golden triangle, symbolizing the Trinity, within which is carved the eye of God. From this triangle emanate many slim rays of golden light. Flanking this symbol and arching toward it are sheaves of wheat and grapevines with clusters of grapes, symbolizing the Eucharist. Slender "clustered columns" comprise the sides of the frame while palm fronds emanate from the capitals and extend upward and inward to create the pointed arch of the frame's upper section. Five symmetrically arranged *putti* adorn this arch, and, decorating the apex, a seven-pointed star rests directly above the head of the centermost angel.[6] In designing this frame with its "basket-arch format and heavily gilded frame," Friedrich was deliberately appealing to the ritual form of "the carved and painted retable altarpiece," which was "a tradition of sacred art reaching back to the fourteenth century."[7] The artist was further highlighting the intended religious function of the painted canvas through its relationship to the ornate gilded frame.

There has been a considerable amount of discussion regarding the initial commission for the *Tetschen Altar*. It is sometimes speculated that Friedrich was inspired to create the painting as a result of a commission from pastor and poet Gotthard Kosegarten.[8] Kosegarten constructed a small chapel on the outskirts of Vitt, a fishing village on the island of Rügen in Germany near Cape Arkona.[9] In summer, Kosegarten preached outside, and when his sermons became increasingly popular, he erected a formal chapel for use during inclement weather.[10] This chapel was indeed built, but Friedrich rejected the commission for

---

[5] William Vaughan, *Friedrich* (London: Phaidon, 2004), 105.
[6] Mitchell, "From Vedute to Vision," 421. Although some scholars, such as William Vaughan and Norbert Wolf, assert that ears of corn are depicted flanking the eye of God on the lowermost part of the frame, they instead appear to be sheaves of wheat, which is more in line with traditional Eucharistic symbolism.
[7] Koerner, *Subject of Landscape*, 47.
[8] Vaughan, *Friedrich*, 23.
[9] Wolf, *Caspar David Friedrich*, 19.
[10] Albert Boime, "Caspar David Friedrich: Monk by the Sea," *Arts Magazine* (November 1986): 59.

the new chapel's altarpiece.[11] Instead, the painter Philipp Otto Runge was commissioned and ultimately painted *Peter Walking on the Waves* to serve as the chapel's altarpiece.[12]

It is possible that Friedrich initially planned to give the painting to Gustav IV Adolf of Sweden. Friedrich was born in the town of Greifswald[13] in Pomerania, "which was intermittently under Swedish rule from the Peace of Westphalia of 1648 to the Napoleonic invasion of 1807."[14] However, Gustav IV Adolf ultimately lost the crown in 1809 when "Sweden's western army organized a coup d'état, overthrew Gustav, and declared his heirs ineligible."[15] Thus, Gustav was never actually given the altarpiece, and there is no evidence that he was ever aware of Friedrich's plan to present him with the work.[16]

Ultimately, the *Tetschen Altar* was purchased by Count Franz Anton von Thun-Hohenstein. Maria Theresa Brühl, who became the count's wife, had seen a similar painting of a cross in the mountains that Friedrich had done in sepia and that had been exhibited in March 1807[17] at the Dresden Academy, and she encouraged the count to purchase it. Instead, Thun-Hohenstein requested that Friedrich create a formal altarpiece based on the small sepia sketch.[18] The count claimed that he intended to use the work as the altarpiece in his own private chapel at Schloss Tetschen in northern Bohemia.[19] As noted, Friedrich had originally planned to give the work to the Swedish king, Gustav IV Adolf, but when the king was deposed, the painter agreed to the count's proposal.[20]

However, contrary to Friedrich's intention for the work, the count and countess did not install the *Tetschen Altar* as the altarpiece of the castle's private chapel since it already had an altarpiece, which the count apparently had no desire to replace.[21] In fact, Joseph Bergler, director of the Prague Art Academy, had created a panel painting

---

[11] Ibid.

[12] Ibid. Runge's *Peter Walking on the Waves* is currently in the collection of the *Hamburger Kunsthalle*.

[13] Wolf, *Caspar David Friedrich*, 27.

[14] Koerner, *Subject of Landscape*, 50.

[15] Ibid., 51.

[16] Vaughan, *Friedrich*, 102–103.

[17] Ibid., 102. Vaughn refers to Maria Theresa Brühl as the Count's fiancée when she saw the sepia cross in the mountains exhibited at the Dresden Academy in 1807, whereas Koerner refers to her as the Count's wife.

[18] Koerner, *Subject of Landscape*, 49.

[19] Vaughan, *Friedrich*, 102.

[20] Koerner, *Subject of Landscape*, 51.

[21] Ibid.

around 1790 that was being used as the chapel's altarpiece.[22] In order to convince Friedrich to sell them the painting, it seems that the count and countess misled Friedrich by falsely indicating that the *Tetschen Altar* would be used as the chapel's altarpiece.[23] In order to maintain the deception, the count and countess invented various excuses to prevent Friedrich from visiting the castle to view his work. Had he actually gone to Schloss Tetschen, Friedrich would have seen that his innovative altarpiece was not being used as the private chapel's altarpiece but had, in fact, been hung "in the bedroom next to an engraving of Raphael's *Sistine Madonna*."[24] Thus, while the work is often called the *Tetschen Altar* rather than *Cross in the Mountains*, it never served as the altarpiece in the castle which was its namesake.

Despite the fact that the *Tetschen Altar* was, ultimately, hung in a domestic context, it must be emphasized that Friedrich had specifically intended the work with its specially designed frame to function in a religious context as an altarpiece. In fact, when the artist first showed the work in his studio around Christmastime in 1808, he closed the windows and placed the painting in its frame on a table draped with a length of black cloth in order to recreate a sacred setting appropriate for an altarpiece.[25]

Indeed, the fact that Friedrich intended the *Tetschen Altar*, a landscape painting, to be a religious altarpiece was the issue most responsible for much of the controversy surrounding the work. At that time, it was unprecedented to use landscape to convey sacred meaning in a devotional painting. It was a strongly and commonly held belief that "landscape should be used to reinforce, augment and strengthen the emotional and moral content of some human event."[26] Many Romantic writers and artists upheld the idea that a landscape should not be the primary signifier of meaning in a painting; it should only play a supporting role by acting as a backdrop for some human narrative. Thus, a painting in which landscape played a lead role in conveying meaning rather than simply being relegated to a supporting, background status was an innovative step, but an altarpiece in which the landscape rather

---

[22] Ibid.
[23] Ibid.
[24] Wolf, *Caspar David Friedrich*, 29.
[25] Ibid., 26.
[26] Mitchell, "From Vedute to Vision," 423.

than human biblical figures communicated the religious significance was distinctly unprecedented.

Friedrich's *Tetschen Altar* flouted the conventions of traditional religious painting. Other than the man-made cross and likeness of Jesus, the landscape is entirely comprised of natural elements that do not indicate human intervention. No actual human figures are depicted in the painting. The figure of Christ on the cross is not intended to represent the actual, physical body of Christ. Instead, it depicts a human-made metal figure created in the likeness of Jesus Christ, attached to a wooden cross. This *Gipfelkreuz*, which literally translates "summit cross," would have been a frequent sight to anyone traveling in the mountains. Friedrich himself was certainly familiar with such crucifixes[27] and he depicted them in various media. However, Friedrich did not depict specific crosses that he had seen in the mountains. Rather, he was inspired and moved by them in general. Thus, the mountain crosses he portrays are generalizations rather than actual images of particular crosses.

The presence of the *Gipfelkreuz* obviously references Christ's suffering and death during his crucifixion, but this historical event is not directly represented. As a result, the landscape also bears significant responsibility for conveying the religious meaning of the devotional altarpiece. Thus, as John Walford notes in *Great Themes in Art*, Friedrich attempted to reveal spiritual truth through the use of natural elements.[28] He did not paint a uniquely miraculous phenomenon or an otherworldly, visionary scene. In fact, Friedrich's *Tetschen Altar* does not depict anything that "could not be empirically recorded in the natural order by a modern observer."[29] Instead, Friedrich used common, everyday mountain sights to symbolically communicate religious truth. The rock that comprises the mountain and upon which the crucifix stands represents "steadfastness," while the fir trees that dot the mountain peak reference "the cycle of humanity."[30] The evergreen fir trees also symbolically communicate the idea of eternal life because they are green all year round. The ivy that coils around the base of the vertical beam of the cross symbolizes "fidelity" because it tenaciously

[27] Ibid., 419.
[28] E. John Walford, *Great Themes in Art* (Upper Saddle River, NJ: Prentice-Hall, 2002), 379.
[29] Ibid.
[30] Ibid.

holds fast to the things around which it grows.[31] The light of the setting sun is associated with "divine presence,"[32] although Friedrich claimed the sun's rays referenced God the Father rather than Jesus Christ.

Friedrich's distinct emphasis on common landscape features in a work of art specifically intended for a religious purpose was a groundbreaking, if not brilliant, artistic innovation according to his supporters, but a grievous offense, if not a sacrilege, to the work's critics. Although the painting aroused ardent support in some of its viewers, others, most notably Friedrich Wilhelm Basilius von Ramdohr, disapproved of Friedrich's religious use of landscape.[33] Ramdohr's objections to the *Tetschen Altar* were so numerous that his twenty-two page long critique was "published in four successive numbers" of the journal *Zeitung für die elegante Welt* (*Journal for the Elegant World*), from January 17 to January 20, 1809.[34] Ramdohr subscribed to the belief that landscape should not be the primary signifier of meaning, especially religious meaning. Instead, he felt that religious themes should be addressed only with human figures as the principal means of communicating sacred significance. He felt that the landscape in religious works should serve only as the backdrop for the actions of human protagonists. With regards to Friedrich's *Tetschen Altar*, Ramdohr contended "that it would be a 'veritable presumption if landscape painting were to sneak into the church and creep onto the altar.'"[35] For the critic, landscape painting and religious painting were two distinct genres, and Friedrich had violated the sanctity of each category by combining them into the religious landscape of the *Tetschen Altar*.[36]

In his lengthy review, Ramdohr also criticized some technical aspects of the painting. For instance, he disliked the lack of a discernible foreground caused by the position of the mountain and felt that the effect of this deficiency was amplified by the manner in which the frame abruptly severs the mountain. In addition, he questioned the ambiguity of the position of the viewer relative to the mountain cross. However, the critic's main objection to the work was that Friedrich did not represent an actual human figure and, thus, did not depict the

---

[31] Ibid.
[32] Ibid.
[33] Wolf, *Caspar David Friedrich*, 26.
[34] Vaughan, *Friedrich*, 108.
[35] Ibid., 7.
[36] Ibid., 109.

actual crucifixion; instead, Friedrich paints a generic mountain cruci-fix in a nonspecific landscape setting in his attempt to convey a specific religious symbolic program. In Ramdohr's mind, the *Tetschen Altar* depicted no clear human protagonist and, therefore, communicated no clear meaning.[37]

Ramdohr's criticisms of the painting and its frame prompted Friedrich to offer his own defense of the *Tetschen Altar,* which was pub-lished in April 1809 in the *Journal des Luxus und der Modern (Journal of Luxury and the Modern).*[38] This was Friedrich's first and last pub-lic explanation of the symbolism of any of his works.[39] According to Friedrich's explanation of the *Tetschen Altar (Cross in the Mountains),*

> Jesus Christ, nailed to the Cross, is turned to the setting sun, here the image of the totally enlivening Father. With Christ dies the wisdom of the old world, the time when God the Father wandered directly on Earth. This sunset and the world were no longer able to apprehend the departed light. The evening glow shining from the pure noble metal of the golden crucified Christ is reflected in gentle glow to the earth. The Cross stands raised in a rock, unshakably firm, as our faith in Jesus Christ. Around the Cross stand the evergreens, enduring through all seasons, as does the belief of Man in Him, the crucified.[40]

While, at first glance, Friedrich's defense of his work might seem satisfactory, upon further reflection it reveals itself to be rather ques-tionable. When the logical outworking of this statement is considered in light of the painting itself and its specially made frame, it becomes clear that the work's function as an altarpiece would have been much better served had Friedrich described the sun as referencing Jesus Christ and the setting rays of the sun as indicating his dying moments on the cross rather than representing God the Father.

While Friedrich's explication is often quoted and might initially seem insightful, in fact, if one thinks through Friedrich's words, his account ultimately appears to have probably unintentional, negative implications. The painter asserted that the setting sun was representa-tive of God the Father. Yet, if this is so, then how is one to interpret the

---

[37] Ibid., 7–8.
[38] Koerner, *Subject of Landscape,* 111.
[39] Mitchell, "From Vedute to Vision," 422.
[40] Quoted in ibid., 422–423.

darkness of night once the sun has set? Would not that darkness imply that God is somehow no longer present? As noted in the Gospels, such as in Mark 15:33, from the sixth hour to the ninth hour during Christ's crucifixion, darkness came over the land. This darkness was symbolic of God the Father removing his presence from Christ after Jesus took the sins of the world in substitutionary atonement. Theologically, God's light has not departed and certainly he has not denied his presence to the world. In the *Tetschen Altar*, when the sun sets, the entire landscape, not just the crucifix, will be cast into darkness. If the sun is representative of God the Father, then this darkness would seem to imply that God will remove his presence from the world, which, as far as orthodox Christian teaching is concerned, is incorrect.

Friedrich attempted to further elaborate on the meaning of the elements in his painting by asserting that, "With Christ dies the wisdom of the old world."[41] Again, the spiritual implications of this statement are illogical. Jesus came to clarify and amplify humanity's understanding of God, and the old world's wisdom certainly did not die as a result of the crucifixion. Both oral and written works such as the Torah and other commentaries were still extant and were accessible to the Jewish people. Christ's death on the cross did not preclude anyone from accessing the Old Testament revelation of God the Father. Furthermore, it was, frankly, nonsensical for Friedrich to assert that the sun was representative of "the totally enlivening Father" only to then contend that, once the sun set, the world was "no longer able to apprehend the departed light." According to these statements, Friedrich seemed to be contending that since the sun was God, once the sun set the world would no longer be able to understand God.

When Friedrich's statements are applied to and analyzed in light of the actual painting, they are hardly conducive to a spiritually touching devotional altarpiece. The more one scrutinizes Friedrich's explanation, the less sense it makes as a theologically sound allegorical or symbolic program. Therefore, it seems that Friedrich probably composed his explanation directly in response to Ramdohr's criticisms and, thus, may not have actually had this particular program in mind when he created the painting and planned the design of the frame. It is entirely possible that Friedrich simply contrived the explanation in

---

[41] Quoted in Mitchell, "From Vedute to Vision," 422.

an attempt to refute Ramdohr's criticisms of the *Tetschen Altar* without completely thinking through the logical and theological implications of the explanatory program he offered in its defense.

Throughout Christian history, Jesus Christ, rather than God the Father, has been compared to the sun. Furthermore, in the New Testament, Christ repeatedly refers to himself using the image of light. For instance, in John 8:12 Christ declares, "I am the light of the world." Therefore, if a symbolic meaning is to be ascribed to the sun in Friedrich's *Tetschen Altar*, it makes more sense and is less theologically troublesome for the sun to refer to Christ instead of to God the Father. Despite Friedrich's own explanation, referencing Christ via the sun is ultimately more in keeping with the tone and intention of the painting and its frame.

Following this suggested meaning for the sun, the *Tetschen Altar* shows a representation of Christ, the Light of the World, hanging on the cross as a substitutionary sacrifice for sinful humanity. The last rays of the sun, as it sets, reference the last moments of Christ's life as he hangs dying on the wooden cross. However, just as the darkness brought by the setting of the sun is not permanent, Christ's death was not ultimate. The sun rises in the morning much as Christ rose from the dead after three days. This interpretation accentuates the symbolic meaning of the natural elements in the painting. The reference to the human life cycle provided by the trees correlates with the death of Christ, while the rock's suggestion of resoluteness and the ivy's symbolic invocation of faithfulness convey a much more hopeful message if they reference the death and subsequent resurrection of Christ than if they refer to God and the implication of his supposed incomprehensibility after Christ's crucifixion.

Furthermore, as this painting does not actually depict Jesus Christ but a metal, man-made figure of Christ affixed to a wooden cross, this particular interpretation, in which the light references Christ, serves to aid the viewer's empathetic reaction and spiritual connection to the work despite the fact that the painting contains no human figures. The *Gipfelkreuz* is positioned in a three-quarter turn away from the viewer, which disrupts the emotional and spiritual connection the viewer might have with a more frontal figure. Moreover, the face of the figure of Christ is further obscured as his left arm, hanging down from the horizontal crossbeam, is positioned in such a way as to prevent a distinct view of Christ's face. Coupled with the rather negative implications of Friedrich's statement, the turning away of the crucifix and Christ's lost profile could seem to invoke a pessimistic mood and even a sense of spiritual abandonment. However, such potentially dark interpretations are avoided if one regards the sun as symbolically pertaining to Christ rather than to God the Father. Even though the sun has slipped below the horizon, the position of its rays seems to indicate that it is situated opposite the viewer. Thus, while the cross appears to turn away from the viewer, the setting sun seems to address the viewer more directly. If the sun is also representative of Christ, there is a clear connection between the sun, its light, and the cross that visually and theologically ties these elements together and creates a more spiritually comforting interpretation than the one offered by Friedrich.

In addition, the symbolic program of the frame reinforces the centricity of Christ and, thus, supports a reading of the *Tetschen Altar* in which the sun and its light are representative of Christ instead of God the Father. The all-seeing eye of God enclosed within a triangle representing the Trinity is positioned in the middle of the frame's bottom panel. The sheaves of wheat and grapevines with clusters of grapes that flank it distinctly reference the body and blood of Christ, which are symbolically consumed during Communion, initiated during the Last Supper, and which were actually sacrificed during the crucifixion. The palm fronds atop the columns that border the sides of the painting could reference Christ's Triumphal Entry into Jerusalem, during which people waved palm fronds. The adoring angels and evening star comprising the upper arch of the frame can also be read as referring to Christ. Adoring angels appeared in the sky after Christ's birth and filled the heavens with celebration. The magi were led to the location of the Christ child by following the radiant light of a star. Thus, the upper portion of the frame highlights the Nativity, the sides of the frame suggests Christ's Triumphal Entry, and the lower panel references both the Last Supper and the crucifixion. The frame provides a condensed, symbolic narrative of the life of Christ, with a particular emphasis on his birth and death.

The program of the frame correlates to the Christ-centered interpretation of the *Tetschen Altar* as it clearly depicts a representation of

Christ on the cross. In addition, the presence of fir trees to represent the cycle of life corresponds with the condensed life of Christ as presented via the symbols on the frame. Further supporting this interpretation is the fact that fir trees are used as *Weinachtsbäume*, "Christmas trees," and Christians celebrate Christ's birth at Christmastime. The trees also allude to Christ's death as the cross on which he was crucified was made of wood, and it is not uncommon to speak of the crucifixion by saying that Christ was "hung upon a tree." In addition, the association of evergreen trees with immortality is evocative of Christ's immortality and coeternality with God the Father as well as, ultimately, of the eternal life that awaits believers after earthly death. Most significantly, the light of the frame's evening star, which alludes to the star that led the magi to Christ and marks his birth, is paralleled by the departing light of the setting sun, which announces his death and the hope his death and subsequent resurrection inspires in those who believe.

It has been said that "nature is the art of God,"[42] and Caspar David Friedrich's *Tetschen Altar (Cross in the Mountains)* seems to agree with this sentiment by declaring that not only does the created world reflect the glory of God, but the natural world can be used to convey profound religious truth. Although the implications of Friedrich's published explanatory program for the *Tetschen Altar* ultimately prove to be unsatisfactory, if the sun is interpreted as being indicative of Jesus Christ rather than God the Father, the spiritual poignancy the artist sought to communicate through the painted landscape and its attendant frame are successfully conveyed. Ultimately, Friedrich's decision to use natural elements in an everyday landscape setting in a religious work of art proves that, in the right hands and with the correct interpretive program, human figures are not always necessary to communicate essential truths of the Christian faith, and the departing light of the setting sun can inspire as much religious contemplation and convey as much spiritual insight as a more conventional crucifixion narrative.

---

[42] Jehiel Keller Hoyt and Kate Louise Roberts, *Hoyt's New Cyclopedia of Practical Quotations* (New York and London: Funk & Wagnalls, 1923), 43. Although the words "Nature is the art of God" are often attributed to Dante Alighieri, in section 16 of his *Religious Medici*, Sir Thomas Brown wrote that, "In brief, all things are artificial, for nature is the art of God."

John Constable, *Dedham Vale*. 1828. Oil on canvas, 57 1/8" x 48". National Gallery of Scotland, Edinburgh.

11

REMEMBER THY CREATOR
John Constable's *Dedham Vale*

ANNE ROBERTS

This beautiful image of the vale of Dedham and the valley of the river Stour by John Constable (1776–1837) represents a pivotal point, both in the artist's own career and in the development of English landscape painting. One of the favorite views of Constable's boyhood, *Dedham Vale* (1828), painted when the artist was in his early 50s, is the climax of a long series of sketches and paintings of this area, dating from the turn of the century. During its completion, in the spring of 1828, Constable's younger brother Abram wrote to him of "the Valley from Langham, that well known (& to me and you) beautiful view."[1] Although rooted in Constable's deep love for the English countryside, the painting also has a European significance. It reflects his early study of seventeenth-century artists such as Claude Lorrain and Jacob van Ruisdael, while at the same time, in its freshness of observation and freedom of handling, it looks beyond the development of French Impressionism to twentieth-century painting.

John Constable's artistic reputation has often been compared to the dazzling career of his contemporary J. M. W. Turner, who had been elected a Royal Academician at the age of only twenty-seven—whereas Constable was made to wait until he was over fifty. Unlike Turner, Constable never traveled outside of England. Not only was he deeply attached to his home landscape, but he had a countryman's intimate knowledge of fields, crops, hedgerows, and riverbanks in every season. As the son of a respected local landowner, he also would have had privileged access to areas where many local folk would have been regarded as trespassers.

---

[1] In R. B. Beckett, ed., *John Constable's Correspondence*, 8 vols. (Ipswich, UK: Suffolk Records Society, 1962), 4:242.

The village of Langham, not far from East Bergholt, where the Constable family lived, straggles along a ridge of higher ground above the Stour valley. Constable's view is taken looking eastward from the lower slopes of the hillside, slightly to the north of Langham church. The church stands apart from the village, in parkland, and can be seen in the background of Constable's painting of 1830, *The Glebe Farm*, now in the Tate Britain. Constable's precise viewpoint over the Vale is inaccessible today, although some features, such as the road bridge toward Stratford Saint Mary, are still recognizable. At the center in the middle distance, the distinctive silhouette of Dedham church tower just cuts the horizon line, and beyond it the sun lights up the water of the Stour, stretching away to Mistley, just before the river opens out toward Harwich harbor.

An earlier view across the Stour valley to Dedham village painted in 1814–1815, now in Boston, is also helpful in locating Constable's position. Here, the tower of Dedham church can be seen in relation to that of Langham, across the valley on higher ground near the top of Gun Hill in the distance. For his paintings of 1802 and 1828, Constable would have used studies made from the lower slopes on the far right-hand side.

Langham had another important significance for Constable. As a young man, in 1798 or 1799, he was introduced to Dr. John Fisher, who had been appointed Rector of Langham in 1790. Dr. Fisher was extremely well connected and, as a canon of Windsor Castle, only visited Langham occasionally. He was on friendly terms with the Royal family, having been a tutor to Prince Edward (the father of Queen Victoria), and was later to become a bishop, first of Exeter and then the more lucrative see of Salisbury. He drew and painted a little himself, became honorary chaplain to the Royal Academy, and was a friend of the Academy's second president, the Anglo-American Benjamin West.[2]

The Fisher family were to become Constable's closest friends. In the autumn of 1811, Dr. Fisher invited Constable to visit Salisbury, where he first met the bishop's twenty-three year-old nephew, also named John Fisher, who had graduated from Cambridge and was soon to be ordained. The two seem to have taken to each other immediately. Fisher, as the younger man, was an eager admirer of Constable's work

---

[2] R. B. Beckett, *John Constable and the Fishers* (London: Routledge & Kegan Paul, 1952), 3–5.

and ideas. The openness of their friendship and correspondence has left a detailed record of Constable's life and thought which is comparable to the letters of Vincent van Gogh half a century later. Both men shared "a deep strain of unaffected piety, in which the enjoyment of landscape was inextricably mixed with gratitude toward its Creator and which was not found to be inconsistent with a fund of healthy ribald humour."[3]

Constable's love of the countryside also reflects his familiarity with Romantic poetry of the late eighteenth century. He sought to make the unique characteristics of English landscape recognized as important for landscape painting in general—just as they had already become for the Romantic poets.[4]

The poems of his contemporary, William Wordsworth, have a close affinity to Constable's work. Although they had no significant personal relationship, the two are known to have met on more than one occasion. For Wordsworth, as for other poets of the Romantic movement, the contemplation of landscape had a moral as well as an emotional significance. He famously wrote of nature as,

> The anchor of my purest thoughts, the nurse,
> The guardian of my heart, and soul
> And all my moral being.[5]

In exhibition catalogs of that time, artists would often supplement the titles of their work with quotations. Constable made use of popular descriptions of nature from James Thomson's "The Seasons"—but the poems and letters of William Cowper appear to have been of greater personal importance to him. "How delighted I am that you are so fond of Cowper," he wrote to his future wife, Maria, "But how could it be otherwise—for he is the poet of Religion and Nature."[6] Cowper had been converted to Christianity in the early 1770s and was befriended by John Newton, vicar of Olney in Bedfordshire, and a leader of the eighteenth-century evangelical revival. Later, Cowper was often

---

[3] Ibid., 16.
[4] John Constable's draft for the introduction to *English Landscape Scenery*, Fitzwilliam MS 39 (Cambridge: Fitzwilliam Museum, 1953). See also the quotation from Constable's prospectus for *English Landscape Scenery* in C. R. Leslie, *Memoirs of the Life of John Constable* (London: Phaidon, 1951), 179.
[5] William Wordsworth, "Lines Composed a Few Miles above Tintern Abbey," from *Lyrical Ballads* (1798).
[6] Letter to Maria Bicknell, June 22, 1812 (in R. B. Beckett, ed., *John Constable's Correspondence*, 8 vols. [Ipswich, UK: Suffolk Records Society, 1964], 6:78).

undervalued or misunderstood because of his Calvinistic beliefs—but these beliefs appear never to have been a problem for Constable. In "The Task," Cowper's most important work in blank verse, published in 1785, some lines could almost be a description of a Constable painting:

> For I have loved the rural walk,
> Through lanes of grassy swarth, close cropped by nibbling sheep,
> And skirted thick with intertexture firm of thorny boughs.

Cowper's love of familiar scenes finds an echo in much of Constable's correspondence, as well as throwing an additional light on his attachment to Dutch painting. Describing the river banks at Olney, Cowper writes,

> Things must be beautiful, which daily viewed,
> Please daily, and whose novelty survives
> Long knowledge, and the scrutiny of years.

Although *Dedham Vale* is recognized as one of Constable's greatest achievements, he left no detailed comments about it, apart from briefly mentioning it, in a letter to John Fisher, as "one of his best." Shown at the Royal Academy exhibition in April 1828, it is very closely based on a smaller painting, made over a quarter of a century earlier in 1802.[7] A juxtaposition of these two images reveals that, although the 1828 version is much larger, the proportion and design of the trees on the right, and the relative height of the horizon line are virtually identical—suggesting that the original design had been carefully traced and squared up—a process which Constable's young assistant John Dunthorne Jr. often carried out for him.[8]

In the 1802 version, the treatment and tone of the foliage reflects Constable's early study of Thomas Gainsborough, who had been born in the town of Sudbury, not far from East Bergholt, and before moving to the more fashionable town of Bath had worked in Ipswich. There, one of his contemporaries was a local artist, George Frost, an ardent admirer who had acquired a significant collection of Gainsborough's drawings. Constable, who visited Frost as a young man, undoubtedly

---

[7] Now in the Victoria and Albert Museum.
[8] Letter from Constable to John Fisher, November 17, 1834; quoted in Leslie, *Memoirs*, 131.

had opportunities to study these, and may have acquired some after Frost's death in 1821. (The parlor at Constable's home in Hampstead was hung with Gainsborough drawings.)[9] It was while visiting Ipswich that he made the famous comment, "I fancy I see Gainsborough under every hedge and hollow tree."[10]

However, a far more important influence was that of the classical landscape painter Claude Lorrain. It is well known that Constable's mother, always eager to further her son's career, had procured an introduction for him to the connoisseur, patron, and amateur painter Sir George Beaumont, whose widowed mother lived in Dedham. It was probably at Lady Beaumont's house that Constable first saw Claude's *Landscape with Hagar and the Angel,* painted in 1646, a treasured acquisition which Sir George often carried with him when he traveled, in a specially designed case. This was to become a painting with which Constable was familiar for the whole of his career. As a student at the Royal Academy, he visited Sir George's London house in Seymour Street, where he was able to make copies and to study the work in depth. Later it hung as part of a group of Claudes in the breakfast room at the Beaumonts' country house at Coleorton, in Leicestershire, from where Constable wrote to Maria, ". . . we do not quit the table immediately, but chat a little about the pictures. . . . We then go to the painting room . . ."[11]

Claude's pastoral landscapes of the Roman Campagna were particularly popular with eighteenth-century English travelers on their Grand Tour of Europe, and many can still be seen in English country house collections. (A prime example of the prevailing taste for classical landscape is the first Earl of Leicester's Landscape Room at Holkham Hall, in Norfolk, in which the paintings can still be seen exactly as they were hung in the late 1750s, and which includes seven Claudes.

Sir George had purchased *Hagar and the Angel* shortly after having first visited Italy with his wife in 1782. It became one of three Claudes which he bequeathed to London's newly formed National Gallery on his death in 1827. In another of these, *Landscape with*

---

[9]Leslie, *Memoirs,* 270.
[10]Letter from Constable to J. T. "Antiquity" Smith, August 18, 1799; quoted in Leslie, *Memoirs,* 9.
[11]Letter to Maria, October 27, 1823; quoted in Beckett, *Constable's Correspondence,* 6:292.

a Goatherd and Goats, the treatment of light and foliage was also important for Constable's early efforts to improve the finish of his work.[12] Later, at Coleorton, he made a careful copy of this painting, which he described as "a little Claude, a grove—probably done on the spot."[13]

Claude's underlying scheme of composition acted as a framework for Constable's own observation of nature. The organization of space in Claude's landscapes operates almost like a traditional stage set, leading the eye back in carefully planned steps—"a dark *coulisse* on one side (hardly ever two) the shadow of which extended across the first plane in the foreground, a middle plane with a central feature . . . and finally two planes, one behind the other, the second being that luminous distance for which he has always been famous."[14] In these paintings the atmosphere is very still and the trees, although their foliage is modeled in the golden light, function principally as silhouettes which frame the view. For Constable, brought up from his earliest childhood to observe the weather, the movement of light and shadow, "which never stand still," must have been a crucial missing element.

Another feature of Claude's system of composition is that the "focal length" of his views is generally very consistent, with small figures and landscape features in the middle distance. The figures, which link the landscape to subjects from either classical literature or the Bible, were often added by assistants, and because of their reduced scale have little sense of character or immediacy. The deep recession of space also means that those rich qualities of surface and texture, which were so important to Constable, become subordinated to the overall design. Claude's subjects appear designed for calm contemplation—the opposite of Constable's devotion to painting as "another way of feeling."

Constable had read Sir Joshua Reynolds's lecture to the students of the Royal Academy,[15] where Reynolds speaks of Claude as a painter who could transport his viewers' minds to higher things, conducting them into the tranquility of Arcadia. Reynolds noted,

---

[12]Leslie Parris and Ian Fleming-Williams, *Constable* (London: Tate, 1991), 60.

[13]Letter to Maria, October 27, 1823; quoted in Beckett, *Constable's Correspondence*, 6:292.

[14]Kenneth Clark, *Landscape into Art* (Harmondsworth, UK: Penguin, 1949), 76–77.

[15]Letter from Constable to John Fisher, October 23, 1821; quoted in Leslie, *Memoirs*, 85.

> Like the history painter, a painter of landscapes in this style . . . sends the imagination back into antiquity; and, like the poet, he makes the elements sympathise with his subject. . . . a landskip thus conducted, under the influence of a poetical mind, will have the same superiority over the more ordinary and common views, as Milton's *Allegro* and *Penseroso* have over cold prosaic narration or description.[16]

Elsewhere in the same lecture Reynolds takes this further: ". . . whatever is familiar, or in any way reminds us of what we see and hear every day, perhaps does not belong to the higher provinces of art, either in poetry or in painting."

Constable, on the other hand, had an instinctive feeling and a passionate visual perception of ordinary things, especially the surroundings associated with his childhood. In a letter to John Fisher he recalled,

> Still I should paint my own places best; painting is with me but another word for feeling, and I associate "my careless boyhood" with all that lies on the banks of the Stour; those scenes made me a painter and I am grateful; that is, I had often thought of pictures of them before I ever touched a pencil.[17]

At the Royal Academy Schools, busy copying Old Master paintings by Annibale Carracci and Claude, he was still homesick for more familiar scenes. "This fine weather makes me melancholy," he wrote to his Suffolk friend John Dunthorne: "It recalls so forcibly every scene we have visited and drawn together. I even love every stile and stump, and every lane in the village, so deep are early impressions."[18] This does much to explain Constable's attraction to the landscapes of Jacob van Ruisdael. He later described Dutch painters as "a stay-at-home people—hence their originality."[19]

It was John Fisher who fondly referred to the Constables's London home, at 1 Keppel Street, as "Ruisdael House."[20] John Walford points out that Constable was making copies of Jacob van Ruisdael over a period of thirty-five years, from 1797 to 1832—almost the whole of his

---

[16] Joshua Reynolds, Discourse 13, December 11, 1786, in Joshua Reynolds, *Discourses on Art* (New York: Collier, 1961), 208.

[17] Letter to John Fisher, October 23, 1821; quoted in Beckett, *Constable's Correspondence*, 6:76–78.

[18] Quoted in Leslie, *Memoirs*, 10.

[19] Third lecture to the Royal Institution; quoted in Leslie, *Memoirs*, 319.

[20] Quoted in Leslie, *Memoirs*, 72.

working life.[21] Even in middle age, he was very reluctant to part with cherished early copies from his student days.[22]

Constable's enthusiasm for Ruisdael dates from the very beginning of his time at the Royal Academy Schools. Prior to that he seems to have known of Ruisdael's work only through etchings loaned to him by the engraver and publisher J. T. Smith (known as "Antiquity Smith"). On the morning of his admission (February 4, 1799), he wrote to John Dunthorne, "I shall begin painting as soon as I have the loan of a sweet little picture by Jacob Ruisdael to copy. Since I have been in town I have seen some remarkably fine ones by him: indeed I never saw him before."[23]

By the following winter, Constable had begun copying "a very fine picture" by Ruisdael which he and a fellow student, Ramsay Richard Reinagle, had purchased in partnership for £70[24]—a very considerable sum at that time. This also tells us much about a student's experience of other artists' work in the days before public galleries. Collectors would sometimes allow access to their homes, or loan a major work to the Academy for study. As the only available reproductions were monochrome engravings or mezzotints, opportunities to copy original paintings were the most important means of developing technique and the use of color. For such copies to have lasting value, intense observation was required, and a mere sketch of the work was insufficient. For Constable, "a sketch . . . will not serve more than one state of mind, and will not serve to drink at again and again."[25]

In *Jacob van Ruisdael and the Perception of Landscape*, John Walford discussed the Dutch seventeenth-century writers' and landscape painters' understanding of nature as "God's second book," reflecting the words of the Confession of Faith of the Netherlands Reformed Churches, where "all created things, both great and small, are like letters, which give us the invisible things of God to behold, namely His eternal power and divinity."[26] At the same time, changing seasons, decay, and death are visual evidence of the consequences of the fall.

---

[21] E. John Walford, *Jacob van Ruisdael and the Perception of Landscape* (New Haven, CT: Yale University Press, 1991), 189.
[22] Leslie, *Memoirs*, 74.
[23] Quoted in ibid., 8.
[24] Ibid., 10.
[25] Letter to John Fisher, November 23, 1823; quoted in Beckett, *John Constable and the Fishers*, 149.
[26] Walford, *Jacob van Ruisdael*, 20.

Constable, with his farming background, would have identified immediately with landscapes by Ruisdael and others where the fertility of the land, with its annual cycle of work, reflects God's providence and care within an uncertain and transient world. In his lectures he also spoke of Ruisdael as enveloping the most ordinary scenes with solemnity and grandeur.[27]

Ruisdael's *View of Haarlem* makes an interesting comparison with Constable's later practice. Like Constable, Ruisdael painted this familiar landscape in both upright and horizontal formats and from different viewpoints. There are no clues as to whether Constable saw any of these versions, although several features—such as the view across the flat polders to the sunlit water beyond, with the silhouette of the Saint Bavo Kerk—suggest elements of *Dedham Vale*. In the distance, workers can be seen moving among the long strips of linen flax, carefully laid out to bleach in the sunlight. At the same time, as John Walford has observed, two-thirds of the canvas is taken up by the drama of the sky where huge clouds are sailing across, and "the juxtaposition of elements within the landscape . . . . conveys a sense of the competing forces of nature and their impact on human life."[28]

It was to be the tension between Claude's structural definition and Ruisdael's contemplation of the everyday world that finally enabled Constable to achieve the breakthrough to his greatest work. In *Dedham Vale*, Constable has framed his landscape with large foreground trees, revisiting the familiar composition of Claude's *Hagar and the Angel*. Sir George Beaumont had died during the previous year, and it is probable that Constable intended this as a farewell tribute to a patron who had also become a valued friend and mentor. The painting is a farewell in another sense; it is the last of Constable's great series of large East Anglian landscapes. The trees that frame the view are full of movement; he has caught the moment, so typical of weather along the east coast of England, when a gust of wind accompanies a driving squall of rain, which can be seen moving away in the distance. The turbulence of the trees and sky is contrasted with the still, small, central point of the church tower and the light beyond it. It has also been suggested that the central positioning of the church could be an indication of

[27] Leslie, *Memoirs*, 318.
[28] E. John Walford, *Great Themes in Art* (Upper Saddle River, NJ: Prentice-Hall, 2002), 332.

England's real source of security against the background of the French revolution and Napoleonic wars.[29]

In the foreground, the lonely figure of the gypsy mother with her child indicates a further reference to the exiled Hagar—and possibly a reminder of rural poverty and unrest in the post-war years. Although seated in the foreground, she is almost indistinguishable in the deep shadow. It has been argued that in painting the rural poor as small figures dominated by the landscape, Constable is literally distancing himself from them as one of the landowning class.[30] She may be included simply as a picturesque figure—but Constable's long study of Ruisdael suggests a possible reference to Dutch landscape, where sunlight is often an indication of the blessing and provision of God, whereas figures immersed in shadow remain outside the place of blessing.

Unusually, Constable's major painting at the 1827 Academy had been a marine subject, *The Chain Pier, Brighton.*[31] He and his family had visited Brighton regularly since 1824, in the hope that sea air would improve Mrs. Constable's failing health. *The Chain Pier* remained unsold, and despite the support of the *Times*, reviews were generally discouraging. During the autumn, Constable made an extended visit to his family in East Bergholt, and this may well have prompted him to return to his favorite subject of Dedham Vale.

Even so, it is extraordinary that such an intensely evocative painting was made when he had been resident in London for many years. Several passages in Constable's letters show a power of recollection that seems to be a combination of deep emotion with a highly developed visual memory. In his well-known description of Ruisdael's *Mill*, now in Rotterdam, he says that "it haunts my mind and clings to my heart, and stands between you and me while I am talking to you."[32] It is almost as if he were seeing all the details on a cinema screen. On another occasion he wrote, "a large, solemn, bright, warm, fresh landscape by Wilson . . . still swims in my head like a dream."[33] These phrases bring alive the power and clarity of Constable's inner vision and explain the urgency of his many oil sketches.

---

[29] Tim Wilcox, *Constable and Salisbury: The Soul of Landscape* (London: Scala, 2011), 15.
[30] John Barrell, *The Dark Side of the Landscape* (Cambridge: Cambridge University Press, 1983), chapter 3.
[31] Now in Tate Britain.
[32] Letter to John Fisher; quoted in Leslie, *Memoirs*, 161.
[33] Leslie, *Memoirs*, 101.

From about 1821, when he was in his mid-forties, Constable had begun to produce exhibition paintings on a far more ambitious scale. However, the process of finishing these large canvases made it increasingly difficult to retain the freshness which he so prized in working directly from nature. In his preparation, Constable resolved the problem by developing a unique method of painting a full-sized sketch. This involved him in free mark-making on a grand scale which anticipates the work of much later painters. In Constable's day, it would have been unthinkable to exhibit these in public—but attitudes have since changed to such an extent that several sketches, such as that for *The Haywain* of 1821, and *The Leaping Horse* of 1826, have become as famous as the finished works. In the case of *Dedham Vale* it seems that, having squared up his composition from 1802, Constable felt no need for a full-sized sketch—yet it is all the more remarkable that he could render the landscape with such precision and intensity.

At this point, Constable had still been denied election as an Academician—despite the fact that *The Haywain* had been much admired, and awarded a gold medal at the Paris Salon four years previously, when the young Eugène Delacroix famously repainted his *Massacre of Scios* as a result. Almost twenty years later Delacroix could write of "Constable, homme admirable . . . . une des gloires Anglaises."[34] The freshness and charm of English painting dwelt in his memory: "[In England] they have a real delicacy of perception and skill that outweighs any tendency to imitate the past,"[35] words that echo many of Constable's own comments on the primacy of firsthand observation. Within Constable's lifetime, the practice of *plein air* painting in oils was gathering pace in France. By the 1830s, the young Theodore Rousseau and his friends were regularly working in the countryside around Barbizon and the Fontainebleau Forest.

Yet for Constable himself, tragedy was about to strike. John Walford has noted a sense of foreboding in *Dedham Vale*. In November 1828, Constable lost his beloved wife Maria after a long struggle with tuberculosis, leaving him with seven children to raise. Within four years John Fisher, his closest friend and encourager, was to die at the age of

---

[34] Quoted in Graham Reynolds, *Constable: The Natural Painter* (London: Evelyn, Adams, & McKay, 1965), 98.
[35] Eugene Delacroix, *The Journal of Eugene Delacroix*, ed. Hubert Wellington (London: Phaidon, 1951), 279–280 (entry for June 17, 1855).

only forty-three. Constable wrote of him, "we loved each other and confided in each other entirely . . . he was a good advisor, though impetuous, and he was a truly religious man."[36]

Rather than an escape from personal grief, Constable's later landscapes increasingly become a vehicle of expression. The gathering darkness reflects his own state of mind, and the looming clouds, unlike his earlier observations of weather conditions, now seem much more personally threatening. He was clearly aware of this himself when he wrote, "every gleam of sunshine is withdrawn from me, in the art at least. Can it be wondered at then, that I paint continual storms?"[37]

The turbulent brushwork from his large sketches now spills over into the finished painting, often aided by the use of a palette knife. Whereas Turner's late paintings appear to dissolve into mists of color, Constable's become heavier and darker. Fresh colors give way to thick, loose strokes of browns, grays, and dark greens picked up with flashes of white. The texture and substance of the paint itself becomes integral to the mood of the picture.

The emotional weight of these late works puts them at one remove from the atmospheric light of French Impressionism, but the obsessive quality of their technique suggests much later twentieth-century paintings by British artists such as David Bomberg and Frank Auerbach. Robert Hughes has written that Constable was Auerbach's exemplar, "because of his obstinacy and wildness: the infatuation with paint . . . . that pervades his late work, and the determination to butt through his experience of Claude to a way of landscape painting that had *not* begun on the Continent among the props of antiquity."[38] Perhaps in his last years Constable became more of a radical than he himself realized. In *Dedham Vale*, the emotional release of his later work is latent, but it is finely controlled. The painting is both a climax and a summing-up of his early attachments and his own artistic development.

In the existing records of Constable's lectures, given toward the end of his life, we have some of his most direct statements about landscape painting. In the last of these, he speaks eloquently of how the painter "must walk in the fields with a humble mind. . . . I would say

[36] Quoted in Leslie, *Memoirs*, 211.
[37] Quoted in ibid., 238.
[38] Robert Hughes, *Frank Auerbach* (London: Thames & Hudson, 1990), 170.

most emphatically to the student, 'Remember now thy Creator in the days of thy youth.'" He goes on to read Milton's moving description in "Paradise Lost" of the amazement of Adam, "his eyes opening for the first time on the wonders of the animate and inanimate world."[39]

Constable's understanding of man in relation to the Creator God was deeply intertwined with his perception of nature. In the same lecture he speaks of man as "the sole intellectual inhabitant of a vast natural landscape. His nature is congenial with all the elements of the planet itself, and he cannot but sympathise with . . . its phenomena in all situations." While consistently expressing a Christian worldview, he rarely articulated this in evangelical language (although this is evident in family letters, especially from two of his sisters). He appears to have become attached to a more intellectual form of Anglicanism, through his close friendship with the Fishers and also possibly Sir George Beaumont, whose regular church attendance and Sabbath observance he was "glad to see" at Coleorton.[40]

A conservative in church affairs as in politics, Constable distrusted radicalism, yet as a painter he almost single-handedly revolutionized English ideas on what constitutes a beautiful landscape.[41] The personal integrity which was so valued by his friends enabled him to see through artificiality and false conventions both in art and in life. In a tribute after his death, the Scottish miniaturist Andrew Robertson, who had been a fellow student, wrote that "he saw clearly, and not through a glass darkly, nor through other men's eyes."[42] His truthful depiction of nature is thus perhaps the most practical outworking of Constable's Christian faith. For him, the importance of landscape painting was that "whatever leads us to a knowledge and love of our Creator leads us to Him, and thus we become both wiser and better men."[43]

---

[39] Lecture at the Literary and Scientific Institution, Hampstead, July 25, 1839 (summary in Leslie, *Memoirs*, 325–331.
[40] Letter to John Fisher, November 2, 1823; quoted in Beckett, *John Constable and the Fishers*, 150.
[41] Hugh Honour, *Romanticism*, Style, and Civilisation (London: Pelican, 1981), 70).
[42] Leslie, *Memoirs*, 268.
[43] Constable's last lecture at Hampstead, 1836; quoted in Wilcox, *Constable and Salisbury*, 17.

Vincent van Gogh, *Sower with Setting Sun*, 1888. Oil on canvas, 12 1/2" x 15 3/4". Van Gogh Museum, Amsterdam (Vincent van Gogh Foundation).

12

WHAT THE HALO SYMBOLIZED
Vincent van Gogh's *Sower with Setting Sun*

JAMES ROMAINE

Sower with Setting Sun (1888) is an iconic painting that manifests Vincent van Gogh's (1853–1890) conception of himself as a Christ-imitating artist working in the modern world. The sower, a recurring motif in his art,[1] is silhouetted against a goldenrod-yellow orb creating the unmistakable presence of a sacred halo. A month prior to painting this work, Vincent, as the artist signed his paintings, had written to his brother Theo,

> . . . in a painting I'd like to say something consoling, like a piece of music. I'd like to paint men or women with something of the eternal, of which the halo used to be the symbol, and which we try to achieve through radiance itself, through the vibrancy of our colors.[2]

This painting evidences four motifs—the sower, the landscape, the sun, and color—that manifest Vincent's conception of his own art. This essay investigates the significance of these motifs in Vincent's art as well as the theological and art historical influences that shaped his artistic development of them.

However, before examining *Sower with Setting Sun*, it is necessary

---

[1] According to Tsukasa Kōdera's study of motifs in Vincent's art, Vincent drew or painted the motif of the sower at least forty-eight times (Tsukasa Kōdera, *Vincent van Gogh: Christianity versus Nature* [Philadelphia: John Benjamins, 1990], 135).

[2] "*. . . dans un tableau je voudrais dire quelque chose de consolant comme une musique. Je voudrais peindre des hommes ou des femmes avec ce je ne sais quoi d'éternel dont autrefois le nimbe était le symbole et que nous cherchons par le rayonnement même, par la vibration de nos colorations*" (L673, September 3, 1888). The most recent publication of Vincent van Gogh's complete correspondence was published in 2009. It is also available online, http://vangoghletters.org/vg/. This website allows the reader to see a facsimile of each letter, a transcription of the letter in its original language, as well as an English translation of the letter. All letters are numbered according to that publication. All translations are by this essay's author from that edition of the letters.

to address the pivotal issue of the relationship between Christianity and art in Vincent's personal beliefs and vocational objectives. It may surprise some enthusiasts of Vincent's art that, between 1876 and 1879, he pursued several vocational paths in Christian ministry, first as an assistant to a Methodist minister in England, then as a theology student in the Netherlands, and finally as a missionary to coal miners in Belgium. Vincent's letters from these years reveal a passion for Christ and Christian service as well as the characteristics, such as a stubborn resistance to social conformity, that would undermine his intentions.

The relationship between Vincent's Christianity and art remains among the most sharply divided points of van Gogh scholarship; it may also be the most consequential. In nearly every case, the scholar's response to this question frames his or her interpretation of Vincent's art. There are essentially four approaches to addressing the potential connections between Vincent's Christian faith and art. Some scholars perceive a disconnect between his life before 1879 and after 1879, the year he took up drawing as his principal occupation; these scholars largely ignore the discussion of Christianity in Vincent's oeuvre. Nevertheless, in omitting the potential influence of Christianity on Vincent's art, these scholars have developed secularized interpretations that may be at odds with the artist's stated intentions. Avoiding the discussion of Christianity in Vincent's art is, inevitably, not a neutral position. Other scholars are adamant that Vincent's artistic career was a refutation of his former self and all that it involved.[3] Many of these studies openly acknowledge that this approach describes Vincent as a person divided, psychologically and spiritually, against himself. Some scholars perceive Vincent's artistic life as a conversion from

---

[3] The first person to put forward this theory of total separation between Vincent's faith and his art was his sister-in-law Johanna van Gogh-Bonger. Although she hardly knew Vincent and met him only a few times, van Gogh-Bonger was, within a year of Vincent's death and following the death of her husband Theo, in possession of most of Vincent's art and correspondence. While everyone who appreciates Vincent's art owes her a great debt for carefully promoting it, it is also true that van Gogh-Bonger was not unprejudiced in what image of Vincent she promoted. In selectively publishing his correspondence, in 1914, it has become evident that, for her own reasons, she attempted to suppress those letters in which Vincent most openly discussed the importance of Christianity to his life and art. (Jesus was not the only person edited out of Vincent letters; van Gogh-Bonger also eliminated any mention of her husband's former mistresses as well as a sister-in-law whom she disliked.) Fortunately, there have been several subsequent publications of Vincent's letters that have brought this connection between art and faith to light. Other scholars who have described Vincent's religious life as a crisis from which he recovered include: Jan Hulsker, *Vincent and Theo: A Dual Biography* (Ann Arbor, MI: Fuller, 1990); Ingo F. Walther and Rainer Metzger, *Van Gogh: The Complete Paintings* (Cologne: Benedikt Taschen, 1990); Albert J. Lubin, *Stranger on the Earth: A Psychological Biography of Vincent van Gogh* (Cambridge: DaCapo, 1996); and W. W. Meissner, *Vincent's Religion: The Search for Meaning* (New York: Peter Lang, 1997).

Christianity to another form of belief.[4] They observe a spiritual current in Vincent's art but do not attribute that to Christianity. Still other scholars recognize a continuity between Vincent's vocation in Christian ministry and his work as an artist.[5] This reading allows for the evolution of thought that might naturally occur in any person's life over the course of several decades, but maintains that Vincent remained basically the same person, with essentially unchanged core beliefs and life purposes. These scholars propose that Vincent found in art a means of realizing those aspirations of spiritual fulfillment and social usefulness that had eluded him in religious ministry.

In 1878, Vincent's theological study and missionary work ended in disappointment. After several months of soul-searching, he set himself on the path to becoming an artist. His letters, written mostly to Theo, in which he described his fundamental objectives, support an argument for recognizing a spiritual and vocational continuity between his years in Christian ministry and his artistic vocation.[6] On June 24, 1880, as he was pondering what direction he should pursue, Vincent wrote Theo a long letter explaining his intentions. He began, "It's with some reluctance that I write to you, not having done so for so long . . ."[7] After not having been in contact with his brother perhaps for as long as a year, Vincent was, in effect, reintroducing himself. Although Vincent prefaced his statements saying, "I must now bore you with certain abstract things," in fact this letter provides insight of unusual depth and detail into Vincent's sense of himself and his present predicament.[8]

One of the recurring themes in this letter is the affinity that Vincent

---

[4]In *Van Gogh and God: A Creative Quest* (Chicago: Loyola University Press, 1989), Cliff Edwards describes him as a Buddhist. In *Vincent van Gogh: Christianity versus Nature*, Tsukasa Kōdera describes Vincent as a pantheist. In both cases, the scholars have drawn connections between motifs in Vincent's art, motifs that could be read in many different ways, and have drawn correspondences with non-Christian philosophies that are unsupported by Vincent's own statements.

[5]Kathleen Powers Erickson, *At Eternity's Gate: The Spiritual Vision of Vincent van Gogh* (Grand Rapids, MI: Eerdmans, 1998); E. John Walford, *Great Themes in Art* (Upper Saddle River, NJ: Prentice-Hall, 2002).

[6]The letters of Vincent van Gogh may be some of the most interesting reading in the history of art. These letters reveal that Vincent was a thoughtful and articulate writer who was very self-aware of his own artistic processes. At the same time, we should read Vincent's letters with the caution that we are reading private correspondence that was not intended for publication. Unfortunately, Vincent archived almost none of the letters that he received. Therefore, the reader is often left to wonder what the other side of the conversation entailed. Nevertheless, these letters are an invaluable source for scholarship on Vincent's life, faith, and art.

[7]L155, June 22 to 24, 1880. This is the first known letter from Vincent to his brother since August 11 to 14, 1879.

[8]In this very letter Vincent wrote, "I'm writing you somewhat at random whatever comes into my pen" (L 155, June 22 to 24, 1880). As in many of his letters, Vincent allowed his thoughts to flow in structure-free style, often returning abruptly to points he had made earlier. This "randomness" should not, however, be read as a lack of seriousness or sincerity. To the contrary, Vincent is revealing himself in an unguarded manner.

identified between the Bible and works of art to address "that something that's called soul."[9] Vincent wrote, "there's something of Rembrandt in the Gospels or of the Gospels in Rembrandt, as you wish, it comes to more or less the same, provided that one understands it rightly."[10] He urged his brother, "Try to understand the real significance of what the great artists, the serious masters, say in their masterpieces; there will be God in it. Someone has written or said it in a book, someone in a painting."[11] That, at this critical and pivotal moment, Vincent drew direct connections between Christianity and art encourages a gospel-informed reading of his own art.

Vincent defined his faith in Christ in terms of love.[12] Belief in God was the power to love and the presence of love evidenced the existence of God. In his June 24, 1880, letter Vincent wrote,

> I'm always inclined to believe that the best way of knowing God is to love a great deal. Love that friend, that person, that thing, whatever you like, you'll be on the right path to knowing more thoroughly, afterwards; that's what I say to myself. But you must love with a high, serious intimate sympathy, with a will, with intelligence, and you must always seek to know more thoroughly, better, and more. That leads to God, that leads to unshakeable faith. To give an example, if someone loves Rembrandt, but seriously, that man will know there is a God, he'll believe firmly in Him.[13]

Vincent addressed the crux of his letter, at this transitional moment, writing, "So you mustn't think that I'm rejecting this or that; in my unbelief I'm a believer, in a way, and though having changed I am the same, and my torment is none other than this, what could I be good for, couldn't I serve and be useful in some way . . . ?"[14] By October 1880, Vincent had decided to pursue art as his principal means of ser-

---

[9] Ibid.
[10] Ibid.
[11] Ibid.
[12] Vincent wrote to Theo, "It should come as no surprise if I tell you, at the risk of your thinking me a fanatic, that I consider it absolutely essential to believe in God in order to be able to love. To believe in God—by that I mean (not that you should believe all those petty sermons of the ministers and the arguments and Jesuitry of the prudish, the sanctimonious, the strait-laced, far from it)—to believe in God, by that I mean feeling that there is a God, not a dead or stuffed God, but a living one who pushes us with irresistible force in the direction of 'Love on'. That's what I think. Proof of His presence—the reality of love. Proof of the reality of the feeling of that great power of love deep within us—the existence of God. Because there is a God there is love; because there is love there is a God" (L189, November 23, 1881).
[13] L155, June 22 to 24, 1880.
[14] Ibid.

vice. His June 1880 letter resumed a correspondence with Theo that would last for the rest of Vincent's life. These letters demonstrate how remarkably consistent Vincent's core beliefs and objectives remained, over the following decade, with those that had motivated his Christian ministry.

Vincent's correspondence, especially his letters to fellow Christian Emile Bernard, further articulates a fundamental and unbreakable connection between art and the gospel. However, the more convincing evidence of the connection between Vincent's Christian faith and art is in the paintings themselves, specifically in the motifs, such as those evidenced in *Sower with Setting Sun*, that recur and develop over the course of his oeuvre. By examining Vincent's use of these motifs, it is possible to discern how the presence of a Christian faith affected his artistic practice.

The sower is one of the most frequently recurring figural motifs in Vincent's art. Joining images of diggers, plowmen, reapers, and harvesters as examples of rural labor in Vincent's art, the sower seems to have had a particularly significant place in Vincent's imagination. Perhaps because of its biblical associations, Vincent imagined the sower as a person of hope and faith, characteristics he also associated with artistic purpose.

Vincent's art and letters articulated an intense affinity with rural labor. He saw the state of the human condition manifested in the plight of the laborers who worked the earth, ate by the sweat of their brows, and were, at last, put to rest, as Vincent put it, "in the very fields that they dug up in life."[15]

Vincent had conceived of his Christian ministry as a means of bringing the consolation and hope found in Christ to those suffering physically, economically, and spiritually. When he became an artist, this same purpose directed Vincent's motif selection. He explained his motivations to Theo, who was in Paris and to whom Vincent was selling his art,[16]

---

[15] L507, c. June 9, 1885.

[16] There is a myth that Vincent sold only one painting. In fact, Vincent sold most of his paintings. Theo van Gogh was a professional art dealer who purchased Vincent's work in return for a stipend. The fact that Vincent's primary collector was his brother is, mostly, beside the point. From Theo's point of view, his collecting of Vincent's art was a business decision, from which he expected to eventually turn a profit. It was not an act of charity. It is, in fact, thanks to their business relationship that we have such an extensive correspondence between the brothers, even if only one side of the correspondence has survived.

There's such a yearning for Religion among the people in those big cities. Many a worker in a factory or shop has had a remarkable, pure, pious youth. But city life often takes away "the early dew of morning," yet the yearning for "the old, old story" remains, the foundation of one's heart remains the foundation of one's heart.[17]

It is noteworthy, even curious, that Vincent painted rural laborers as his subjects but considered urban workers as his viewers. Vincent wanted to create paintings that could hang in the rooms of urban laborers that would, by reminding them of their rural youth, give them temporal comfort and eternal hope.

According to Jan Hulsker's authoritative catalog raisonné, Vincent's first work of art was a copy of an image of a sower by Jean-François Millet.[18] It is not surprising that someone intent on teaching himself to draw would start by copying the work of another artist. Vincent had spent nearly seven years as an art dealer and knew the work of countless artists; that he began by copying an image of a sower by Millet, a work he described as having "more soul than in an ordinary sower in the field," reveals an artistic character that he intended to imitate.[19]

A devout Christian, farmer's son, and artist committed to dignified representations of peasant life, labor, and piety, Millet inspired Vincent as a model of an artist motivated by faith. In 1883, Vincent wrote to his brother, "The longer I think about it the more I see that Millet believes in a something on High."[20] Vincent paid Millet perhaps the highest compliment when he wrote to Bernard that, while Eugène Delacroix and Rembrandt van Rijn had succeeded in painting the image of Christ, "Millet has painted . . . Christ's doctrine."[21] By this, he meant that Millet painted with, not only in his motifs but in his method, the values of faith, love, and humility that Vincent considered most Christlike.

Vincent believed that the artist's responsibility was to declare that presence of God which had been hidden, that which had been revealed

---

[17] L082, Friday, May 12, 1876. Vincent was quoting from a hymn by Arabella Catherine Hankey called "The Old, Old Story." It goes, in part, "Tell me the old, old story, Of unseen things above, Of Jesus and His glory, Of Jesus and His love. Tell me the story simply, As to a little child; For I am weak and weary, And helpless and defiled."
[18] Jan Hulsker, *The New Complete Van Gogh: Paintings, Drawings, Sketches* (Philadelphia: John Benjamins, 1996), 13.
[19] L298, January 3, 1883.
[20] L401, October 31, 1883.
[21] L632, June 26, 1888, ellipses his.

to the humble and poor peasant but concealed from the proud and wise clergy. While Millet may be called a "realist" in that he remained both faithful to the appearance of things and true to the sociohistorical life of his subjects, the truth that Vincent found in Millet's work was that "all reality is also symbolic at the same time."[22] Vincent wrote, "It seems to me that a painter has a duty to try to put an idea into his work. I was trying to say this in this print—but I can't say it as beautifully, as strikingly as reality, of which this is only a dim reflection seen in a dark mirror—that it seems to me that one of the strongest pieces of evidence for the existence of 'something on high' in which Millet believed, namely in the existence of a God and an eternity . . ."[23] At the genesis of his artistic project, Vincent rooted his creative means and ends in God. He affirmed this divine source for his creativity in a letter to Theo, written only a few months before the artist's death, confessing, "It requires a certain dose of inspiration, a ray from on high which doesn't belong to us, to do beautiful things."[24]

For Vincent, the work of art achieved a state of beauty through its spiritual yearning. In a letter to Anthon van Rappard, Vincent encouraged this fellow artist, whom Vincent suspected was more concerned with technical issues than with the moral imperative of being an artist, to embrace,

> the positive awareness that art is something larger and loftier than our own skill or learning or knowledge. That art is something which, although produced by human hands, is not wrought by the hands alone but wells up from a deeper source in our soul, and that I find something in dexterity and technical knowledge about art that reminds me of what, in religion, they'd call self-righteousness.[25]

In Vincent's estimation, the artist who was motivated by "something on high" could develop the necessary technical skills, but the academician would never produce art.

Becoming an artist was, for Vincent, a moral choice. Christ was

---

[22]L533, October 4, 1885.
[23]L288, November 26 to 27, 1882. It is noteworthy that in 1882, after Vincent had, according to some scholars, abandoned Christianity, he was referencing 1 Corinthians 13:12. In fact, his letters continued for the rest of his life to include references to the Bible. In most instances, Vincent would paraphrase or partly quote a text. This suggests that the Bible was a foundational part of Vincent's thinking, that evidenced itself almost involuntarily.
[24]L850, February 1, 1890.
[25]L332, March 21, 1883.

not only an inspiring figure; the imitation of Christ was Vincent's *raison d'être* for being an artist. This is articulated in a letter to Theo in which Vincent lamented, "mother simply cannot comprehend that painting is *a faith*."[26] (To interpret this statement as a claim by Vincent that art had become a substitute faith replacing Christianity doesn't make sense, since Vincent and Theo's mother, a devout Christian, would never have accepted art as a substitute faith. Vincent's wish that his mother would agree with his perspective suggests that he still intended to be a true believer.)

While Vincent's vocational shift from Christian ministry to artistic production was not a declaration of unbelief, it did evidence a crisis of religion. Vincent attributed the failure of his theological studies and missionary work to an academic religious elite authority who, in his view, had abandoned the truth of the gospel.[27] Vincent considered his break with institutional religion an embrace of Christ, who was less likely to be found in church but was still present in the lives and deaths of the peasant faithful.

In 1885, Vincent found his doubts and faith mirrored in the demolition of a local church. Vincent had drawn or painted this church more than thirty times, and he painted it one last time with its tower removed. Describing this painting, entitled *The Old Church Tower at Nuenen (The Peasants' Churchyard)*, Vincent wrote,

> I wanted to say how this ruin shows that *for centuries* the peasants have been laid to rest there in the very fields that they dug up in life—I wanted to say how perfectly simply death and burial happen, coolly as the falling of an autumn leaf. . . . And now this ruin says to me how a faith and religion moldered away, although it was solidly founded—how, though, the life and death of the peasants is and will always be the same, springing up and withering regularly like the grass and the flowers that grow there in that churchyard. Victor Hugo, whom they've also just buried, said Religions pass, God remains.[28]

---

[26] L490, April 6, 1885 (emphasis his).

[27] Vincent wrote Theo saying, "You must know that it's the same with evangelists as with artists. There's an old, often detestable, tyrannical academic school, the abomination of desolation, in fact—men having, so to speak, a suit of armor, a steel breastplate of prejudices and conventions. Those men, when they're in charge of things, have positions at their disposal, and by a system of circumlocution seek to support their protégés, and to exclude the natural man from among them" (L155, June 22 to 24, 1880).

[28] L507, c. June 9, 1885. In fact, Vincent meant to quote Jules Michelet, not Victor Hugo. Perhaps it was not necessary, but it is noteworthy that Vincent did not remind Theo that their father, the Reverend Theodorus van Gogh, had been buried in that very churchyard only a few months previously.

The Old Church Tower continues a central theme in Vincent's art, a use of agrarian labor—sowing and reaping—as a metaphor for the cycle of life and death. In the rising flowers that grow up year after year, Vincent found an expression of a resilient faith, even after the church tower had come down.

In evoking Victor Hugo's name, Vincent framed his own personal contentions with institutional religion within a broader context. Vincent was keenly aware of the historical moment in which he was working. He recognized this as a crossroads between an age of faith and an age of modernity. This tension between a desire to preserve the faith of the peasants and to embrace the ideas of the modern world was a persistent theme of Vincent's letters and art.

Preceding *Sower with Setting Sun*, the painting *The Old Church Tower* evidences an identification with the landscape; this tie to the land was something that Vincent admired about rural laborers. For Vincent, this boundedness to the land combined a consciousness of the cyclical process of growth and decay in nature with a connection to place.[29]

Vincent was, of course, much more than a painter of landscapes; nevertheless, the landscape held a distinct and significant place in his art. *Sower with Setting Sun* is, conceptually and visually, an encounter between the figure and the landscape. Bernhard Mendes Bürgi, Nina Zimmer, and Walter Feilchenfeldt, in *Vincent van Gogh: Between Heaven and Earth: The Landscapes*, discuss the changing relationship between figures and the landscapes they inhabited (and worked) in Vincent's art. They note that Vincent's art from the Netherlands, "depicts people as simple laborers who must submit to a natural God-given order [of the cycles of nature] but for whom that order is also a sanctuary."[30] They add,

> In Arles, Van Gogh returned to the laborers of his early paintings, albeit under the aegis of a different iconography. Figures like the sower, the reaper, the laborer in a vineyard are now informed with

---

[29] The visual manifestation of a spiritual connectedness to place in Netherlandish art is discussed in Henry Luttikhuizen's "The Shape of Place: Joachim Patinir's *Landscape with Saint Jerome*," chapter 5 in this book.
[30] Bernhard Mendes Bürgi, Nina Zimmer, and Walter Feilchenfeldt, "Introduction," in Carel Blotkamp et al., *Vincent van Gogh: Between Heaven and Earth: The Landscapes* (Ostfildern, Germany: Hatje Cantz, 2009), 16.

biblical and mythological imagery, lending an emblematic significance to landscapes.[31]

Vincent's landscape painting was rooted in his conception of the
human condition as a state of pilgrimage and his perception of nature
as a creation and revelation of God. The theme of pilgrimage is perhaps
most clearly expressed in the text of a sermon he delivered on Sunday,
October 29, 1876, at a Wesleyan Methodist church in Richmond,
England. Vincent said,

> It is an old faith and it is a good faith that our life is a pilgrim's
> progress—that we are strangers in the earth, but that though this
> be so, yet we are not alone for our Father is with us . . . there is
> only a constantly being born again, a constantly going from dark-
> ness into light.[32]

Vincent's conception of the person as a pilgrim whose path to eternal
joy and life first had to wind through a temporal period of sorrow and
death was rooted in his reading of *The Imitation of Christ* by Thomas à
Kempis and John Bunyan's *The Pilgrim's Progress*. If Vincent's conception of the human condition found description in the suffering pilgrim,
his faith was in Christ as consoler. For Vincent, faith was a creative
practice of imitating Christ and transforming sorrow into joy. His
notion of life as a pilgrimage led Vincent to focus on natural motifs that
manifested transience; his belief in God led him to treat these motifs
with a sense of permanence. This paradox of mortality and eternity
gives Vincent's landscapes a vibrancy and mystery.

One of the most significant influences on Vincent's own conception of how a painter should treat landscape was the work of Jacob van
Ruisdael, whom he mentioned in at least forty-two letters.[33] The first
mention of Ruisdael is in a letter dated 1875, nearly five years before
Vincent seriously considered becoming an artist, and the last mention is from a letter posted in 1889, well after Vincent had reached
artistic maturity. Therefore, it can be proposed that Ruisdael was an

---

[31] Ibid.

[32] Vincent had written this sermon out in its entirety and included it in a letter to Theo (L096, Friday,
November 3, 1876). In this quoted passage, he refers to: 2 Corinthians 6:10; John 3:3; 1 Peter 1:23; and
1 Peter 2:9.

[33] As was common in the nineteenth century, Vincent spelled the artist's name "Ruysdael."

overarching influence that, in part, shaped Vincent's conception of his own artistic vocation.

Vincent named the seventeenth-century Dutch painters Jan van Goyen, Isaac van Ostade, and Ruisdael as models for landscape painting, writing, "Do I want them back, or do I want them to be imitated? No, but I do want the honesty, the naivety, the faithfulness [of their art] to remain."[34] Did the influence of Ruisdael have any impact on Vincent's works, such as *Sower with Setting Sun*, painted in Arles? In fact, as Carel Blotkamp suggests, in an essay entitled "Ruisdael in Provence," the influence of this seventeenth-century landscape painter was, perhaps, even *more* pronounced in Vincent's work made in the south of France.[35] From Arles, Vincent wrote, "Here—except for a more intense color, it reminds one of . . . the Holland of Ruisdael and Hobbema and Ostade."[36] Although Vincent was moving south in search of more brilliant color, what he found was a landscape that reminded him of the north.

Vincent described a version of Ruisdael's *View of Haarlem*, at the Rijksmuseum in Amsterdam, as one of his favorite works.[37] *View of Haarlem* evidences a vision of interconnectivity and harmony, between heaven and earth, between humanity and nature.[38] Ruisdael's spiritual composure was the manifestation of an artistic method that John Walford calls "selective naturalism," one of finding and depicting motifs with a sense of spiritual presence.[39] Walford notes that Ruisdael's perception of landscape was rooted in a belief that God's presence is visible in his creation. Walford writes, "Selective naturalism may thus embody a religious and contemplative attitude towards observed reality . . . [an]

---

[34] L291, December 4 to 9, 1882.

[35] Carel Blotkamp, "Ruisdael in Provence," in *Between Heaven and Earth*, 75.

[36] L630, June 23, 1888. Vincent had also compared the landscape in Arles to Ruisdael in a previous letter (L623, June 12, 1888). He would mention this comparison twice more (L639, July 13, 1888; and L644, July 17 to 20, 1888). Although his letters assume that the reader, Theo, knows what he means by calling a landscape "so Ruisdaelesque," it is clear that Ruisdael's paintings had strongly informed how Vincent looked at the landscape.

[37] The version of Ruisdael's *View of Haarlem* in Amsterdam's Rijksmuseum that Vincent admired is only minimally different from the version at Zurich's Kunsthaus (featured on the cover of this book and discussed in the introduction). It is evident from the angles and spacing of the skyline of Haarlem's church towers that Ruisdael painted these two works from different but proximate places on the dunes.

[38] Of Ruisdael, Walford writes, "there is a sense of order, of well-being, and of everyday activity, and, in the landscapes of Ruisdael and others, a peaceful harmony between man and his environment despite a prevailing consciousness of the ultimate transience of life" (E. John Walford, *Jacob van Ruisdael and the Perception of Landscape* [New Haven, CT: Yale University Press, 1991], 20).

[39] Ibid., 18.

intertwining of material and spiritual levels of reality."[40] Similarly, this ability to see, and make seen, the transcendent within the temporal was, for Vincent, the artist's highest objective.

In addition to *View of Haarlem*, one of the works by Ruisdael that Vincent most studied was a painting in the Louvre Museum entitled *The Bush*.[41] This image is visually dominated by a tree (or very large bush) that rises along the painting's central axis. Typical of many of Ruisdael's trees, this "bush" evidences a life of growth through strife. While it is not possible to directly link Ruisdael to the tree in Vincent's *Sower with Setting Sun*, Ruisdael significantly shaped Vincent's notion of the tree motif as a metaphor for spiritual resilience.

Describing an 1882 drawing, entitled *Roots, Study of a Tree*, of a tree growing up beside a river, Vincent wrote,

> I've tried to imbue the landscape with the same sentiment as the figure. Frantically and fervently rooting itself, as it were, in the earth, and yet being half torn up by the storm. I wanted to express something of life's struggle . . . in those gnarled black roots with their knots. . . . I tried without any philosophizing to be true to nature, which I had before me, something of that great struggle has come . . . almost inadvertently.[42]

In *Sower with Setting Sun*, Vincent painted the tree as if it were a figure. It grows up beside the river, stretches out its limbs, and leans toward the sower. The tree establishes both forward space and time in the painting. The tree occupies the place, beyond the picture's lower edge, toward which the sower is moving. It also forecasts the potential of organic growth toward which the sower is working. If the seed falling into the ground may be read as a metaphor for death, the tree is a symbol of resurrection.

The seventeenth-century Dutch artist who most profoundly affected Vincent was, certainly, Rembrandt. The formal, conceptual, and theological influences of Rembrandt's art on Vincent remain among the least examined dimensions of a life and oeuvre that has been exhaustingly scrutinized. Perhaps scholars have not yet found the right words to describe their relationship. As Vincent himself noted, "Rembrandt goes

---

[40] Ibid.
[41] Vincent mentioned Jacob van Ruisdael's *The Bush* in five letters between 1875 and 1885.
[42] L222, May 1, 1882.

so deep into the mysterious that he says things for which there are no words in any language."[43] Vincent resonated with Rembrandt's art on several levels; perhaps most significantly, Rembrandt's use of value, the light and darkness of a color, agreed with Vincent's theology. He wrote to Theo, "You surely know that one of the root or fundamental truths, not only of the gospel but of the entire Bible, is 'the light that dawns in the darkness.' *From darkness to Light*."[44] Vincent directly connected this theme to Rembrandt. Describing Rembrandt's rendering of Christ with Mary and Martha, Vincent wrote, "I hope not to forget that drawing, nor what it seemed to be saying to me, 'I am the light of the world: he that follows Me shall not walk in darkness, but shall have the light of life.'"[45]

In many of his early paintings, such as *The Potato Eaters*, Vincent depicted figures seen by lamplight in the evening, what he called "Rembrandtesque effects."[46] In these paintings, the lamp hangs over the figure(s) like a halo. *Sower with Setting Sun* advances this strategy in using the sun as a halo. The frequency of Vincent's depiction of the sun in his paintings in the south of France, compared to his work in the Netherlands, has led Tsukasa Kōdera to suggest that the sun had become a substitute for Christianity in Vincent's art. However, there is no evidence for this in Vincent's letters. Rather than imagining the sun as a replacement motif, it is more in keeping with Vincent's own statements to consider the sun as a further development of the theme of "light in the darkness" that he admired in Rembrandt's art.

Sower with Setting Sun evidences a Netherlandish inclination for disguised symbolism, an artistic method by which common motifs, whether man-made or natural, were depicted in a way that suggested deeper meaning. Just as Vincent's art conceptually bridged faith and modernism, his artistic strategy evidenced a dual commitment to naturalism and symbolism. However, while *Sower with Setting Sun* manifests an unmistakable presence of symbolism, Vincent's own description of this painting emphasized his use of color. Indeed, one of the most noticeable differences between *The Potato Eaters* and *Sower with Setting Sun* is the use of color transformed by the intervening year in Paris.

In 1885, intent on exploring what his own art might gain from

---

[43]L534, October 10, 1885.
[44]L148, November 13, 15, or 16, 1878 (emphasis his).
[45]L131, September 18, 1877.
[46]L445, April 30, 1884.

contact with what was the center of the contemporary art world, Vincent joined Theo in Paris. In Paris, Vincent developed friendships with artists including Henri Toulouse-Lautrec, Paul Gauguin, and Bernard. Although Vincent's relationship with Gauguin has drawn the most attention, in both scholarly and popular interest,[47] in fact, Vincent's correspondence with Bernard is more insightful.[48] Bernard, a devout Catholic, and Vincent developed a friendship based on a common search for a modern visual language that conveyed faith.

Because of his appropriation of the vibrant colors of Impressionism, Vincent has been called a "post-impressionist," with a suggestion that his art originated from Impressionism. This francocentric interpretation fails to recognize that Vincent had already matured significantly as an artist before encountering Impressionism. It was not Impressionism that inspired Vincent's use of color; it was Vincent's artistic enterprise that found in Impressionist coloring a useful motif.

Vincent experimented with Impressionist and Pointillist methods but, as *Sower with Setting Sun* demonstrates, he developed a method of color application that was uniquely his own. Vincent began to apply unmixed primary and secondary colors side by side in order to create specific visual and spiritual effects. Although, in 1887–1888, the visual character of Vincent's art evolved rapidly, sometimes markedly changing from one week to the next, its themes and objectives remained basically unchanged. This consistency of artistic purpose is explained, in part, by the fact that his sense of himself as an artist remained rooted in his faith.

In *Sower with Setting Sun*, Vincent employed color as a motif revealing the soul's yearning for "something on high." In subordinating color's mimetic function and, thereby, elevating color as a subject, Vincent

---

[47] Perhaps the best scholarly treatment of the Vincent-Gauguin relationship is Debora Silverman, *Van Gogh and Gauguin: The Search for Sacred Art* (New York: Farrar, Straus & Giroux, 2000). The most infamous "popular" treatment of their relationship is Irving Stone's *fictional* biography *Lust for Life* (New York: New American Library, 1934). In 1956, this was made into a movie staring Kirk Douglas as Vincent and Anthony Quinn in an Oscar award–winning role as Gauguin. Given the depiction of Vincent, in *Lust for Life*, as mentally and violently insane, no discussion of Vincent van Gogh's art can, unfortunately, escape questions of the episode on December 24, 1888, in which he mutilated his ear. Perhaps the best discussion of this incident and its relationship to Vincent's mental health is found in Erickson's *At Eternity's Gate*. Her conclusion is that Vincent suffered from a hereditary form of temporal lobe epilepsy. This was also the diagnosis of Dr. Felix Rey, the physician who personally treated Vincent in Arles. The first occasion of this epilepsy was brought on by an argument with Gauguin. The subject of this argument is a matter of scholarly speculation. Most significantly, Erickson finds no direct connection between Vincent's epileptic episodes and his art.

[48] It may be that Paul Gauguin was too self-focused to have an interesting relationship with anyone else.

distinctly broke with Impressionism, in which color functioned as an effect of the eye's physiology. Vincent's use of color as an expressive motif, autonomous from visual description, may be his most significant contribution to late-nineteenth and twentieth-century art. That this "Modernist" artistic innovation developed out of Vincent's Christ-inspired method is noteworthy.

In fact, the artist who perhaps most distinctly influenced Vincent's Christ-oriented theory of color, Eugène Delacroix, had been deceased for three decades before Vincent arrived in Paris.[49] Mentioned in at least one hundred letters, Delacroix was an artist whom Vincent deeply admired. From reading about Delacroix and studying his paintings, Vincent learned Delacroix's method of placing complementary primary and secondary colors together in order to heighten their visual sensation. (For example, placing a red next to a green.) But Vincent's interest in Delacroix was not primarily technical. Vincent was impressed with Delacroix's paintings of Christ. In fact, he listed Delacroix and Rembrandt as the only two painters who visually manifested Christ as "the light of the world."[50] Rembrandt achieved this through his contrast of value, heightening a certain area of light surrounded by a usually larger area of darkness. Delacroix achieved this through his contrast of colors.[51] Vincent wrote, in a letter predating *Sower with Setting Sun* by a few months, that Delacroix's *Christ Asleep during the Tempest*, "speaks a symbolic language through color itself."[52]

Responding to this work, Vincent wrote,

> The question remains this—Christ's boat by Eugène Delacroix and Millet's sower are of entirely different workmanship. Christ's boat— I'm talking about the blue and green sketch with touches of purple and red and a little lemon yellow for the halo, the aureole—speaks a symbolic language through color itself. Millet's sower is a colorless *grey*. . . . Can we now paint the sower with color . . . ?[53]

---

[49]Vincent had read about Delacroix's theories of the effects of using primary and secondary colors together in Charles Blanc's *Grammaire des arts du dessin* and in his *Les artistes de mon temps*.
[50]Vincent wrote to Emile Bernard, "The figure of Christ has been painted—as I feel it—only by Delacroix and by Rembrandt . . . . And then Millet has painted . . . . Christ's doctrine" (L632, June 26, 1888, ellipses his).
[51]Vincent wrote to Emile Bernard, "Rembrandt works with values in the same way as Delacroix with colors. Now, there's a gulf between the method of Delacroix and Rembrandt and that of all the rest of religious painting" (L649, July 29, 1888).
[52]L634, June 28, 1888.
[53]Ibid.

In *Sower with Setting Sun*, Vincent answered his own "question," in bringing together those elements that he admired from Delacroix and Millet, as well as Ruisdael and Rembrandt. Like Rembrandt, Vincent painted numerous self-portraits; these are prized for the artist's ability to reveal his inner personhood through the appearance of his features and the qualities of his art. However, if any painting might be called a portrait of Vincent's conception of a Christ-imitating artist, *Sower with Setting Sun* visually manifests the artistic endeavor as a creative act of faith.

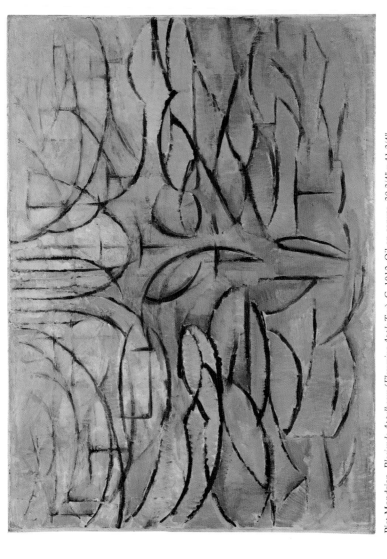

Piet Mondrian, *Bloeiende Appelboom (Flowering Apple Tree)*. C. 1912. Oil on canvas, 30 3/4" x 41 3/4". Gemeentemuseum, The Hague. © 2011 Mondrian/Holtzman Trust c/o HCR International, Washington DC.

13

EVOLVING A "BETTER" WORLD
Piet Mondrian's *Flowering Apple Tree*

GRAHAM BIRTWISTLE

In his chapter on early-twentieth-century Modernism in *Great Themes in Art*, John Walford discusses the Dutch artist Piet Mondrian (1872–1944) under the category of "Spirituality." Of the artists Walford deals with under this theme, only the French Catholic Georges Rouault, in his sensitive portrayals of vulnerable people on the margins of society, clearly based his spiritual values on a traditional Christian understanding of sin and redemption. By contrast, Vassily Kandinsky, Robert Delaunay, Constantin Brancusi, and Mondrian himself sought to define new kinds of spirituality and used their art as a means to represent impersonal cosmic forces and the pure essence of things. This led them, in very different ways, on paths toward abstraction.

In Mondrian's case, Walford shows how the artist's spirituality was linked to a process of abstraction by comparing two of his paintings, which depict the same basic motif of a single tree: *The Red Tree* (1909) and *Flowering Apple Tree* (1912). While both works reflect Mondrian's concern with the tree's inner structural principles rather than with its outward appearance, Walford notes that in the painting of 1912 "the natural motif is almost entirely relinquished in favor of the universal forces suggested in the earlier painting."[1] In taking *Flowering Apple Tree* as its subject, this essay will look more closely at the formal composition of this painting before expanding upon Walford's interpretation of its spiritual content in the light of what we know about Mondrian's beliefs and intentions. But there is another issue that arises from

---

[1] E. John Walford, *Great Themes in Art* (Upper Saddle River, NJ: Prentice-Hall, 2002), 445.

Walford's comparison of the two paintings. Their markedly different styles, in the space of only three years, make it clear that Mondrian was developing his art rapidly. In fact, *Flowering Apple Tree* of 1912 was in its turn a stepping-stone toward later and more abstract works, much as *The Red Tree* had been three years earlier. *Flowering Apple Tree* therefore repays consideration both in its own right and as one more stage in what Mondrian called the "evolution" of his work. To see where that evolution led him, we shall also need to take account of developments that came after *Flowering Apple Tree*.

It would indeed be difficult to ignore the works that Mondrian went on to make after 1912. He is one of several artists who, for better or worse, have provided Modernist art with its equivalent of what in the business world are major brand names. The name "Pollock," for instance, conjures up for many people the intricate swirls of dripped paint that typified Jackson Pollock's work from the late 1940s on. Similarly, "Mondrian" has become synonymous in cultural discourse with certain features that derive from a particular phase in the artist's oeuvre. Around 1920, Mondrian began to use black grid lines to enclose rectangles and squares of white, gray, and primary colors in paintings that have come to represent one of the most familiar brands in modern art. My Dutch newspaper recently devoted a page to demonstrating the pervasiveness of Mondrian's iconic images, not only in museums across Europe, North America, and Japan, but in commercial adaptations such as Mondrian sneakers and T-shirts, Mondrian pottery and placemats, Mondrian pen sets and clocks, and even a Mondrian designer dress (Yves Saint Laurent, 1961).[2] The commercialization of Mondrian's later style may seem obtrusive, particularly when contrasted with the artist's own notable disinterest in worldly success, but it forces us to acknowledge the existence of a widespread conception of how a "Mondrian" should look. Since *Flowering Apple Tree* does not fit that widespread conception, it is worth considering the inevitable question about how it relates to Mondrian's most famous works.

For most buyers of popular Mondrian-ware, the attraction lies simply in the striking grid forms and bright colors associated with his art. However, a good many critics and art historians have also focused

---

[2] "Mondrianer dan ooit/Mondriaans in musea," *NRC Handelsblad Cultureel Supplement* 28 (January 2011).

their attention on the formal characteristics of Mondrian's art, either ignoring his spiritual concerns or mentioning them only as a coda to his achievement as a pioneer of modern pictorial methods. We see the latter, for instance, in H. H. Arnason's *A History of Modern Art*, since 1969 a widely used course book for students in art history. Arnason is one of several writers who prefigured Walford by comparing *The Red Tree* with *Flowering Apple Tree*, but in doing so Arnason was primarily concerned with tracing Mondrian's stylistic development: "one can see his progress from naturalism through Symbolism, Impressionism, Post-Impressionism, Fauvism, and Cubism, to abstraction."[3] Since Mondrian's art has lent itself to cogent discussion in purely formal or stylistic terms, that approach is a good place to start.

What most obviously distinguishes *Flowering Apple Tree* from *The Red Tree* is its Cubist style. Gone are the intense, Expressionistic colors and Symbolist draftsmanship of 1909 and in their place have come muted coloring and an overall system of interlocking shapes and lines. These are composed in such a way that they define strong formal tensions across the picture plane, but they only vaguely suggest the organic shape of the tree. Mondrian has here adopted a pictorial method first developed by Pablo Picasso and Georges Braque, the leading Cubists working in Paris, who had stimulated one another in developing an alternative to the long Renaissance tradition of painting an illusory window on the world. Picasso and Braque began in 1907 by shattering the traditional window into fragmented shapes, which in Braque's early experiments looked cube-like (hence a critic's remark which gave the new style its name). In subsequent years, they gradually refined the fragmented forms into a seemingly autonomous visual language that escaped complete abstraction only by a few strategic clues to everyday reality. They generally avoided strong colors, using a palette of subdued tints that did not distract from their experiments with line and form. In all these respects, Mondrian has followed their example.

Mondrian first saw Cubist paintings for himself in 1911, possibly in the spring, when he briefly visited Paris, and certainly in the fall, at an exhibition held at the Stedelijk Museum in Amsterdam by the Moderne Kunst Kring (Modern Art Circle).[4] As a founding member

---

[3]H. H. Arnason, *A History of Modern Art* (London: Thames & Hudson, 1988), 202.
[4]Carel Blotkamp, *Mondrian: The Art of Destruction* (London: Reaktion, 1994), 57–58.

of this circle, Mondrian helped design its exhibition to give Dutch aspirant Modernists (of which Mondrian himself was one) firsthand knowledge of the international art scene. Through contacts in Paris, such as Lodewijk Schelfhout (the first Dutch Cubist), the exhibition included more than thirty works by minor Parisian Cubists and seven and three paintings respectively by Picasso and Braque, which an installation photograph shows to have been examples of early Cubism from around 1907–1908. The exhibition must have whetted Mondrian's appetite. Close to forty, and already an experienced painter, he now decided to move to the forefront of modern art development. By January 1912 he had left Amsterdam to join Schelfhout and others who were trying to make their mark in Paris as Cubist painters. To improve his chances he modified his family name Mondriaan to the internationally more acceptable Mondrian.

Mondrian's paintings and drawings of 1912 show him exploring the potential of Cubism, in some cases closely following the example of Picasso and Braque in using still life as his subject. Mondrian was not accustomed to painting still lifes, but among his earliest Cubist works of 1912 are two versions of *Still-life with Ginger-Jar*. In other cases, Mondrian returned to subjects that were familiar to him, such as figures, buildings, seascapes (and dunes), and landscape elements, notably trees, which he now began to paint in a Cubist style. One painting entitled *Trees* (Carnegie Museum of Art, Pittsburgh) has a strongly vertical format. Long straight tree-trunk forms thrust to the top of the canvas, where the foliage is represented by greenish and ocher patches enclosed in arching Cubist shapes with heavy contours that suggest leaded stained-glass windows. For many commentators, this composition evoked Gothic church architecture. In two other tree paintings from 1912, however, the format is horizontal, only a single tree is represented, and there are no apparent Gothic references. These two paintings, *Gray Apple Tree* and *Flowering Apple Tree*, have similar dimensions (within one inch) and share the same basic composition, with a relatively short and curved tree trunk in the lower center and an emphasis on the sideways spread of the branch forms.[5] *Flowering Apple Tree* is therefore closely related to *Gray Apple Tree*, also in the same collection of The Hague's Gemeente Museum. The Mondrian scholar

---

[5]For illustrations of the three tree paintings, see ibid., 69, 72.

Carel Blotkamp has discussed the possibility of their being companion pieces, probably based on the same drawing of a tree, but he is cautious since Mondrian showed only *Flowering Apple Tree* at the 1912 exhibition of the Modern Art Circle in Amsterdam.[6] It seems likely that *Gray Apple Tree* was painted first, as its sketchier brush strokes and fuller naturalistic detail suggest that it might have been the closer of the two to a preliminary drawing from nature. *Gray Apple Tree* still retains vestiges of the Symbolist draftsmanship that we saw in *The Red Tree* of 1909. *Flowering Apple Tree*, on the other hand, is considerably more refined and goes a step further toward abstraction. Of the two, it is the more thoroughly Cubist painting and as such it points to Mondrian's future development, rather than to his past.

Which stylistic characteristics of *Flowering Apple Tree* did Mondrian go on to develop further? And which did he leave behind? In general, he continued diminishing the role of recognizable natural forms in his paintings in favor of an increasingly pure and abstract play of lines. Links between the Cubist shapes and the organic forms of his subject are already quite tenuous in *Flowering Apple Tree*, and in subsequent works of 1913–1914 such links become even more difficult to ascertain. Mondrian's subject matter shifts from trees to seascapes and city facades (some are simply entitled *Composition*), allowing a change in formal emphasis from the curved to the rectilinear. In *Flowering Apple Tree* the centrally placed, curved forms of the tree-trunk anchor the composition, while the many straight and intersecting lines pull in vertical and horizontal directions. In works made during the following two years, curved lines gradually disappear and make way for an overall pattern based solely on the intersections of short vertical and horizontal lines. But the curve takes on a new function. Mondrian borrows from Picasso and Braque the practice of creating an oval composition within a rectangular (canvas or paper) ground, often using curved contour lines to define its boundary. The beginning of his interest in an oval-shaped Cubist composition can already be seen in *Flowering Apple Tree*, where the central tree-forms are richer in color and more clearly delineated than the forms closer to the edge of the canvas. This creates a roughly discernible oval area of sharp focus in the middle of

---

[6] Ibid., 71.

the picture, so that we see the painting as a formal construction rather than as a window on reality.

Mondrian's further development was influenced by another change in his circumstances. In the summer of 1914, he was visiting the Netherlands when the First World War broke out—as unexpectedly for Mondrian as for many other people. He did not return to Paris till after the war had ended in 1919. As events unfolded, the Netherlands managed to maintain its neutrality, becoming relatively isolated from the rest of Europe but offering a haven for artists in exile from war-torn France and Belgium.[7] The war years spent back in the Netherlands were not without benefit for Mondrian. While he had received scant recognition in Paris, he now gained a number of Dutch supporters, such as the influential art critic H. P. Bremmer. In comparison with his previous two years in Paris, Mondrian's productivity during 1914–1916 dropped, though in the works that he did make, he took new strides. Still using elemental linear forms as his basic pictorial units, he initially worked in black and white or monochrome and then reintroduced an emphasis on color. Rectangular patches of pastel blues, reds, and ochers also became part of the overall structure. In 1917, he briefly abandoned lines entirely, making compositions out of rectangular color planes that dance irregularly across the surface. But, in 1918–1919, Mondrian gave line its definitive role in shaping rigorous checkerboard and grid patterns to enclose rectangles of white, blue, red, and yellow. The iconic "Mondrian style" (his own term for it was Neo-Plasticism) was now almost complete, save for his refinement of the blues, reds, and yellows into intense primary colors in 1920. Since 1915, all these developments had been catalyzed by new contacts, such as the Dutch artists Theo van Doesburg and Bart van der Leck, who were similarly developing a more abstract style in their paintings. Together with these and other artists and architects, Mondrian helped found and run the periodical *De Stijl*, which from 1917 to its demise in 1928 gave its name to a new and influential movement in art and architecture.

Flowering Apple Tree is one of the first paintings to show Mondrian mastering the Cubist techniques that set the course for his systematic

---

[7] See Graham Birtwistle, "World Wars I and II," in S. D. Muller, ed., *Dutch Art: An Encyclopedia* (New York and London: Garland, 1997), 450–453.

abstraction process of the next eight years. Indeed most art historians have called *Flowering Apple Tree* a Cubist painting. But it is noteworthy that, in January 1914, Mondrian wrote to Bremmer, defining his views on Cubism and Futurism (which glorified modern technology using a Cubist-influenced pictorial language). Mondrian judged these movements by the yardstick of modernity, their relation to "the spirit of the time," and found them both wanting. If Futurism was truly modern in its subject matter, it was old-fashioned in arousing only fleeting emotions, while the problem with Cubism was its limitation to traditional subject matter such as figure-studies and still lifes. Mondrian wrote, "Cubism has taken the great stride toward abstraction and is for that reason modern and future-oriented: it is therefore not modern in content, but modern in technique. As far as I am concerned, I do not belong to either but I feel the spirit of the time in both, and in myself."[8] So, for all his earnest exploration of Cubist techniques, Mondrian did not regard himself as a Cubist. He preferred to steer by his own compass. *Flowering Apple Tree* is not simply a Cubist painting; it affirms Mondrian's own inner sense of spiritual direction.

Through the years, writers on Mondrian have remarked on his "strict Calvinist" upbringing, often implying that this was an unlikely milieu to produce a great modern artist. Mondrian's family was indeed Dutch Reformed, but far from hostile to art. His father (a head teacher with a diploma in art) and his uncle Frits Mondriaan (a landscape painter) encouraged him to qualify as an art teacher, which he did. After moving from Winterswijk to Amsterdam in 1892, to study at the State Art Academy, Mondrian lodged for three years in the household of the publisher J. A. Wormser, a close friend of the theologian and statesman Abraham Kuyper who led the recently formed *Gereformeerde* Church. In 1893 Mondrian himself became a communicant member of their *Gereformeerde* Church in Amsterdam.[9] Clearly, Calvinist faith was for the young Mondrian a matter not only of upbringing but also of choice. Though mainly a landscape painter, he undertook some Christian commissions, in 1898 designing panels for the pulpit of

---

[8] Quoted in Els Hoek, "Piet Mondriaan," in *De beginjaren van De Stijl 1917–1922* (Utrecht: Reflex, 1982), 55 (my translation from the Dutch).

[9] J. M. de Jong, "Piet Mondriaan en de gereformeerde kerk van Amsterdam," *Jong Holland* 3 (1989): 5, 20–23. Some eighty years and various church schisms later, John and Maria Walford and I were to become guest members of a successor to this church in Amsterdam.

the English Reformed Church in Amsterdam (in the Begijnhof, well-known to tourists).

Around 1900, Mondrian experienced a crisis in his faith and ceased to participate in Reformed church life. He continued to feel a spiritual kinship with certain Roman Catholic artists and, as some Catholics had done in the 1890s, he turned to more esoteric kinds of spirituality. In particular, he valued his friendship with theosophical artists, such as Cornelis Spoor. Mondrian's interest in theosophy reached a turning point in 1908 after he attended lectures given in Amsterdam by Rudolf Steiner, then a leading theosophist and in later years the originator of influential anthroposophical theories on art and architecture. Hearing these lectures initiated Mondrian's lifelong regard for Steiner (the feelings were never reciprocated) and, more directly, it led to Mondrian's decision to join the Theosophical Society in May 1909.

Briefly stated, theosophy created a synthesis of world religions, historic philosophies, and modern scientific knowledge, based on the ideas and methods of Helena P. Blavatsky in her books *Isis Unveiled* (1877) and *The Secret Doctrine* (1888).[10] Blavatsky drew extensively on Eastern (mainly Hindu and Buddhist) religious texts, symbols, and practices, and vegetarianism and yoga were widely practiced in the movement. Some theosophists also turned to occult, mediumistic practices. Mondrian did not become vegetarian but was sometimes seen holding yoga positions. He was curious about occult experiences but, wary of their dangers, did not seek them out. His main interest was in the worldview of the movement, the cosmogonic myths postulated by Blavatsky. These hold that all life is a single and malleable whole, "The Plastic Essence" (cf. Mondrian's own term Neo-Plasticism), which is subject to fundamental laws of involution and evolution (destruction followed by regeneration). At the core, the Father and Mother of life continually spin their web of spirit (male) and matter (female), which creates the reality we experience. So the theosophist believes in the destruction of what exists to make way for the evolution of what is new and better. And he believes reality to be the product of a continual interaction of spirit with matter, male and female principles that are constantly reshaping their relationship. Everyday "nature" is, for the

---

[10]I draw here on information from the PhD thesis of M. T. Bax, *Het Web der Schepping. Theosofie en kunst in Nederland van Lauweriks tot Mondriaan*, VU University Amsterdam, April 2004.

theosophist, marked by tragedy, but behind it he discerns an unseen "Nature" that calls him to a higher spiritual level.

By 1908, Mondrian's theosophical beliefs were becoming evident in his works, with female figures depicted frontally and rigidly, at prayer or in devotion, and also strongly vertical (male) forms of lighthouses or church towers. He simplified and flattened his compositions to suggest mystical meaning.

Mondrian's most overtly theosophical painting, a triptych of 1911 entitled *Evolution*, depicts a stylized female figure, accompanied by theosophical symbols, in three stages of spiritual enlightenment. From left to right to center, she begins in a tragic state of materiality, is enlightened, and ultimately passes into spiritual radiance in the raised central panel. The triptych's theosophical content was clear enough to those who saw it in 1911 (many of Mondrian's contemporaries were also theosophical artists), but during later decades knowledge of, and interest in, Mondrian's theosophical beliefs diminished. In 1971, Robert Welsh published his influential article on "Mondrian and Theosophy," analyzing *Evolution* and other works in a manner that pointed Mondrian scholarship back to an understanding of the artist's beliefs.[11] In 1986–1987, the blockbuster exhibition and catalog *The Spiritual in Art: Abstract Painting 1890–1985* (Los Angeles, Chicago, The Hague), to which Welsh and Blotkamp contributed, claimed much media attention by demonstrating the significance of theosophy and other esoteric beliefs for the paintings of Mondrian, Kandinsky, and many other key artists. However, some Mondrian scholars, such as Kermit Champa, continued to maintain a formalist approach. Only in 2004, when Blotkamp's student Marty Bax defended her PhD thesis in Amsterdam, were Mondrian's theosophical principles finally explored in considerable detail.[12]

Mondrian showed his overtly theosophical triptych *Evolution* at the same 1911 exhibition of the Modern Art Circle in Amsterdam where he saw the Cubist works from Paris. Shortly afterward, he moved to Paris to acquaint himself with Cubism. Then at the 1912 exhibition of the Modern Art Circle he showed his *Flowering Apple Tree*, a Cubist

---

[11] Robert P. Welsh, "Mondrian and Theosophy," in *Piet Mondrian 1872–1944: Centennial Exhibition* (New York: Solomon R. Guggenheim Foundation, 1971), 35–51.
[12] See note 10.

painting. There is a revealing symmetry to these events. During 1912, Mondrian had not lost interest in theosophy but had found a better, more modern way of representing his beliefs. Welsh suggests that "Mondrian's adoption of the Cubist style was in part due to his conviction that it embodied the greatest potential for evolving a truly spiritual form of art."[13] Welsh quotes from a speech given at the opening of the 1911 exhibition in which Jan Toorop, an older Catholic artist respected by Mondrian, called for a new, spiritual style "simplified into straight or quietly undulating vertical or horizontal lines."[14] Mondrian may or may not have consciously heeded that call, but his *Flowering Apple Tree* certainly resembles Toorop's description.

Mondrian himself has helped us to understand the spiritual content of *Flowering Apple Tree* in one of his rather tortuous theoretical texts published in *De Stijl*. He describes "the evolution of the founders of Neo-Plasticism" (i.e., his own art) as "liberation from the indefinite (the visual appearance of things) in order to reach a pure image of the definite (where the proportions are balanced)."[15] In this somewhat obscure terminology he is justifying his evolution from naturalistic to abstract art and his gradual process of penetrating beyond material appearances to reach the spiritual essence of things. The balanced proportions he refers to are those between the vertical (male/spiritual) and horizontal (female/material) principles derived from his theosophical worldview. Mondrian goes on,

> Is it pure chance that they [i.e., Mondrian] preferred the rectilinear, that they defied ordinary visual appearances by daring to paint a forest with only vertical tree-trunks? And when they had abstracted the tree-trunks to lines or planes, is it strange that they then introduced the horizontal—which in nature is scarcely visible—in order to bring the vertical into balance?[16]

These passages clarify Mondrian's intentions in his Cubist tree paintings of 1912—the vertical Pittsburgh painting *Trees* and the two paintings from The Hague, which restore horizontality. What Mondrian did

---

[13] Robert P. Welsh, "Sacred Geometry: French Symbolism and Early Abstraction," in *The Spiritual in Art: Abstract Painting 1890–1985* (New York: Abbeville, 1986), 83.
[14] Ibid.
[15] Piet Mondrian, "Het bepaalde en het onbepaalde," *De Stijl* 2 (1918): 2, 14–19, 17 (my translation from the Dutch).
[16] Ibid. (my translation from the Dutch).

not clarify is the thematic link between the two horizontal paintings. Here, Blotkamp has pointed to Mondrian's longstanding interest in natural cycles in relation to the theosophical doctrine of involution and evolution, death and regeneration. This had already led him to themes such as dying flowers in works of 1908. *Gray Apple Tree* shows the suspended life of winter, while *Flowering Apple Tree* represents the renewed vigor of spring, the evolution of new life.[17]

Flowering Apple Tree is scarcely convincing simply as a depiction of a tree, as John Walford pointed out. It does indeed depict universal forces, as Walford observed, but not only that. To perceive Mondrian's spirituality in this painting, we should note the way in which he has constructed vertical and horizontal forces in supreme balance. This balancing of forces in the composition affirms Mondrian's spiritual project of evolving a higher and better world through art. Does this make *Flowering Apple Tree* a theosophical painting? Fortunately not. Were Mondrian to have continued painting in the direction of his *Evolution*, which is unequivocally a theosophical work, he would probably have reached only a niche public of like-minded viewers. By turning to the visual structure of Cubism in 1912, he both satisfied his own spiritual-artistic demands and created paintings that ultimately appealed to many who did not share his beliefs. *Flowering Apple Tree*, like all good art, retains a certain ambiguity about its character and purpose. That is why it offers itself for analysis on different levels, to different kinds of perception.

As early as 1913, the Parisian poet and chronicler of Cubism Guillaume Apollinaire sought to define the qualities peculiar to Mondrian's Cubism. Apollinaire noted that Mondrian was a Dutchman, and though he had apparently undergone the influence of Picasso, "his personality has remained intact. His trees and his female portrait display a sensitive cerebral quality. This kind of cubism clearly follows a different path from that of Braque and Picasso, artists whose 'recherche de matière' is presently arousing such interest."[18]

In later years, Rudi Fuchs, director of Amsterdam's Stedelijk Museum, similarly affirmed Mondrian's great ability to remain himself. Fuchs saw no break between the early and the late Mondrian,

---

[17] Blotkamp, *Mondrian: The Art of Destruction*, 71.
[18] Guillaume Apollinaire, *Chroniques d'art 1902–1918*; quoted in ibid., 19–20.

since even in an international context Mondrian stayed true to the Dutch tradition in which he had begun: "The firm, precise construction, taut but at the same time light, which characterizes the whole oeuvre of Mondrian, is probably particularly Dutch."[19] Fuchs argued that Mondrian's "sensitive, Dutch eye" always prevailed over schematic and theoretical tendencies in abstraction, allowing Mondrian to maintain into the twentieth century the Dutch painterly tradition of "refined and quiet observation" that in the seventeenth century had made Dutch art so distinct from Italian Baroque and French Classical art.[20]

In this context, we can add a factor that John Walford has mentioned in his writings on Dutch seventeenth-century landscape art: "Ideally Dutch landscapists were concerned with combining their observations of landscape with an understanding of its essence."[21] If the sensitive Dutch eye was crucial for Mondrian's art, as Fuchs has argued, then so, too, was an understanding of the essence of what it observed. For many seventeenth-century Dutch artists, such as Jacob van Ruisdael, that understanding was, as Walford points out, "inspired by the widely-held perception of the world as 'God's second book of revelation', as [H. L.] Spiegel, [Constantijn] Huygens, and others called it."[22] Both in the Dutch Calvinist circles in which the young Mondrian initially moved and in the nineteenth-century Romantic landscape tradition which formed his first artistic habitat, the art and literature of the Dutch seventeenth century were constantly held up as models. After his conversion to theosophy, the understanding of spiritual meanings behind natural appearances took on an even greater significance for Mondrian. Walford's distinction between two seventeenth-century approaches to landscape painting can elucidate the particular way in which Mondrian understood nature: "The many Italianate landscape paintings, like pastoral poetry, evoked an idyllic world, timeless and immutable, quite foreign in inspiration to the images of transience and decay produced by [Jacob van] Ruisdael and others."[23] In Walford's contrast of approaches, there can be no doubt that Mondrian belongs

---

[19] Rudi Fuchs, "Piet Mondriaan," in *Tussen kunstenaars: Een romance* (Amsterdam: De Bezige Bij, 2003 (1988)), 47–60, 52 (my translation from the Dutch).
[20] Ibid., 57 (my translation from the Dutch).
[21] E. John Walford, *Jacob van Ruisdael and the Perception of Landscape* (New Haven, CT: Yale University Press, 1991), 19.
[22] Ibid.
[23] Ibid.

to the tradition of Ruisdael. Though he represented universal forces in highly abstract works, Mondrian did not paint an idyllic or immutable world. As we have seen, his theosophical beliefs brought an emphasis on destruction and evolution, decay and regeneration, and on the natural cycles of change. His *Flowering Apple Tree* represents anything but a timeless and unchanging world. Its Cubist painterly technique would soon be superseded as Mondrian evolved his art ever further. And, pointedly, it takes as its subject matter life's changes: a tree now in bloom that had seemed dead in winter and sometime later would seem lifeless again. Mondrian, as the painter of both the wintry and bare *Gray Apple Tree* and the *Flowering Apple Tree*, would surely have concurred with the early eighteenth-century Dutch poet Claas Bruin, who wrote: "Nature loathes things that always stand before her, she loves change."[24]

---

[24]Ibid., 24.

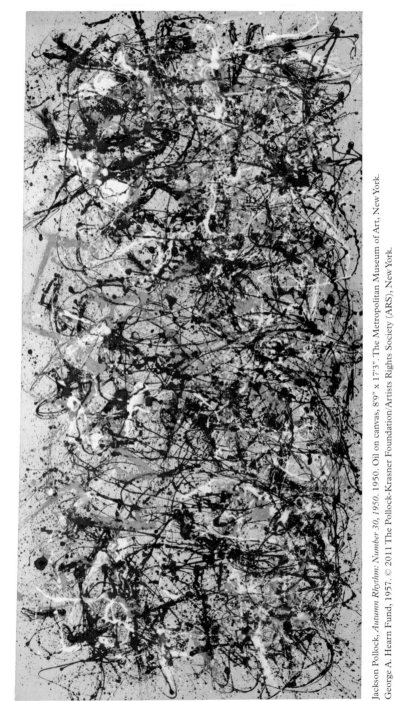

Jackson Pollock, *Autumn Rhythm: Number 30, 1950*. 1950. Oil on canvas, 8'9" x 17'3". The Metropolitan Museum of Art, New York. George A. Hearn Fund, 1957. © 2011 The Pollock-Krasner Foundation/Artists Rights Society (ARS), New York.

14

SPIRITUALLY CHARGED VISUAL STRATEGY
Jackson Pollock's *Autumn Rhythm*

LINDA STRATFORD

Jackson Pollock's *Autumn Rhythm*, at eight-and-three-quarters by seventeen-and-one-quarter feet, is as physically imposing as it is visually affecting. At first, *Autumn Rhythm* may appear singularly unintelligible, a brazen tangle of paint. However, viewers willing to study *Autumn Rhythm* will discern the delicate mesh of complex rotations and revolutions that covers its surface. Swirling arcs of white, brown, and turquoise enamel paint appear to have spontaneously landed atop a snakelike coil of black. Revolving skeins create a dense forest of pigment, in a complex play of overlapping trails and paths. At proximity, pools of color surface, surrounded by pigment poured, dripped, and splashed. The work evidences "autumnal" tones, a connection to its October 1950 conception, that season in which trees bare their black silhouettes and leaves are spontaneously buoyed in complex rotations. There is a wildness and animation to the piece, and at the same time a structural unity afforded by the dominant undergirding of lyrical black loops and a perimeter of bare, unprimed canvas offering a self-imposed border.

John Walford's *Great Themes in Art* explores works of art as visual manifestations of spiritual perception. In similar manner, this essay will demonstrate the ways in which Pollock's *Autumn Rhythm* may be seen as an allegorical representation of spiritual rebirth, and indeed, resurrection. Twentieth-century abstract painting, through mid-century, sought to provide a corrective to the materialist preoccupations of the modern age, freeing viewers from materialist representation in order to stimulate spiritual awareness. However, works such as *Autumn Rhythm*, tethered to corporeal, bodily movement, served a corrective role within the disembodying nature of fully abstract painting. In the leaping, dipping, and swinging of Pollock's gestural strokes would be provided allegorical representation of life beyond the limits of time and space. Whether in regard to the incarnation, the resurrection, the Eucharist, or simply the notion of the human being as "body-soul," such pieces provided metaphoric representation of salvific "spirit" animating "flesh."

Autumn Rhythm's break with the picturing function of art at the time this work was carried out was, and still is, startling. For centuries, since the Renaissance, the paradigm of imitation had been central to the notion of aesthetic experience, inspiring illustrations of idealized beauty and re-creations of important historical events. Beginning in the late-nineteenth and into the early-twentieth century, from the Impressionists to the Symbolists and through the fully abstract experiments of Wassily Kandinsky, Piet Mondrian, and Kasimir Malevich, artists began to replace depiction of recognizable objects from the natural world with less-than-naturalistic experiments in abstraction. The historical break with the picturing function of art allowed artists to pursue a more experiential orientation, one in which the work of art was meant not so much to depict, as to evoke, experience. This experience would increasingly be that of a transcendent, spiritual sort. Such is the visual language with which Pollock constructed *Autumn Rhythm*.

An iconic example of Abstract Expressionism, *Autumn Rhythm*'s "abstract" and "expressionist" tenets are clear. Pollock's painterly plasticity points back to the near abstraction of Claude Monet's later paintings.[1] In his *Great Themes in Art*, Walford describes Monet's *Poplars* in a manner that could quite easily be applied to a work like *Autumn Rhythm* or Pollock's *Blue Poles* of 1952. Walford writes,

> Monet once explained his impressionistic procedure as an effort to forget the identity of the object in front of [him]. . . . In *Poplars*, Monet focused almost exclusively on gradations of light and color, and heightened their abstract pictorial qualities. In the contrasting rhythm of near and far trees, and the sensuous dance of color on the surface of the canvas, Monet transformed actual optical sensation into something almost trance-like.[2]

---

[1] Paul Hayes Tucker et al., *Monet in the Twentieth Century* (Boston: Museum of Fine Arts, 1998).
[2] E. John Walford, *Great Themes in Art* (Upper Saddle River, NJ: Prentice-Hall, 2002), 423.

Sensations within landscape stimulated Monet's reveries, the experience of which, as in the case of Pollock, translated into abstract skeins of paint. Monet's painterly responses to his *plein air* immersion relied on an instinctual communion with the landscape, a communion that has been referred to as "mysterious and infinite." While Monet was a naturalist, his works are anything but naturalistic; rather, his works suggest the spirituality of Monet's communion with nature.[3] Similarly, in the case of Pollock, works such as *Autumn Rhythm* would allow the artist to make visible, through painterly sensation, the unseen world of inner spiritual experience.

Autumn Rhythm's compositional provocation is also indebted to the early-twentieth-century breach with picture-function practiced by Georges Braque and Pablo Picasso, whose Cubist works deconstructed "form and space into flat, interlocking planes set at varying angles that rupture traditional expectations for illusionistic representation."[4] Cubism introduced this startling and new form-shattering role for painting. It removed from optical sensation its prior commitment to precise and objective depiction, replacing it with that of subjective, experiential vision. Materialism now became the "target" of the painter rather than his or her objective.

Autumn Rhythm's debt to the expressive wing of modern art is also clear, with borrowings from Vincent van Gogh and Paul Gauguin through the German Expressionists and Surrealists. Distancing from naturalism, through varying degrees of abstraction, allowed late-nineteenth- and early-twentieth-century Symbolists and Expressionists to evoke emotional intensity through expressive color and simplified, flattened forms. German Expressionists, such as Ernst Ludwig Kirchner, Erich Heckel, and Emil Nolde incorporated self-consciously "primitive" figures in forest settings and treatments to pursue direct, unmediated compositions designed as a foil to an overly civilized bourgeois society.[5] Their works appeared unfinished; colors were distorted and figures made angular. This disruption bore with it an element of protest against bourgeois norms and academic convention; it in turn was

---

[3] Michael Leja, "The Monet Revival and New York School Abstraction," in *Monet in the Twentieth Century*, 103.
[4] Walford, *Great Themes in Art*, 449.
[5] Gill Perry, "Primitivism and the Modern," in Charles Harrison et al., *Primitivism, Cubism, Abstraction* (New Haven, CT: Yale University Press, in association with the Open University, 1993).

intended to open the path to a more pure and instinctual way of life, the way of life encountered in the mysticism of primitive peoples. Walford noted, "At the heart of Modernism was the feeling that Western culture and the values that sustained it had become bankrupt."[6] The art of "primitive" cultures, it was believed, harbored and promised a return to mankind's inner spiritual light.

In 1905 Kirchner, Heckel, and others formed a group known as *die Brücke*, "the bridge." They pursued varying degrees of departure from naturalism, especially in their use of color, while still including figuration. *Fully* abstract work would be pursued in the years preceding World War I. Between 1911 and 1914, Wassily Kandinsky and Franz Marc led a group known as *der Blaue Reiter*, "the Blue Rider."[7] *Der Blaue Reiter* was less primitivistic in its interests than *die Brücke*; Kandinsky and Marc embraced cosmopolitan influences, including those of the dynamic paintings of Robert Delaunay. Walford noted that Delaunay's work evoked a "heightened awareness of the essential life-force and cosmic order that lifts us beyond the reach of the material world."[8]

Of all these early Modernists, Kandinsky made the most complete break with representation as he began to allow his colors to unfold in a bold, organic style, working in an improvisational manner. He wrote, with missionary zeal, of his vision in his 1911 essay "Concerning the Spiritual in Art." He described the corrective role played by abstract art—an urgent role, he claimed, given the materialist preoccupations of the modern age. Abstract painting, he explained, was the artist's attempt to realize visually the spirit's "inner necessity."[9]

Kandinsky's idealist, Neoplatonic orientation remained when, upon returning to his native Russia at the outbreak of World War I, he began to pursue a more geometric abstraction, nurtured there by avant-garde interest in the concept of sacred geometry. Whether organic or geometric, the importance of fully abstract art, for Kandinsky, rested on its ability to distance from the "imperfections of material reality," pointing to a higher realm.[10]

Piet Mondrian likewise transformed his work into fully abstract

[6] Walford, *Great Themes in Art*, 440–441.
[7] Rose-Carol Washton Long, "Expressionism, Abstraction, and the Search for Utopia in Germany," in *The Spiritual in Art: Abstract Painting 1890–1985*, ed. Maurice Tuchman (New York: Abbeville, 1986).
[8] Walford, *Great Themes in Art*, 446.
[9] Wasily Kandinsky, *Concerning the Spiritual in Art*, trans. M. T. H. Sadler (New York: Dover, 1977), 26.
[10] Walford, *Great Themes in Art*, 443.

compositions, moving after the First World War to highly reduced imagery of flat rectangles of primary color. Like Kandinsky driven by Neoplatonic philosophical beliefs, Mondrian opined on the spiritual role of fully abstract art.[11] No longer confined to the role of particular representations, he argued, works of art were now free to express true reality—that of a higher, transcendent realm. Kasimir Malevich, like Mondrian and Kandinsky, also experimented in pure abstraction. Shortly after World War I, Malevich exhibited his flat polygonal shapes in red and black, followed by an even more radical *White on White* series of white squares on white ground. For Malevich, as for Kandinsky and Mondrian, abstract paintings were not exercises in design but an integral means of pictorially communicating transcendent, spiritual occupations.[12] Evoking not body, but soul, their purpose was to heighten awareness of things infinite and transcendent, beyond the material.

As American Abstract Expressionism emerged in the 1940s, exemplified in the work of Adolph Gottlieb, Barnett Newman, Jackson Pollock, and Mark Rothko, it drew from diverse Modernist precedents of abstraction and expressionism. However, Abstract Expressionism was also significantly impacted by Surrealist émigrés fleeing Europe.[13] Many of these artists were influenced by Carl Jung's theories about dreams, psychic automatism, and the exploration of a collective unconscious via cultural myths and symbols. Visually, this influence of Surrealism made for the reinsertion of degrees of recognizable imagery and figuration. Thus, Pollock's work, between c. 1938 and 1945, represented a step away from the disembodying nature of geometric abstraction, to include figuration, as he incorporated imagery drawn from the North American Indian, ancient Assyrian, Egyptian, and Mayan civilizations.[14] This imagery explored mystical forces of creation, birth,

---

[11] The intent of Mondrian's "Neoplasticism" was to signify spiritual harmony. In his 1920 manifesto, "Neoplasticism," Mondrian described his goal of freeing line and color from natural appearance in order to explore the dynamic of equilibrium. In so doing, art is freed to express "true reality" and "true life" (Piet Mondrian, "Neo-Plasticism," *Abstraction-création* 1 (1932): 25; "Neo-Plasticism," *Abstraction-création* 2 (1933): 31.

[12] Charles Harrison, "Abstraction," in *Primitivism, Cubism, Abstraction*.

[13] Salvador Dali, Max Ernst, Leonora Carrington, Stanley William Hayter, André Masson, Roberto Matta, Gordon Onslow Ford, Wolfgang Paalen, Kurt Seligmann, Yves Tanguy, and Surrealist poet-spokesman André Breton fled Paris for the United States during the Second World War (Martica Sawin, *Surrealism in Exile and the Beginning of the New York School* [Cambridge, MS: MIT Press, 1995]).

[14] Pollock's interest in Jung included his own Jungian analysis. His interest in Jung was heightened by meeting painter and theorist John Graham in 1940. Graham had written on Picasso and primitive art and encouraged Pollock's interest in North American Indian art (John Golding, *Paths to the Absolute: Mondrian, Malevich, Kandinsky, Pollock, Newman, Rothko, and Still* [Princeton, NJ: Princeton University Press, 2000]). Elizabeth Langhorne has written on the healing power of images and automatist drawings encouraged and

death, and resurrection that would later be realized in *Autumn Rhythm* in a more pure and material form.

By the fall of 1950, when Pollock painted *Autumn Rhythm*, he had moved away from Jungian-inspired abstraction to employ a radically different approach. In this approach painterly abstraction replaced any trace of figuration.[15] Harold Rosenberg coined the term "action painting" to describe this new method, explaining, "At a certain moment the canvas began to appear to one American painter after another as an arena in which to act—rather than a space in which to reproduce . . ."[16] A 1950 film by Hans Namuth is a record of Pollock's process. Carried out close to the time that Pollock was working on *Autumn Rhythm*, the film shows the artist painting on unstretched canvas laid flat on the floor, moving about the piece. Holding the paint can with one hand, Pollock scatters paint with the other, dripping and flinging the material as he moves.

Pollock described his method, saying,

> My painting does not come from the easel. . . . [Painting] on the floor I am more at ease. I feel nearer, more a part of the painting, since this way I can walk around it, work from the four sides and literally be *in* the painting. . . .
>
> When I am *in* the painting I am not aware of what I am doing. It is only after a "get acquainted" period that I see what I have been about. I have no fear of making changes, destroying the image . . . because the painting has a life of its own. I try to let it come through. It is only when I lose contact with the painting that the result is a mess. Otherwise there is pure harmony, an easy give and take, and the painting comes out well.[17]

Clement Greenberg, perhaps the leading American art critic of that time and an early champion of Pollock's art, spoke of Pollock's break

analyzed by Pollock's therapists in Jungian analysis. Her article has appeared in German as "Jackson Pollock und das Sakrale: Das Kirchenprojekt," trans. Karsten Harries, in *Sakralität und Moderne*, ed. Hanna-Barbara Gerl-Falkovitz (Munich: Hawel, 2010), 110–144.

[15] Pollock's approach has been linked to that of Monet's late work. Leo Steinberg wrote of Monet's late *Water Lilies*, "You can invert the picture or yourself at will, climb upwards with slow, sinking clouds or drift with lily leaves across a nether sky; lie cheek to cheek with the horizon, search among opaque waters for diaphanous shrubs, and find the source of light at its last destination. . . . in the *Water Lilies*, the law of gravity—that splendid projection of the human mind too firmly lodged in its body—is abrogated, as in the underwater movies of Cousteau . . ." ("Month in Review," *Arts* [February 1956]: 46–48).

[16] Harold Rosenberg, "The American Action Painters," *Art News* 51 (September 1952): 22–23, 48–50.

[17] Jackson Pollock, *Possibilities I*, ed. Robert Motherwell and Harold Rosenberg, 1947–1948 (only one issue appeared), emphasis his.

with the picturing function of art as the fulfillment of a "Modernist" impulse. In his essay "Modernist Painting," Greenberg defined the essence of this paradigm as a strategy of self-interrogation. He wrote,

> The essence of Modernism lies, as I see it, in the use of characteristic methods of a discipline to criticize the discipline itself, not in order to subvert it but in order to entrench it more firmly in its area of competence. . . . It quickly emerged that the unique and proper area of competence of each art coincided with all that was unique in the nature of its medium.[18]

For Greenberg, this impulse manifested itself in painting as a movement from pictorial representation to emphasis upon the medium itself:

> Realistic, naturalistic art had dissembled the medium, using art to conceal art; Modernism used art to call attention to art. The limitations that constitute the medium of painting—the flat surface, the shape of the support, the properties of the pigment—were treated by the Old Masters as negative factors that could be acknowledged only implicitly or indirectly. Under Modernism these same limitations came to be regarded as positive factors, and were acknowledged openly.[19]

In Greenberg's view, Pollock's break with the picturing function of art freed art to call attention to its own material conditions, rather than calling attention to spiritual preoccupations that had earlier in history been the impetus for full abstraction.

Countering this formalist reading of Pollock's art, Harold Rosenberg sought to frame the art in existentialist terms. Rosenberg claimed that action painting was an "autobiographical act of self-creation," likened to "existential theatre."[20] Rosenberg described the innovation of action painting:

> The innovation of Action Painting was to dispense with the *representation* of the state [the artist's psychic state or tension] in favor of

---

[18] Clement Greenberg, "Modernist Painting," in *Art in Theory 1900–2000: An Anthology of Changing Ideas*, ed. Charles Harrison and Paul Wood (Malden, MA : Blackwell, 2003), 755.
[19] Ibid.
[20] Quoted in Stephen Polcari, *Abstract Expressionism and the Modern Experience* (New York: Cambridge University Press, 1991), 357.

enacting it in physical movement. The action on the canvas became its own representation. This was possible because an action, being made of both the psychic and the material, is by its nature a sign—it is the trace of a movement whose beginning and character it does not in itself ever altogether reveal . . . yet the action also exists as a "thing" in that it touches other things and affects them.[21]

Other art historians have continued to counter Greenberg's formalist interpretation of Pollock's action painting as a type of essentialism misrepresenting the work. Irving Sandler, for example, maintained that Pollock and other gestural painters remained preoccupied with meanings that related to "the whole of human experience."[22] Others throughout the next two decades continued to find the High Modernist position difficult to accept.[23] For example, standing before *Autumn Rhythm* in 2002, T. J. Clark, in a continuing critique of Greenberg's perspective, insisted that Pollock's gestural abstraction signified a desire to communicate experiential subject matter. Exchanging views with Modernist critic Michael Fried in front of the piece, Clark suggested that the point of dispensing with the figure was "to try to discover a complete 'other' to figuration," compelling the viewer to read the picture and its surface in an absolutely new way requiring an unnerving loss of "connotational habits."[24]

Nevertheless, despite their break with traditional methods of visual description, Abstract Expressionists, such as Pollock, Mark Rothko, and Adolph Gottlieb, insisted that their work communicated urgent spiritual content. While their art did not depict an illusion of reality, Pollock and his colleagues insisted that their art evoked or materialized a reality that was more true to human experience than illusion.

Rothko articulated this assertion in a 1956 conversation with Selden Rodman, in which he disputed the suggestion that his paintings were "abstract." Rothko said,

---

[21] Harold Rosenberg, "American Action Painters," *The Tradition of the New* (New York: Horizon, 1959), 27 (the chapter cited is a reprint of Rosenberg's article by the same title published in 1952 and cited in note 16, above; the quote cited here is from a footnote that did not appear in the original article).
[22] Irving Sandler, "Introduction," in *The Triumph of American Painting: A History of Abstract Expressionism* (New York: Harper & Row, 1970).
[23] Jonathan Harris, "Modernism and Culture in the USA, 1930–1960," in *Modernism in Dispute*, ed. Paul Wood et al. (New Haven, CT: Yale University Press, in association with the Open University, 1993).
[24] *Jackson Pollock: Michael Fried and T. J. Clark in Conversation*, 26 min, 2002, produced by the Open University.

I'm interested only in expressing basic human emotion—tragedy, ecstasy, doom, and so on—and the fact that lots of people break down and cry when confronted with my pictures shows that I *communicate* those basic emotions. . . . The people who weep before my pictures are having the same religious experience I had when I painted them. And if you, as you say, are moved only by their color relationships, then you miss the point![25]

Gottlieb went further than Rothko in debating the "abstractness" of his painting. Gottlieb wrote, in language that evidences the influence of Jung,

Certain people always say we should go back to nature. I notice they never say we should go forward to nature. It seems to me they are more concerned that we should go back, than about nature.

If the models we use are the apparitions seen in a dream, or the recollection of our pre-historic past, is this less part of nature or realism, than a cow in the field? I think not. The role of the artist, of course, has always been that of image-maker. Different times require different images. Today when our aspirations have been reduced to a desperate attempt to escape from evil, and times are out of joint, our obsessive, subterranean and pictographic images are the expression of the neurosis which is our reality. To my mind certain so-called abstraction is not abstraction at all. On the contrary, it is the realism of our time.[26]

Gottlieb's "realism of our time" suggests that there is, in any given moment of history, a contemporary way(s) of seeing, strategies of perception that organically and necessarily respond to the urgency of the human experience of that historical time. Pollock echoes this conception of a distinctly "contemporary" art in telling William Wright, in a radio interview, "Modern art to me is nothing more than the expression of contemporary aims of the age we are living in. . . . All cultures have had means and techniques of expressing their immediate aims—the Chinese, the Renaissance, all cultures."[27] Pressed to describe his own painting technique in "contemporary" terms, Pollock said, "It

[25] Rothko, Mark. "Notes from a conversation with Selden Rodman, 1956," in *Writings on Art* (New Haven, CT: Yale University Press, 2006) 119–120.

[26] Adolph Gottlieb, quoted in "The Ides of Art: The Attitudes of Ten Artists on Their Art and Contemporaneousness," *The Tiger's Eye* 1/2 (December 1947).

[27] Jackson Pollock, "Interview with William Wright," in *Jackson Pollock: Interviews, Articles, and Reviews*, ed. Pepe Karmel (New York: Museum of Modern Art, 1999), 20.

seems to me that the modern painter cannot express this age, the airplane, the atom bomb, the radio, in the old forms of the Renaissance or of any other past culture. Each age finds its own technique."[28] Finally, Pollock explained in a 1950 interview,

> The modern artist, it seems to me, is working and expressing an inner world—in other words—expressing the energy, the motion, and other inner forces . . . . the modern artist is working with space and time, and expressing his feelings rather than illustrating.[29]

In summary, those who opposed purely formalist readings of Abstract Expressionism contended that, while fully abstract art does not depict, it does in fact embody content.[30] If action painting may then be seen as a practice of abandoning depiction while yet *representing*, what might *Autumn Rhythm* represent? Better put, to what does *Autumn Rhythm* give representation?

Much has been written about the search for spiritual regeneration following the Second World War, and humanity's spiritual struggle therein.[31] Critics and historians, in particular, have often addressed postwar action painting in religious terms. For example, John Golding described Pollock's turn to action painting as a personal, salvific event, describing his gestural paintings as a quasi-religious "breakthrough," affirming that Pollock was doing more than producing paintings; he was seeking "salvation."[32] Those close to Pollock at mid-century recognized that Pollock's quest included spiritual expression. Betty Parsons observed that Pollock was "extremely intrigued with the inner world. . . . He had a sense of mystery. His religiousness was in those terms—a sense of the rhythm of the universe, of the big order . . ."[33] Pollock's wife, Lee Krasner, recounted the artist's spiritual interest as well, explaining, for example, that when they were married he, not she, insisted on a church wedding. She says Pollock was raised in a family

---

[28] Ibid.
[29] Ibid., 21.
[30] In fact, the varieties in abstract art grow out of the varying philosophical positions represented by various abstract movements. One must consider the influence of Neoplatonism on early abstract artists, and at the same time anti-idealist rather than materialist views arising in the Soviet Union around abstraction, especially in the work of the Constructivists (Harrison, "Abstraction," 200).
[31] See, e.g., Polcari, *Abstract Expressionism and the Modern Experience*; and Golding, *Paths to the Absolute.*
[32] Golding, *Paths to the Absolute*, 137.
[33] Quoted in E. A. Carmean, "The Church Project: Pollock's Passion Themes," *Art in America* 70/6 (Summer 1982): 115.

that was "violently anti-religious," that he felt a sense of "great loss" because of this, and that at the time of their marriage he was "tending more and more to religion."[34] Kirsten Hoving noted, "While Pollock was not religious in the conventional sense, he was, by many accounts an intensely spiritual man."[35] Elizabeth Langhorne has claimed that Pollock's art evidenced "a spiritual quest,"[36] going on to explain, "The very forms that so fascinated Greenberg in Pollock's work were in fact the products of a spiritual quest of just the sort Greenberg dismissed."[37]

In fact, when Jackson Pollock painted *Autumn Rhythm*, he was in the midst of discussions about a church design project that would centrally incorporate his action paintings. In the summer of 1950, just months before the completion of *Autumn Rhythm*, he had begun meeting with Tony Smith, who was then a practicing architect, and Alfonso Ossorio, who had recently been engaged in painting a large mural for a church in the Philippines, for extended discussions of a design intended for a Catholic church proposed to be built on Long Island. These discussions continued until the project was abandoned in 1952 after Pollock, Smith, and Ossorio presented it to a group of prominent Catholics interested in modern art who might have sponsored construction.[38]

Elizabeth Langhorne has followed this relatively unknown story with questions about the suitability of Pollock's poured paintings for a Christian worship setting. Her questions center on the absence of Christian metanarrative in Pollock's works, and the absence of singular Christian belief on the part of the artist. E. A. Carmean earlier agreed that, "The idea of placing paintings executed in the same style as *Autumn Rhythm*, *One*, and *Lavender Mist* in a church setting was stunning."[39] What would Pollock's all-over paintings have to say to Christian worshipers? It is helpful in answering this question to return to the earlier question, "to what does *Autumn Rhythm* give

[34] Lee Krasner, "Interview with Francine du Plessix and Cleve Gray," in "Who Was Jackson Pollock," *Art in America* 55/3 (May–June 1967): 48–51; reprinted in *Jackson Pollock: Interviews, Articles, and Reviews*, 31.

[35] Kirsten A. Hoving, "Jackson Pollock: Outer Space and Artist's Space in Pollock's Cosmic Paintings," *American Art* (Spring 2002), 92.

[36] Elizabeth Langhorne, "The Magus and the Alchemist: John Graham and Jackson Pollock," *American Art* 12/3 (Autumn 1998): 48.

[37] Ibid., 46–67.

[38] Elizabeth Langhorne, "Jackson Pollock and Religion: The Church Project" (paper presented at the Association of Scholars of Christianity in the History of Art (ASCHA) symposium, New York, February 8, 2011).

[39] Carmean, "Church Project: Pollock's Passion Themes," 12.

representation?" To what invisible presence or spirit does *Autumn Rhythm* give visible form? Alan Kaprow described the posture necessary to absorb Pollock's work:

> I am convinced that to grasp a Pollock's impact properly, one must be something of an acrobat, constantly vacillating between an identification with the hands and body that flung the paint and stood "in" the canvas, and allowing the markings to entangle and assault one into submitting to their permanent and objective character.[40]

As described earlier, the particular dashes and spills found throughout *Autumn Rhythm* indicate the painter's path and gestural movements. If Monet translated optical experience into movement, Pollock made the energy of movement optically visible. The viewer follows the outline of movement, becoming aware of a path, or trail, of activity. A rhythmic dance is suggested, evident at points where the artist walked or leapt. Pollock's exertion comes to mind—the sheer physical task of weighing in against this work's scale and looming horizontality, willing the weight of the bucket against the force of gravity; and carving from deep within the delicately controlled muscular exertion required to rhythmically fling pigment. Breathing in and out, the artist would have stretched, dipped, and flung in determined execution, at moments throwing, dripping, or sprinkling paint, at other junctures trickling a slow pour. The work's diverse marks suggest varying tempo, where lines trail thick or thin; heavy or delicate; and straight or curved. One imagines the physical effort and circulatory rhythm by which the artist's body crossed these routes. If the spectator tries to comprehend this work by focusing on individual and disparate points of contact, the work fails to make sense. Its imagery is tethered to corporeal, bodily movement across the whole expanse of the canvas, testifying to dynamic, rhythmic encounter with its overall expanse.

Looking at *Autumn Rhythm*, it is one thing to apprehend that Pollock's mid-century gestural work suggested dance and bodily movement, something that contemporary critics immediately grasped.[41] It

---

[40] Allan Kaprow, "The Legacy of Jackson Pollock," *Art News* 57/6 (October 1958): 24–26, 55–57.

[41] Robert M. Coates, "The Art Galleries: Extremists," *The New Yorker* 26 (December 9, 1950): 109–111. Coates reviewed Pollock's November 1950 exhibit at the Betty Parsons Gallery, in which *Autumn Rhythm* was displayed: "In Pollock's work . . . the drawing is irregular and sinuously curved, while the composition, instead of being orderly and exact, is exuberant and explosive. Both suggest the organic . . ."

is another to consider that action painting, according to Pollock's own claims about contemporary practices, was meant to illustrate "inner spirit," or as Rosenberg termed it, to "touch other things." In other words, Pollock's action paintings, anything *but* "fleshless," bore potential to convey, as well, the ethereal and numinous. This begs a return to the questions at hand: "to what does *Autumn Rhythm* give representation, and, more pointedly, in consideration of the church project, to what end would Pollock's poured paintings be included in a specifically Christian worship setting?" and "What would be the point of ushering such corporeal energy into a holy place?"

As soon as this question is framed, its answer begins to emerge. In many ways a church setting, more so than a museum setting, would have allowed Pollock's action paintings their fullest imagistic impact. Within the proposed church project, Pollock's poured paintings were to have been mounted, or perhaps suspended, around the altar, forming a kind of "sacred enclosure."[42] Here the Eucharist, a ceremony in which, according to Catholic belief, the bread and wine *become* the body and blood of Christ, would be celebrated. Here other matter-spirit mysteries would be preached, such as the virgin birth, holy miracles, and Christ's resurrection. Here as well, beneath Pollock's drip paintings, would be celebrated the notion of Christ as the embodiment of God in human form, according to the doctrine of the incarnation.[43] Christian worship is uniquely centered on teachings regarding the interpenetration of spirit and matter. Pollock's action paintings would provide representation for these and other Christian convictions difficult to grasp without imagistic statement. One might ponder resurrection in the metaphoric account of revolving skeins, overlapping trails, and lyrical loops signaling the celebratory dance of a spiritually animated body.[44] In the leaping, dipping, and swinging of Pollock's works would be provided allegorical representation of life beyond the limits of time and space. Whether in regard to the incarnation, the resurrection, the Eucharist, or simply the notion of the human being as "body-soul," Pollock's action paintings would bear an epistemic potential uniquely

---

[42] Elizabeth Langhorne, "Jackson Pollock and the Sacred: The Church Project," 3 (unpublished English manuscript version of "Jackson Pollock und das Sakrale: Das Kirchenprojekt").

[43] Athanasius, *The Incarnation of the Word of God* (New York: MacMillan 1946). Translation of Saint Athanasius's fourth-century treatise.

[44] "But some one will say, How are the dead raised? and with what manner of body do they come?" (1 Corinthians 15:35, ASV).

accentuated within a Christian framework. The metaphoric representation of salvific "spirit" animating "flesh" found in works such as *Autumn Rhythm* suggests an aptness for church.

Pollock was of course not limited to explicitly *Christian* references in pursuing the "body-soul" nature of existence; nor was he unaware of extra-Christian interest in the transmutation of spirit into bodily form. The relationship between matter and spirit that so preoccupied Pollock had drawn him to multiple sources, including Jung, as mentioned above, but also shamanism, ritualistic art, and the mysteries of alchemy. The latter interest was particularly nurtured by his friendship with John Graham, who Pollock claimed was the one person who really understood his art.[45] Elizabeth Langhorne has described Pollock's and Graham's shared interest in esoteric ideas, including "religious ideas that Greenberg disliked," recounting how after initially reading Graham's writings, Pollock uncharacteristically wrote to Graham and paid him a visit. Pollock recalled, "I knocked on his door, told him I had read his article and that he *knew*."[46] What was it that Graham knew? Pollock seemed especially interested in Graham's studies of matter-spirit transference based on esoteric explorations of alchemy, an ancient practice believed to be on one level physical, in line with original alchemist interest in turning lead into gold, for example, and on another, metaphysical. Langhorne suggests, "For artists who took the premises of alchemy seriously, it could become a vehicle for investing spiritual and emotional meaning in the act of painting . . ."[47]

The act of painting, as expressed in works including *Autumn Rhythm*, carried forward the spiritual legacy of abstraction. Pioneers of abstraction had expanded the definition of the art object from that which provided depiction to that which through abstract means evoked experience. The move from depiction to experience that inspired Pollock stretched to Monet, whose late work explored the feeling of being in spiritual communion with nature, rather than witness to its depiction.[48] From Monet's late Impressionism, through Expressionism,

---

[45] Langhorne, "Magus and the Alchemist," 48.
[46] Quoted in ibid., 49.
[47] Ibid., 52.
[48] Leja, "Monet Revival and New York School Abstraction," 103. Leja cites William Seitz's claim that Monet's belief in a nonmaterial reality constituted an essential stage in development from the physicalist theory of Courbet, to the metaphysical naturalism motivating Monet and Kandinsky. Leja also contends that "Seitz's Monet resonated better with the spiritual and psychological interests of the abstract expressionists than did Greenberg's Monet" in accounting for the revived interest in late Monet in the 1950s.

and the fully abstract experiments of Kandinsky and others, artists began to replace the depiction of recognizable objects from the natural world with less-than-naturalistic experimentation. The break with the picturing function of art was intended to open the path to works of art that would obviate the materialist preoccupations of modern life, allowing artists, in Kandinsky's words, to realize, visually, the spirit's "inner necessity." Abstract painting suggested a means of pictorially communicating the transcendent, spiritual realm.

However, Pollock's work signaled a step away from the disembodying nature of early abstract painting, reinserting corporeal action. While Rosenberg claimed that action painting was an "autobiographical act of self-creation," others maintained that Pollock and other gestural painters remained preoccupied with meanings that related to "the whole of human experience." Action painting compelled the viewer to read painting in an entirely new way, a way calling attention to its materiality while yet conveying spiritual preoccupations.

T. J. Clark has suggested that the importance of the piece was its complete "other" to figuration. It deployed its abstract elements of line, color, and surface in "an absolutely new way."[49] Action painting indeed holds a unique epistemic potential: it yields not only to the body, but also to the soul, offering metaphoric representation of salvific "spirit" animating "flesh."

While a certain hierarchy of values continues to affect the reception of *Autumn Rhythm*—first and foremost, academic disinterest in things religious—the work continues to speak to those willing to listen. Its physical girth, painterly expression, and scope of vision make it difficult to ignore. While a disregard for religious influences has contributed to a certain obviation of its religious merits, a theologically nuanced reading of Jackson Pollock's *Autumn Rhythm* invites imaginative understanding by which truths central to Christian creedal convictions are given representation through particular Expressionist strengths. *Autumn Rhythm* continues to suggest connection not only to the spiritual heritage of abstract painting in general, but to Christian belief in particular.

---

[49]T. J. Clark, in *Jackson Pollock: Michael Fried and T. J. Clark in Conversation*, video, 26 min., produced by the Open University (New York: Films Media Group, 2002).

Joseph Beuys, *Coyote: I Like America and America Likes Me.* Photo of performance at Rene Block Gallery, New York, 1974. Photo © Caroline Tisdall. Courtesy Ronald Feldman Fine Arts, New York/www.feldmangallery.com.

15

THE LIBERATING MYTH
Joseph Beuys's *I Like America and America Likes Me*

JAMES WATKINS

Coyote: I Like America and America Likes Me (1974) is a performance (or what he called an "action") by Joseph Beuys (1921–1986) that combines elements of art and life into a contemporary myth.[1] On May 21, 1974, Beuys was flown to John F. Kennedy airport in New York City. Upon arrival, his plane was met by an ambulance. He was wrapped in white felt, laid onto a rolling stretcher, and placed inside the ambulance. With lights flashing, the ambulance drove through New York City until it parked outside the René Block Gallery on East Broadway. Beuys was carried to a room where the felt was removed. Inside the room, a coyote waited inside a cage. Beuys spent the next three days in the room with the coyote, and, for periods of time, allowed the coyote to be released from the cage. On film recordings of the action, the two can be seen interacting in various ways: the coyote sniffing curiously at Beuys, the two sitting on a mat of straw, the coyote playing with Beuys's gloves, and so on. Beuys had only a gray felt blanket, a cane, a musical triangle, and copies of the *Wall Street Journal*. The dialogue between Beuys and coyote was a silent one—apart from an occasional series of three notes on the triangle followed by the noise of a turbine engine briefly blasted from a tape recorder. On May 25, the ambulance returned, and Beuys was again wrapped in white felt and placed on a stretcher. The ambulance drove him through New York City to the airport, where he boarded a plane for Germany.

---

[1] *I Like America* is documented in a black-and-white film, with sound, that runs approximately thirty-five minutes, and in photographic images. Although this description of *I Like America* stands outside of dialogue with various interpretations of the piece and is intended to present the reader with those elements of the action that are most significant, it is, nevertheless, doubtful whether this sketch can avoid becoming an interpretation.

Beuys's action *I Like America* has all the qualities of a great myth. It is mysterious, complex, and suggestive of multiple layers of meaning. It seems to exist both inside and outside of the "ordinary" world of time. Beuys and the coyote appear to be locked in a confrontation full of psychological, social, and spiritual depth. This essay will now explore how one's perspective on Beuys's personal mythology directly influences one's perception of *I Like America*'s mythical character.

Because of the personal nature of this iconic action, the meaning ascribed to *I Like America* is interwoven into and inseparable from Beuys's own mythology and persona. As a result, any interpretation of the work is dependent upon how one regards Beuys's myth making. The nature of myth in Beuys's work and persona is one of the most divisive issues among scholars of his art. In fact, each scholar's response to "the story,"[2] as it is referred to in the literature on Beuys's art, reveals as much about the scholar as it does about the art.

At the heart of the debate over Beuys is what may be called a "myth of origins." Beuys's principal myth is "the story" he told about himself as a German dive-bomber pilot during World War II. During the winter of 1943, Beuys's plane was hit by Russian anti-aircraft fire while he was flying over the Crimea and was forced to make a hard landing. The crash killed his copilot and severely injured Beuys. As Heiner Stachelhaus relates,

> It was a miracle Beuys survived; and he owed his survival to a group of nomadic Tartars who discovered the wrecked Stuka and its badly injured pilot in deep snow. They took him into one of their tents, devotedly tended the mostly unconscious man for eight days, salved his massive injuries with animal fat, and wrapped him in felt to warm him and help him conserve body heat. They fed him milk, curds, and cheese.[3]

"The story" is deeply connected to Beuys's oeuvre. For example, his recurring use of the materials fat and felt is connected to his experiences with the Tartars.[4] Furthermore, the other mythologies that

---

[2] For an in-depth discussion of "the story," see, Peter Nisbet's "Crash Course: Remarks on a Beuys Story," in *Joseph Beuys: Mapping the Legacy*, ed. Gene Ray (New York: D.A.P., 2001).
[3] Heiner Stachelhaus, *Joseph Beuys*, trans. David Britt (London: Abbeville, 1987), 22.
[4] Even those who hold to the veracity of Beuys's myth of origins, however, are sometimes careful to explain that those elements in Beuys's work that closely relate to his experience with the Tartars do not only refer

Beuys created in his works, including *I Like America*, originated from "the story."

The disagreements over how one should approach the mythical quality of his persona and art are highly polarized. The Beuys literature evidences, at least, five distinct perceptions of this method of mythologizing, each of which will be critically discussed in greater detail. There are some scholars who embrace "the story" and Beuys's mythologizing at face value. There are other critics who entirely reject "the story" as a fabrication and Beuys as a dangerous charlatan. Between these two more extreme positions, there are scholars who neither believe the story nor reject it. These scholars embrace Beuys's method of mythologizing as having psychological, social, and/ or spiritual usefulness. In exploring these different perspectives, it will become clear that no critic interprets *I Like America* with an innocent eye, but that all of these interpretations are based on previous commitments. One of the most significant commitments that critics make when interpreting *I Like America* is to a concept of myth. While each of these perspectives opens up rich veins of exploration in *I Like America*, none of the critics, nor even Beuys himself, puts forward a robust concept of myth that can defend Beuys's myth making from the criticism that it is a deceit. This essay concludes by briefly considering J. R. R. Tolkien's thought on myth and arguing that the mythical quality of *I Like America* should be interpreted as a liberating, rather than deceiving, element of Beuys's action.

Some scholars accept Beuys's mythology as factually true. They embrace "the story" of death and resurrection as evidence of his prophetic and shamanistic role. These believers view *I Like America* as Beuys playing the role of *shaman*. One of Beuys's earliest American champions was Caroline Tisdall. Tisdall curated a major exhibition of Beuys's art at the Guggenheim Museum in 1979 (five years after *I Like America*). It was in the catalog to that Guggenheim Museum show that Beuys recounted "the story" in detail. Discussing *I Like America*, Tisdall described Beuys's dramatic entrance in New York City on a stretcher as pointing toward "a trauma in mankind's state of being."[5]

---

to that experience but also take on new layers of meaning within his work as a whole. See Caroline Tisdall, *Joseph Beuys* (New York: Solomon R. Guggenheim Foundation, 1979), 17.
[5] Ibid., 24.

Alain Borer, similarly, describes Beuys, with his cane (or crook), as a mythical shepherd who "leads his disciples to a place only he knows of (the promise of a higher state)."[6] Or one might interpret the action mythically as a story of a wounded man from the "old world" who seeks out healing within an element in the "new world."[7] The shepherd staff, which was a regularly featured element in Beuys's art, could be variously interpreted as an instrument for fending off predators (and perhaps disagreeable critics) and/or corralling the flock (and devotees).

It is also significant that the coyote is an important symbol within Native American mythology, and so Beuys's action also raises questions about woundedness within the American historical psyche.[8] All of these critics raise the significance of *I Like America* to mythical proportions.

As Taylor Worley points out, one of the significant problems for those who regard Beuys as a shaman is their tendency to assign impossibly grand aims to Beuys's art. As an example, Worley quotes Götz Adriani, who writes,

> Beuys seeks in his life and work the restoration of the lost unity of nature and spirit, of cosmos and intellect, and places against goal-determined rationalism a way of thinking which includes archetypical, mythical, and magical-religious associations.[9]

As Worley insightfully remarks, these critics "appear to take Beuys fully at his word and reverence him as the healer rather than the sign of the healer."[10] For these scholars, Beuys's myth making opens new possibilities—perhaps even a new reality—for humankind. They see Beuys's work as both a critique of modern secularism as spiritually vacuous and a way to re-enchant Western culture by healing its spiritual trauma. But one wonders if their vision of re-enchantment is merely a juxtaposition of premodern magic against modern sophistication.

Equally passionate in their perception of Beuys are those critics

---

[6] Alain Borer, *The Essential Joseph Beuys*, ed. Lothar Schirmer (London: Thames & Hudson, 1996), 23. Borer's understanding of myth in relation to Beuys's work is nuanced such that he lets go of any claim for historical accuracy, but he still believes the myth is necessary for understanding Beuys's work.

[7] Lucrezia De Domizio Durini, *The Felt Hat: Joseph Beuys: A Life Told*, trans. Howard Roger MacLean (Milano: Edizioni Charta, 1997), 52.

[8] As is often noted, Beuys's inclusion of animals in his work is directly related to his interest in various traditional mythologies. See Stachelhaus, *Joseph Beuys*, 54–60.

[9] Götz Adriani, in Götz Adriani et al., *Joseph Beuys: Life and Works* (Woodbury, NY: Barron's Educational, 1979), 2.

[10] Taylor Worley, "Theology and Contemporary Visual Art: Making Dialogue Possible," (PhD diss., University of Saint Andrews, 2009), 175.

who outright reject "the story." They regard Beuys's myth making as deceptive and dangerous. Benjamin Buchloh, in an essay responding to Beuys's Guggenheim retrospective, disproved Beuys's myth of origins. Buchloh deconstructed "the story," element by element. For example, responding to photographic evidence of Beuys's crashed plane, photographs first published in Götz Adriani's book, Buchloh asked, "And who took the photographs? The Tartars with their fat-and-felt camera?"[11] By suggesting that it is a compensation for the facts of a life that Beuys cannot, or does not, want to live with, Buchloh describes "the story" and Beuys's myth making as an attempt to "deny his participation in the German war and his citizenship."[12] Ultimately, argues Buchloh, Beuys uses myth making like a child who hides his eyes from the horror. Buchloh's devastating, and very personal, attack upon Beuys leaves little room for more critical appraisal of his work. Without Beuys's personal mythology intact, all of his other mythologies deteriorate: *I Like America* appears to be little more than a sham calculated to ensure the continued worship of his devotees.

Although Mark Rosenthal shares Buchloh's skepticism regarding Beuys's personal mythology, he moves beyond this skepticism by considering Beuys's body of work in terms of its formal relationships.[13] He focuses his interpretation of *I Like America* on Beuys's theory of sculpture. Movement is the central feature of his theory: Beuys considers his work to exist within a movement between chaos and order, organic and crystalline, hot and cold, etc. When turning to *I Like America*, Rosenthal highlights the relationship between the roaring turbine noise and the musical triangle as a dipolar aspect of the action pointing toward chaos and order. He quotes Beuys, who says that the triangle "was intended as an impulse of consciousness directed towards the coyote—it helped to restore his harmonized movements."[14] Perhaps the action as a whole can be interpreted as a movement from estrangement to reconciliation in the relationship between the coyote and Beuys, who also, as Rosenthal notes, form a bipolar relation of innocence and experience.[15]

---

[11] Benjamin Buchloh, "Beuys: The Twilight of the Idol," in *Joseph Beuys: Mapping the Legacy*, 202.
[12] Ibid., 203.
[13] Mark Rosenthal et al., *Joseph Beuys: Actions, Vitrines, Environments* (Houston: Menil Foundation, 2004).
[14] Quoted in ibid., 42.
[15] Ibid., 64. Rosenthal, in fact, suggests that the theme of innocence and experience in Beuys's work is rooted in "the story" because Beuys portrayed himself as the experienced and cultured European who is nursed to health by the Tartars and so returned to a state of innocence.

The formal relationships of the action aside, Rosenthal is still attentive to the deep irony betrayed by the title because, as he notes, Beuys offered little evidence that he appreciated America, and in 1974 there was still little serious American engagement with his work.[16]

Although Buchloh proves "the story" to be factually unbelievable, his absolute rejection of Beuys's myth making leaves him no strategy of engaging works such as *I Like America*. Is it best to dispense with Beuys's myth making altogether, and so also his social, political, economic, and religious aspirations, and to regard his work as a complex aesthetic of formal relationships? Rosenthal's formal analysis of Beuys's work is helpful because it locates significant elements in a body of work that, at first glance, may appear chaotic. But his tendency to separate Beuys's theory of sculpture from his political thought, or what Beuys actually called Social Sculpture, seems artificial.[17] Is it possible to offer a more positive assessment of Beuys's myth making practice while not placing impossible expectations upon *I Like America*?

In his essay "Joseph Beuys: Between Showman and Shaman," Donald Kuspit attempts to maintain a skeptical attitude toward Beuys's myth of origins, and yet to deflect Buchloh's negative criticisms.[18] Kuspit points out that Beuys's persona is actually an antihero, and not an object worthy of worship, as Buchloh suggests. Kuspit sees Beuys's myth of origins in a positive light by suggesting that "personal mythology is a way of dealing with trauma, and as such is necessary for psychological survival."[19] Thus, he views Beuys's art, in general, as a form of self-healing from the trauma of World War II, and also as Beuys's wish to heal others from the same trauma. He writes, "In general, artistic action reveals the communal character of personal trauma. Artistic action makes it part of collective mythology. Artistic action does not avoid history, but heals its victims."[20] Kuspit grants to Beuys's myth of origins, and to his persona as an artist, a

[16] Ibid., 89.
[17] For Beuys, this connection appears to have been obvious. He says, "the true foundation of Action Art is the element of movement . . ." See "Joseph Beuys in Conversation with Friedhelm Mennekes," in Joseph Beuys, *In Memoriam Joseph Beuys: Obituaries, Essays, and Speeches,* trans. Timothy Nevill (Bonn: Inter Nationes, 1986), 33.
[18] Donald Kuspit, "Joseph Beuys: Between Showman and Shaman," in *Joseph Beuys: Diverging Critiques,* ed. David Thistlewood (Liverpool, UK: Liverpool University Press, 1995), 27–50.
[19] Ibid., 28.
[20] Ibid., 29.

psychological significance, or what Kuspit calls a "subjective realism," that sidesteps Buchloh's and Rosenthal's critical remarks about Beuys the trickster.

Interpreting *I Like America*, Kuspit emphasizes the way that the action is therapeutic for Beuys as a dialogue between victim and victimizer. He suggests that Beuys plays the roles of both victim (even symbolizing all victims) and victimizer. But unlike most victimizers, Beuys approaches his victim with empathy: "In a gesture of empathy, the victimizer's guilt leads him or her to lend his or her life to the victim, which means that the victimizer feels what it would be like to live and die as a victim."[21] The difficult task of developing empathy for the victim, which inevitably produces strong feelings of guilt in the victimizer, is the healing regimen "that Beuys demands of his German audience."[22] Kuspit also interprets the coyote psychologically as an infantile version of Beuys's self. Here he explicitly draws a connection between Beuys's myth of origins and *I Like America*:

> He survived it [the war] by internalizing the warmth and support of the Tartars, and above all by identifying with the Tartar leader, a shaman who became his spiritual mother. Similarly, in *I Like America and America Likes Me*, Beuys the concerned shepherd mothers Beuys the infantile captive, symbolized by a hunted wild animal in need of guidance and care to survive.[23]

According to Kuspit, *I Like America* is a ritual or rite of passage through which Beuys seeks wholeness instead of woundedness, and through which he offers the same possibility for others.

Kuspit's emphasis on the psychological significance of Beuys's work provides a viable alternative to the skepticism of Buchloh and Rosenthal, but has he really defended Beuys's myth making? Kuspit places the various myths that Beuys creates at the service of his psychological healing, and so he prefers to view myth pragmatically. Therefore, although Kuspit rescues Beuys's mythology, he does so only for the time being until the healing is accomplished and the world can dispense with Beuys's myth. Furthermore, it would seem that much

---

[21] Ibid., 39.
[22] Ibid.
[23] Kuspit, "Between Showman and Shaman," 47.

of Beuys's work is inescapably social and political, and so cannot be captured within Kuspit's psychological framework.

Some scholars perceive Beuys's myth making through the prism of his own self-described social, political, and economic thought. Thierry de Duve, for example, considers Beuys through the lens of Marxism.[24] He describes Beuys in Marxist terms as the proletarian: the one who simultaneously embodies a utopian vision of the future but also presently suffers under modern capitalism. According to Duve, Beuys hopes to move beyond the problems of the proletarian by emancipating the creative potential latent in all human beings.[25] Thus, Duve makes a further connection between Marx and Beuys: where Marx speaks of labor, Beuys speaks of creativity.[26] Beuys's declaration that "everyone is an artist" is a statement of political liberation that seeks to steal back human creativity from an oppressive capitalist system and return it to the masses.

Linda Weintraub organizes her essay on Beuys as a commentary on Beuys's document *Organization for Direct Democracy through Referendum (Free People's Initiative) June, 1971.*[27] Thus, she is primarily interested in the way that Beuys's political thought influenced his art. Like Duve, she observes that Beuys's call for everyone to be an artist, or what he also called Social Sculpture, plays a central role in his thought. When she addresses *I Like America*, she applies Beuys's political vision, which included founding the *Political Party for Animals* in 1974, to the action, saying, "in Beuys' world view, all living creatures possess creative potential. Animals, for instance, can help people reactivate their repressed creativity. . . . [In *I Like America*...] Beuys communed with a representative of the animal realm."[28] Significantly, Weintraub also highlights that the René Block Gallery is located in an affluent area of New York City, and she suggests that this contrasts with the juxtaposition Beuys is making between civilization and nature. She believes

---

[24] Thierry de Duve, "Joseph Beuys, or the Last of the Proletarians," in *Joseph Beuys: The Reader*, ed. Claudia Mesch and Viola Michely (Cambridge, MA: MIT Press, 2007), 134–150.

[25] Ibid., 141. Duve is rather pessimistic about Beuys's utopian vision: "For this tragic and optimistic Janus is above all pathetic; both his faces are turned backward, towards the modernity he brings to a close. It could not be otherwise, since that which Beuys promised by creativity is what all of artistic modernity never ceased to promise, to hope for, to invoke as the emancipatory horizon of its achievement."

[26] That Beuys might have made this connection himself can be seen clearly in his silkscreen lithograph *Creativity = Capital* (1983).

[27] Linda Weintraub, "Joseph Beuys: Political Reformation," in *Art on the Edge and Over* (Litchfield, CT: Art Insights, 1996), 177–183.

[28] Ibid., 182.

that the key to interpreting *I Like America* lies in Beuys's choice to dispense with the normal (civilized) means of dealing with a wild animal and borrow a strategy from the coyote's own behavior. And conversely, Weintraub suggests, "the coyote displayed what in humans would be called moral consciousness"[29] by not harming Beuys. In this way, *I Like America* disrupts the oppressive victim-aggressor relationship, and points toward the possibility of greater creative freedom.

Social, political, and economic interpretations of *I Like America* are appealing because they bring to light what is clearly a dominant theme in Beuys's work as a whole. But these interpretations are also dissatisfying because they tend to reduce the mythical quality of his *I Like America* into social, political, or economic ideals, and they do not pause to consider the motivation behind Beuys's vision for the future of humanity in creative freedom. Is Beuys motivated purely by a political ideology, or does his vision for society have deeper roots within a much broader system of values for humanity and the cosmos as a whole? As Beuys's maxim "everyone is an artist" suggests, it appears that he is working with a concept of the nature of humanity, and, as some scholars suggest, this concept cannot be wrested from its theological framework.

Some scholars choose to critically embrace Beuys's myth making through the lens of Christian theology. Friedhelm Mennekes, a Jesuit priest and director of a center for contemporary art (Kunst-Station Sankt Peter) in Cologne, views Beuys's Christology as the foundation of his artistic practice. Mennekes writes,

> [T]he Christology of Joseph Beuys is not a theory, but rather a real, fundamental Christo-Praxie, i.e. a decision for Christ, a discipling of the self. For Beuys, Christ is the actual representative of humanity since the Resurrection. There is no other possibility for the individual except to assume the role of Christ. Here lies the possibilities for humanity; life is brought to completion through death.[30]

Beuys was also very interested in Rudolf Steiner's anthroposophy, and especially his notion of the "Christ impulse." Beuys describes the Christ impulse in this way:

---

[29] Ibid.
[30] Friedhelm Mennekes, *Joseph Beuys: Christus Denken* (*Thinking Christ*) (Stuttgart: Katholisches Bibelwerk, 1996), 110.

So now it is dead, the earth is dead. But now, how can this death be surpassed, how can it be renewed, or regenerated. . . . And this charges humankind with the total responsibility for the fate of the earth and for humankind's possibility for life on earth. . . . There is a possibility for humankind's development. And this is the secret, or this mystery, or this mystic, existing in Christianity, or in the impulse of Christ.[31]

Beuys may have moved beyond Steiner's understanding of the Christ impulse, but what he seems to have principally gained from Steiner is a developmental view of humanity as participating in the fate of the cosmos. Drawing upon Mennekes's writing, Taylor Worley suggests that spiritual re-enchantment, of both art and human society, is a helpful framework through which to interpret Beuys.[32] Significantly, he suggests that Beuys's myth of origins can be interpreted through the lens of Christ's death and resurrection. He draws interesting parallels between Beuys and his fellow German Dietrich Bonhoeffer, who struggled to find room for Christianity within a "religionless" society. By focusing on Beuys's relation to Christian theology, both Mennekes and Worley provide a theological framework for Beuys's artistic practice.

Mennekes and Worley suggest that Beuys's Christology impacts his artistic practice in at least two significant ways. First, it influences Beuys's decision to explore the use of mundane and even foul materials. Worley helpfully suggests that where Marcel Duchamp denigrates art by exalting the banal, Beuys chooses to discover the extraordinary within the ordinary.[33] In view of Christ's incarnation, the entire world takes on a sacramental character latent with spiritual energies and possibilities. Second, Beuys's Christology influences his claim that everyone is an artist. His actions are often open-ended, so that they call upon the audience to participate in or complete the performance, and so also assume their responsibility of creatively shaping the world.

Exploring *I Like America* in light of Beuys's theological commitments seems, at first, a frustrating task because the action lacks any obvious Christian imagery, other than the shepherd's crook. Both

---

[31] Joseph Beuys, in *Joseph Beuys Talks to Louwrien Wijers* (Amsterdam: Kantoor Voor Cultuur Extracten, 1980), 45.
[32] Worley, "Theology and Contemporary Visual Art," 170–216.
[33] Ibid., 198.

Mennekes and Worley privilege Beuys's action *MANRESA* (1966) because, taking place at the historical center of Spanish Ignatian spirituality and including a large cross, it lends itself more easily to such a perspective.[34] By contrast, *I Like America* is more obviously influenced by Native American mythology. But the inclusion of other religious mythologies is not necessarily grounds to dispense with a Christian interpretation. As Mennekes and Worley suggest, Beuys's choice to include nontraditional materials, which they argue is a direct application of his understanding of the incarnation, is just as operative in *I Like America* as it is in the rest of his work. *I Like America* also has a very incarnational quality as it is a meeting of two rather different sorts of beings: a human and a coyote. Weintraub's suggestion that Beuys sometimes takes on the behavior of the coyote corroborates this view, as does Beuys's appearance as a shepherd, for Jesus is also portrayed as the good shepherd. Furthermore, the suggestion made by several thinkers that *I Like America* is a form of healing, whether psychological, spiritual, or social, accords with Beuys's own interest in the healings and miracles of Jesus.[35] But one wonders how far it is possible to stretch this interpretation because it seems clear that Beuys comes to the coyote for *his own* healing, and so perhaps this is not an image of the Christian God assuming human flesh to heal it. At this point, Worley's connection between Beuys and Bonhoeffer is illuminating because both stress the importance of God choosing to suffer with humanity in the person of Jesus, and both emphasize that God's glory is hidden in creation. In other words, the incarnation is an event of remarkable paradoxes in which God is both revealed and concealed. Jesus presents himself as Lord of the cosmos, but also as a human being who is in need—who on the cross can say, "I thirst."

Beuys's persona as theologian, of all his personas, has been most underappreciated. By drawing out the theological influence upon Beuys's work, Mennekes and Worley highlight certain aspects of his work that might otherwise go unnoticed. Furthermore, by placing Beuys in conversation with Bonhoeffer, Worley elucidates what is surely one of Beuys's overall aims: to overthrow the modern secularism

---

[34] See Friedhelm Mennekes, "Joseph Beuys: *MANRESA*," in *Joseph Beuys: Diverging Critiques*, 149–164; and Worley, "Theology and Contemporary Visual Art," 209–211.

[35] Mennekes, *Christus Denken*, 8.

that led to the destruction and despair of World War II. But even in Worley's theological perspective, Beuys's myth making remains open to Buchloh's critique that by coloring history with myth Beuys is simply choosing not to look at the facts as they are. Even if Beuys's myth making can be interpreted through the lens of Christian theology, one could still argue that Christianity is just another myth implicated in Beuys's self-delusion.

How one perceives Beuys's complex personal mythology greatly influences the way that one interprets *I Like America*. One biographer describes Beuys's oeuvre as a many-sided diamond that is complex, but unified.[36] Each of the five personas discussed in this essay attempt to provide this unity for Beuys's work as a whole, and so also a key to the interpretation of any one particular work. Some personas leave more questions than others, but all examine important and relevant aspects of *I Like America*. While it is tempting to arbitrate between these different interpretations, it may be more true to Beuys's totalizing and inter-disciplinary vision of reality to see these different perspectives as evidence of the multi-valent and complex nature of *I Like America*. There still remains, however, the question of whether Beuys's myth making should be understood as liberating or as deceiving, and on this issue there appears to be little room for equivocating. We have seen a variety of ways to deal with Beuys's myth making, but lacking in the Beuys scholarship is a robust concept of myth as more than mere distortion of historical fact.

In interpreting Beuys, J. R. R. Tolkien may be a valuable dialogue partner who can offer such a concept of myth. Tolkien is most well known for his massive fantasy novels such as *The Silmarillion*, *The Hobbit*, and *The Lord of the Rings* trilogy. These books represent a remarkable achievement of mythological writing. Tolkien and Beuys might have found much in common: both were Catholic, both vehemently opposed modern secularism, both experienced the devastation of war, and both were intensely interested in northern European mythology. But Tolkien was an academic and scholarly writer, and so it is not surprising that we find in Tolkien a more complex and subtle concept of myth.

Tolkien develops his concept of myth most fully in his essay "On

---

[36] Durini, *Felt Hat*, 9.

Fairy-Stories."[37] According to Tolkien, myth and reality are inseparably related. He uses the image of a bubbling cauldron into which the
figures of myth and history are placed to mingle and season. At the
same time, however, myth opens up another world distinct from reality that—if it is well made—prompts readers to "believe" in it, and not
merely to suspend disbelief. The possibility of the other world that
myth generates, says Tolkien, is predicated upon "the hard recognition that things are so in the world as it appears under the sun; on a
recognition of fact, but not a slavery to it."[38] Ironically, myth would be
impossible if one were not able to distinguish it from the way things
really are. Following from this relationship between myth and reality,
is the benefit of myth as allowing one to see things anew. Tolkien's suggestion is that, as things in the world become familiar, human beings
take possession of them, but myth grants humanity freedom from that
possessiveness. He writes that myth,

> because it is mainly trying to do something else (make something
> new), may open your hoard and let all the locked things fly away like
> cage-birds. The gems all turn into flowers or flames, and you will
> be warned that all you had (or knew) was dangerous and potent,
> not really effectively chained, free and wild; no more yours than they
> were you.[39]

In other words, the very act of myth making reminds one of the givenness of reality, and also that one cannot possess this givenness—the
historical fact of one's past and history—because one receives it as a
gracious gift. It is a feature of the graciousness of this gift that it does
not enslave humanity. This understanding of givenness is central to
Tolkien's view of humanity as sub-creators: creatures who make secondary worlds within the primary world of their Creator.

In light of Tolkien's understanding of myth, one could suggest that
Beuys's myth making is not an attempt to hide from the cold, hard
facts of his complicity in World War II, but that his ability to accept
and comprehend those facts allows him to explore the meaning of his
past through mythology. The creation of other mythologies throughout
his work, such as the action *I Like America*, is related to the liberating

---

[37] J. R. R. Tolkien, "On Fairy-Stories," in *Tree and Leaf* (London: George Allen & Unwin, 1964), 11–70.
[38] Ibid., 50.
[39] Ibid., 53.

power of Beuys's own personal mythology, and also extends this power to those who participate in his actions. Once again we meet the force of the theological interpretation, for ultimately the liberating power of Beuys's myth making cannot reside in Beuys himself, but it must ultimately lie, as Tolkien says, in the gracious gift of the Creator to the sub-creator. True creative freedom, it might be said, does not derive from the human desire for autonomy, but from the joyous acceptance of a gracious gift. This view of creative freedom is present in Beuys's *I Like America*, especially in his relationship to the coyote. As Beuys himself suggests, when he hands the coyote his gloves to play with, he is also symbolically granting the coyote the power of possession that humans arrogate to themselves.[40] The relationship between Beuys and coyote is more like one of equals—even though Beuys as shepherd has a unique role to play—who allow themselves both to possess and to be possessed by the other. In his meeting with the coyote, Beuys finds ways to meet the coyote on its own terms, as wild and not domesticated, even though they meet in a space constructed by human hands. Through the exercise of his freedom to know the wild animal as wild, and so not to know the coyote as a possession, Beuys's myth making points toward the sort of freedom that can "let all the locked things fly away like cage-birds." Both *I Like America* and Beuys's myth making, in general, offer a vision of how one might live in the world that is deeply resonant with Tolkien's suggestion that human beings are sub-creators who creatively accept the gracious gift of their Creator.

---

[40] Caroline Tisdall, *Joseph Beuys: Coyote* (London: Thames & Hudson, 2008), 15.

Portrait of John Walford: Number 2, 2009. Photo by Steven Jaehnert.

AFTERWORD
A Portrait of E. John Walford

JOEL SHEESLEY

Painting a portrait of John Walford is an exciting challenge. It calls for both an objective reckoning and a subjective interpretation that infuses dispassionate observation with subjectivity, life, and purpose. Walford is a visually striking subject and so a sense of motif or graphic focus is ready at hand. But such strong features can invite one into an easy and superficial caricature. His charisma must be balanced with a diffidence whose visual appearance is harder to represent. Somehow the picture must tell a candid story, but it should also acknowledge evidence of life's interruptions and subplots. I pick up my brushes with caution but with hope that my thirty-year working relationship with John Walford will give me the perspective I need and allow me to shed some valuable light on the person I have come to respect and love.

The first part of my picture I draw not from life but from photographs. It's the foundational "blocking-in," but I must depend on secondary sources. The picture here is of an aristocratic and privileged young man growing up on a country estate in England. It is the story of that person's coming of age in the revolutionary youth culture of the 1960s; of his disillusionment with the system of wealth and the high-society future that he saw rushing forward to overwhelm him; ultimately of his despair of life itself. It is also the story of his discovery of a truly abundant life found not in the posh yet mind-numbing status quo of an elite social class, but in the adventure of answering God's vocation; God's call to an indeterminate yet grace-filled journey leading not to an end, but to constant new beginnings. The subject of my picture thus first appears roughly outlined in the early stages of his bold and yet humbly accepted undertaking to follow his perception of God's call, to leave his attachments in Britain and Europe and come to America.

In the summer of 1981 a mid-thirtyish John Walford arrived in Wheaton, Illinois. He had been hired to teach art history and to assume the chairmanship of the art department at Wheaton College. Just prior to his appointment, the college president, Hudson Armerding, had harbored serious reservations about whether Wheaton College could support a department of art. He presented his doubts in the form of a proposal to the faculty to drop the college's art major. When the college faculty voted unanimously to retain the major, Armerding's strategy turned to finding what he considered dependable leadership for the department.

John Walford had studied art history with Hans Rookmaaker at the Free University of Amsterdam, and then completed a PhD in art history under the supervision of Michael Jaffe at Cambridge University. At Cambridge's Wolfson College he had been granted the Speelman Fellowship, dedicated to the study of Dutch and Flemish art. He wrote his dissertation on Jacob van Ruisdael. In all of his scholarship John Walford applied the insight of his mentor H. R. Rookmaaker: that the worlds of culture and nature, deeply profound within themselves, are imbued with and also revelatory of spiritual realities that are of consequence to everyone.

President Armerding's experience with the practicing artists in the Wheaton College art department had left him unconvinced of their capacities to act as strong departmental leaders. In Walford, Armerding found a different kind of person. Walford was a historian who held a prestigious academic degree. Well-known evangelical leaders attested to his Christian faith. Further, his commitment to the task of leading the art department was assured by his willingness to leave Britain for the United States. John Walford seemed to embody everything for which Hudson Armerding was looking.

Armerding himself was an esthetically sensitive man. But he was also a man of somewhat austere principle for whom military service had been extremely influential in shaping his conception of leadership and institutional responsibility. He had difficulty accepting strains of Romanticism and twentieth-century Modernism. Perhaps most importantly, Armerding also represented the mindset typical of many of the College's board of trustees and a significant segment of the College's broader constituency. This group perceived art with suspicion. Art could not compete with theology and the sciences for a position of central intellectual importance.

For Walford, art and theology were best understood as natural partners whose historic cooperation had sadly begun to unravel sometime in the Enlightenment. But even that unraveling continued to offer a rich perspective on the ceaseless longings of the human spirit. At its weakest, Armerding's outlook advised a kind of retreat from emerging conventions of contemporary art. Walford, schooled in the thinking of H. R. Rookmaaker, had learned a healthy skepticism for the programs of late Modernism, but he also had absorbed Rookmaaker's penchant for engagement rather than retreat. This set the stage for a respectful but persistent tension with the College administration as John Walford began to take leadership of his new department.

Walford's mixed stance toward Modernism also set the stage for some tension between John Walford and the practicing artists who constituted the art department. For these artists, the tenets of Modernism were foundational assumptions in the practice of art. Furthermore, some forms of Christian belief, not founded on a Reformed theological outlook, discovered affinities rather than discontinuities between the motives of Modernist aesthetics and Christian vision. Walford's early skepticism of Modernist aesthetics met a regular challenge from his artist colleagues, a challenge that John Walford would later describe to be "as unpleasant as chewing on sand." Walford would have to find a way to bargain amiably with both the College administration and his new artist colleagues.

Other obstacles had to be met head on. Walford was the only art history professor in a department that had never before hired, nor been led by, a full-time art historian. The visual resources for teaching art history were extremely limited, and what existed had been drawn together for teaching the most general kind of survey courses. As he prepared for his fall semester classes, Walford found himself in a very difficult situation. He had to teach courses for which the art department proved to have a significant deficit of good quality slides, the primary visual resource upon which art history pedagogy depends. Where and how to procure these things, in an unfamiliar culture, where John had yet to develop contacts with fellow art historians to whom he might turn for help, proved daunting. What's more, his new colleagues hardly appreciated his predicament since the department's slide collection had proven adequate for their needs.

Furthermore, John Walford the seventeenth-century Dutch specialist was now responsible for teaching the whole history of Western art. At Wheaton College, art history had traditionally been offered as little more than a general background for the work of studio artists.

No thought had been given to the concept of art history as a major field of study in itself. Walford's vision was larger. But his larger vision only placed a larger burden on his own shoulders. As a result he found himself in a ceaseless state of preparation, working on lectures about periods and styles of art far from his area of specialization, and constantly frustrated by the lack of adequate visual resources to convey his work. Though the first years at Wheaton brought John Walford to near intellectual and emotional exhaustion, burning his candle at both ends, this stress does not show itself much in our portrait. Walford met these pressures with enthusiasm and a mature sense of duty.

Walford's mind, however, could not rest solely on the daunting task of developing the art history curriculum. As the chair of a studio art department he also had to learn and defend the logic of a studio curriculum. Further, he would have to learn to appreciate the working habits of studio artists whose scholarship bore little resemblance to that of art historians. Colleagues outside of the art department hardly understood nor could offer much consolation. Years after the College began to acknowledge his accomplishments in scholarship, teaching, and administration, it was still not uncommon for faculty from other departments to ask John questions about what kind of *artist* he was. It was thanks to John's forbearing and gregarious nature that he was able to find a few understanding friends.

My portrait now needs to reflect some sign of this gregarious wit (perhaps in the lifting of that eyebrow . . . there) because all of John's British sense of duty might have broken down in the absence of a good sense of humor. In fact, through that humor, relationships with his art colleagues and the College administration began to produce more pleasure and fellowship than confrontation and pain. Collegiality among art department faculty became legendary on campus. In the mid-1980s, Walford had achieved sufficient stature at the College to persuade the administration to substantially renovate the art facilities in Adams Hall.

Within a few years he had developed and refined an art history curriculum that he could teach without draining away every ounce of his creative energy. Eventually his vision of training art historians and not just practicing artists began to bear fruit. Among so many of his students, the Wheaton graduates contributing essays to this volume are shining examples of his mentorship.

Walford also found time to attend to his own research and, in 1991, Yale University Press published *Jacob van Ruisdael and the Perception of Landscape*, based on John's dissertation. He became well known as an insightful and entertaining lecturer and in 1997 was awarded Wheaton College's Senior Teacher of the Year Award. He was also noticed for his analytic mind, and he began to be invited as a consultant to help evaluate and make recommendations to art departments at other universities.

John recognized his own gift as the ability "to state complex problems in simple terms." Based on that insight he undertook what would be one of the most demanding intellectual and organizational projects of his career, the writing of *Great Themes in Art*, an introductory art history textbook published by Prentice-Hall in 2002. The demands of writing a nationally marketed textbook that carried the marks of John's conviction about the importance of art's spiritual and religious significance at a time of intense theoretical and political upheaval in the art world proved a substantial task. *Great Themes* is a stunning achievement that offers a holistic approach to understanding the long run of art history. Given the limiting requirements and vested interests imposed by so many different stakeholders in the contents of such a textbook, the book is as much a wonder of diplomacy as it is a shining example of integrative art historical thinking. In response, Wheaton College awarded Walford the Senior Scholar Achievement Award.

John Walford, who always conducted his public persona in a very visible way, was, at this point, his most visible as a scholar, teacher, mentor, administrator, and public speaker. So my portrait begins to take on the appearance of so many pictures of accomplished men whose self-assured looks convey a comfortable self-confidence. Upon completion of *Great Themes*, and after twenty-one years of serving first the needs of artists, John Walford resigned the position of chair of the art department to concentrate more fully on teaching and research.

It is time to give my subject a rest from his pose, but as he steps off the modeling stand I look carefully and somewhere (Is it in his shoulders?) I am surprised to see the slightest sign of being ill at ease. Maybe the discomfort has been there all along and I am just noticing it now, but as he steps out of the light and relaxes from his pose as extroverted and confident administrator, scholar, and leader it seems he moves into an alien space. It is as if a strange room has opened up before him and now invites him in to confront a long-standing emotional fragility. For the first time, I begin to perceive my subject as vulnerable. On two occasions during the next ten years John Walford would have to take extended leaves of absence from his teaching obligations to address debilitating bouts of deeply set personal anxiety.

In typical Walford fashion, John's response to these periods of discouragement was to face them head on. He sought recourse to the healing power of the Christian faith and prayer that have always sustained him. He also actively sought psychological help and applied himself directly to recommended therapy. One consequence of this therapy was John's rediscovery of photography as a medium of personal expression. The advent of digital technology had removed the obstacle of the wet darkroom and its inhibiting logistics. John quickly absorbed the possibilities of digital cameras and of image manipulation made so feasible through Photoshop. He soon realized that his fascination with the visual images he began to produce bore a direct relationship to the history of images that he had so long studied as an art historian.

Photographic pairings of art historical images with images from everyday life present possibilities of formal and iconographic connection that now offer John a new format for art historical thinking. Based on formal parallels and sometimes iconographic dissonances, Walford began to create polyptychs, images composed of several discreet photographs that interact to create meaning much as traditional Christian diptychs and triptychs have. Through these images he is exploring, now in nonverbal terms, an interaction with art history on a new level. He has also begun to explore new avenues of comment on consumer culture, current events, and more traditional themes of art such as the journey of life and the enigmatic relationships of beauty, desire, lust, and greed. Much of this work has been collected in *An Art Historian's Sideways Glance*, published in 2009 by Piquant Editions.

But our picture of John Walford now must morph further to depict him as a fully connected cyberspace aficionado. Walford has established an active presence on Flickr.com. Here he interacts freely with a wide community sharing his art historical (and now artistic) insights in a "classroom" quite unimaginable when John first took up the challenge to teach art history. Indeed through digital photography and Flickr.com, Walford may have found his ideal pulpit combining virtual involvement in a social network with the opportunity to share insights gained over a lifetime of looking and thinking about art.

Retirement is something of a non sequitur in John Walford's world. Remember that to retire, or retreat, goes against one of the first principles John learned from Rookmaaker: the principle of engagement. But engagement for John has always had its price. It has come at a cost. Depiction of the cost or toll exacted on a vibrant and well-lived life is often the most moving dimension of a well-made portrait. The artist who can somehow represent this wear and tear, holding it in tension and locating it within a sense of wholeness, does a great thing. We look so often to the eyes in such a portrait to communicate this admixture of the working of law and grace in a life. In fact, it is borne throughout the entire body.

So I see John Walford as I once tried in vain to paint him. He is a tall, warm-skinned man wearing a tweedy jacket and tie, and standing near his office door, his thin, wiry torso curves to his left as he leans a forearm on a tall gray filing cabinet. A large Michelangelesque left hand droops heavily over the cabinet top. His jacket swings open as the other arm hangs loosely across his protruding right hip. There is tension and energy in this *dehanchement* or weight shift. I am reminded of *The Virgin of Paris*, whose springy body spritely supports the Christ child, but Walford's hand has all the languid weight of *David*. These opposing energies interact and support a head with something of a lion-like nose and bearded muzzle. I perceive two very differently shaped eyes. He is immediately photogenic, and to me almost entirely unpaintable.

What I see before me is this amazing body, this vulnerable honest man so willingly looking out at me, inviting me to witness his own witness. This spiritually enlivened, awkwardly postured pose begs me to get it right, to find the way to represent the history of tensions in its muscles and bones, the objective secrets it bears on its skin, and its hopeful anticipation of the future. These two different eyes look out under heavily shaded brows and sparkle quietly like dark jewels. I try. I try hard, but in the end my painting simply does not do him justice. I have been unable to pull all the parts together. My painting fails to point away from itself and toward my model's searching curiosity and persistent vitality. All the sessions end in my frustration and embarrassment. Finally we abandon the project. I am remorseful to have wasted his time. He, somehow, remains optimistic and quietly forgiving.

CONTRIBUTORS

Dr. James Romaine is a New York based art historian who has published extensively on the history of Christianity and the visual arts. He is president of the Association of Scholars of Christianity in the History of Art (ASCHA; http://christianityhistoryart.org/). Dr. Romaine earned a PhD in art history from the Graduate Center of the City University of New York. He is an associate professor of art history and chair of the department of art history at Nyack College.

Dr. Graham Birtwistle gained degrees in art history at Manchester University (1964) and the VU University Amsterdam (1970, 1986). He subsequently taught and researched in modern art and theory at the VU University (initially under Dr. H. R. Rookmaaker) from 1971 till his retirement in 2004. Since the 1970s, his main research theme has been twentieth-century primitivism, and out of this has grown a specialization in European artists of the mid-century Cobra movement. Many of his publications deal with Cobra and its associated artists such as Asger Jorn, Karel Appel, Constant, and Corneille.

Dr. William Dyrness is professor of theology and culture at Fuller Theological Seminary and founding member of the Brehm Center for Worship, Theology, and the Arts. His current research focuses on the visual culture of Islam, Buddhism, and Christianity, and on the influence of Christianity on modern art. His most recent books are *Poetic Theology: God and the Poetics of Everyday Life* (2011), and *Primer on Christian Worship* (2009).

Linda Møskeland Fuchs investigates the development of Christian imagery in late Roman art. She serves as president of the governing board of Chesterton House, a Christian study center affiliated with Cornell University, and on the community advisory board of the Herbert F. Johnson Museum of Art at Cornell. Her background in art, art history, biblical studies, and education includes degrees from Wheaton College, Trinity Evangelical Divinity School, the University of Chicago, and Cornell University.

Marleen Hengelaar-Rookmaaker is editor-in-chief of ArtWay (www.artway. eu), an online resource about the visual arts for individuals and congregations. She did her studies in musicology at the University of Amsterdam. For many years, she worked as an editor, translator, and writer. She edited the *Complete Works* of her father, art historian Hans Rookmaaker, contributed to several books, and wrote numerous articles about popular music, liturgy, and the visual arts. She lives in Zwolle in the Netherlands.

Dr. Rachel Hostetter Smith holds the Gilkison Chair in Art History at Taylor University. The recipient of the Best Article of the Year Award from the journal *Explorations in Renaissance Culture*, Smith publishes on a wide range of topics in the arts including art, architecture, literature, and film. She is project director and curator of the international exhibition *Charis: Boundary Crossings—Neighbors Strangers Family Friends* and is developing a follow-up project in

South Africa with the Nagel Institute for the Study of World Christianity. Smith is the 2009–2010 recipient of the Franklin W. and Joan M. Forman Distinguished Faculty Scholar Award.

Dr. Rachel-Anne Johnson earned her PhD at the University of California, Santa Barbara in 2012. She received her MA in art history from the University of Toronto and her BA in English literature and art history from Wheaton College. Her dissertation, "Suburban Bruegel: Chorography and Rhetoric in Pieter Bruegel's Series of the Months," was supported by the American Association of University Women, the Metropolitan Museum of Art, and the Social Sciences and Humanities Research Council of Canada. Dr. Johnson has lectured frequently on Bruegel's agricultural landscape paintings and is currently working on a monograph based on her dissertation.

Dr. Henry Luttikhuizen is professor of art history at Calvin College. He is coauthor of the second editions of *Northern Renaissance Art: Painting, Sculpture, the Graphic Arts from 1350 to 1575* (Prentice-Hall, 2005) (with James Snyder and Larry Silver); and *Art of the Middle Ages* (Prentice-Hall, 2006) (with James Snyder and Dorothy Verkerk). He recently curated the exhibition *The Humor and Wit of Pieter Bruegel the Elder* (Calvin College, 2010). He is currently completing a book manuscript examining the relationship between visual imagery and devotional practices in late fifteenth-century Holland.

Kaia Magnusen is a doctoral candidate in art history at Rutgers University. She received her bachelor's degree from Wheaton College and her master's degree from the Institute of Fine Arts, New York University. She has taught art history at Rutgers University, Hunter College, and Middlesex County College. She has been a curatorial intern at the Whitney Museum of American Art, the Museum of Modern Art and the Museum of Biblical Art in New York, and the Museo dell'Opera del Duomo in Florence. She has been awarded a Baden-Württemberg Scholarship at the Universität-Konstanz in Konstanz, Germany.

Dr. Matthew J. Milliner is assistant professor of art history at Wheaton College. He studied theology at Princeton Theological Seminary (MDiv) and art history at Princeton University (MA and PhD), where he specialized in Byzantine art.

Anne Roberts is a painter, illustrator, and art historian who has taught for many years at the College of West Anglia in King's Lynn, UK. She trained at Camberwell School of Art, the Royal Academy Schools, and the University of Cardiff, and holds an MPhil from the University of East Anglia for her study on the early-twentieth-century English painter Harold Gilman.

Dr. Calvin Seerveld earned a BA from Calvin College, an MA from the University of Michigan, and a PhD in philosophy and comparative literature at the Free University of Amsterdam. After teaching at Belhaven College (Jackson, MS) and Trinity Christian College (Palos Heights, IL) he became senior member in philosophical aesthetics at the graduate Institute for Christian Studies, Toronto (1972–1995). Older Testament studies and art history are two of his hobbies.

Joel Sheesley is a painter. He graduated with a BFA in painting and drawing from Syracuse University School of Art, and from the University of Denver School of Art with an MFA in painting and printmaking. He teaches art at Wheaton College. His work has been exhibited regularly in Chicago, including at the Chicago Cultural Center in 2010, and in other cities across the country. Mr. Sheesley received an Illinois Arts Council fellowship in 2002. In 2008 Mr. Sheesley's painting was the subject of a major retrospective exhibition at the Brauer Museum of Art at Valparaiso University.

Dr. Jan Laurens Siesling studied art history at the Free University of Amsterdam, where for four years he was an assistant professor, specializing in sixteenth-century Dutch art. He taught for more than twenty years in the international program of the University of Syracuse (NY) in Strasbourg, France, and in the international program of the University of Southern Mississippi in Pontlevoy, France. His publications, in French, Dutch, and English, concern French and Dutch art of the nineteenth and twentieth centuries. In 2007 he was appointed director of the art museum at the University of Southern Mississippi, where he is an assistant professor of art.

Dr. Linda Stratford has a PhD from the State University of New York (Stony Brook) and is an associate professor at Asbury University. She has produced numerous publications and presentations that draw upon cross-disciplinary training in art history, aesthetics, anthropology, and sociology. Her continued interest in the ways in which ideological constructs not only arise from but themselves confine historical narratives is central in her forthcoming manuscript *Artists into Frenchmen*. A cofounder of the Association of Scholars of Christianity in the History of Art (ASCHA), she is completing, with coeditor James Romaine, an edited collection entitled *Methodologies of the History of Christianity in the Visual Arts* (Wipf and Stock).

Matthew Sweet Vanderpoel is a PhD student in the history of Christianity at the University of Chicago Divinity School. He earned his BA in art history and history at Wheaton College. Afterward, he served as a visiting instructor at Université Chrétienne Bilingue du Congo in the Democratic Republic of Congo. His research interests revolve around connecting devotional practices, both popular and elite, to academic theological discourse in the context of late medieval Europe.

James Watkins is a PhD student at the University of St. Andrews, where he participates in the Institute for Theology, Imagination, and the Arts. His dissertation is titled "God, Artist, and Material: Toward an Ethical Paradigm for Artistic Creativity." He is also assistant editor of "Transpositions," a blog and online resource for those interested in the relationship between Christianity and the arts. He holds a BA in studio art from Wheaton College and a MCS in Christianity and the arts from Regent College.

INDEX

Page numbers in *italics* indicate photographs.

Abbot Suger of Saint Denis, 61, 62, 68

Abstract Expressionism, 240, 242, 246–247, 248, 248n30; emergence of American Abstract Expressionism, 243–244; impact of surrealism on, 243

academia, "religious turn" of, 92, 92n4, 97–99

Acts of Peter (apocryphal), 51

Adolf of Utrecht (Apostle of the Frisians), 158

Adriani, Götz, 259

Aeneid (Virgil), 174

Aesop's fables, 116

aevum (eternal time of the visionary state), 60, 68

Alberti, Leon Battista, 94

alchemy, 252

Alpers, Svetlana, 27, 31, 140–141

American Society for Eighteenth-century Studies, 168n6

Amiens Cathedral, labyrinths of, 70

Analysis of Beauty (Hogarth), 169

Antal, Frederick, 166

Antwerp, 112, 139, 140, 144, 148, 149

Apollinaire, Guillaume, 235

architecture, as music in space, 68, 68n26

Armerding, Hudson, 272

art: as an "anachronism," 101, 101n69; evangelical view of as idolatry, 16; existentialist view of, 245–246; as a gift of the Holy Spirit, 34; openness of the church to, 19; status of, 19; as a visual realization of inherent meaning, 31. *See also* art, Christian

art, Christian, 41, 41n1, 105–107; and biblical hermeneutics, 43

Art of Describing, The (Alpers), 140–141

Art Historian's Sideways Glance, An (Walford), 276

art history, 93; Calvinism's role in, 33–34; and Christianity, 35; content-oriented method of, 36, 37; dilation of, 91–92; focus of on iconographic decoding, 31–32; and the providence of God, 32–33; Renaissance art history and the marginalization of art as an expression of religious devotion, 99–100; trends in, 18–19; Vasari's approach to, 94–95; Vienna School of, 96

As You Like It (Shakespeare), 176

Association of Scholars of Christianity in the History of Art (ASCHA), 20, 98

Assumption of the Virgin (Titian [1516–1518]), 37

Audran, Claude, III, 174

Augustus of Primaporta, 48

Autumn Rhythm: Number 30, 1950 (Jackson Pollock [1950]), *238*, 249–250; as an allegorical representation of spiritual rebirth, 239–240; "autumnal" tones of, 239; and the break with the picturing function of art, 240, 244–245; composition of, 241; critical reception of, 253; debt of to other artists, 241; gestural and dance movements within, 250–251; as an iconic example of Abstract Expressionism, 240; size of, 240

Baillods, Jules, 132

Baldass, Ludwig von, 113

baptism, 55

Bassus, Junius, 44–45; funeral of, 45, 45n12

Bassus, Junius Annius, 44, 44n11

Bax, Marty, 233

Beaumont, George, 201

Beckmann, Max, 171

"Beggars' Opera, The" (Gay), 171

Belles Heures (Beautiful Hours [Limbourg brothers]), 77

Belting, Hans, 100

Bening, Simon, 138

Benjamin, Walter, 98, 131

Berengaudus, 65; on John's falling down at the beginning of his revelation when face to face with God, 66

Bergler, Joseph, 183

Bernard, Emile, 211, 220

Beuys, Joseph, 255; on "Action Art," 260n17; Christology of, 263, 264; critics who reject his myth or "the story," 258–259; inclusion of animals in his works, 258, 258n8, 263; interest of in Steiner's concept of the "Christ impulse," 263–264; Marxist interpretation of his work, 262; myths and mythologizing of, 256–258, 256–257n4, 264, 266, 267–268; persona of as a theologian, 265–266; psychological significance of his work, 261–262; as a shaman, 258; theme of innocence and experience in his work, 259, 259n15; theory of movement in sculpture, 259

Bible, the, 170, 210

Blavatsky, Helena P., 232

Bloeiende Appelboom (Piet Mondrian [1912]), *224*, 225–226, 237; Cubist style of, 227–230, 230–231, 234; showing of at the Modern Art Circle, 233–234; stylistic characteristics of, 229–230; Walford's view of, 235

Blotkamp, Carel, 217, 229, 233, 235

Blue Poles (Pollock [1952]), 240

Body of the Dead Christ in the Tomb, The (Hans Holbein [1521]), 124, 132

Boleyn, Anne, 126

Bonhoeffer, Dietrich, 264, 265

books of hours, 77–78, 141–142

Borer, Alain, 258, 258n6

Bosch, Hieronymus, 113

Botticelli, 169

Boucher, François, 169, 173

Bouguereau, William-Adolphe, 171

Brancacci, Felice Michele, 92, 104

Brancacci Chapel (Masolino, Masaccio, and Filippino Lippi [15th century]), *90*, 92; debates concerning who painted the frescos in, 96–97; depiction of Ananias and Sapphira in, 104; effect of the "religious turn" in academic scholarship on scholarship concerning the Brancacci Chapel, 99; as the first view of the modern world, 104–105; image of *Madonna del Popolo*

as the visual and spiritual focus of, 92–93, 92n7, 99–102, 100n62, 106 (see also *Vita*, of Blessed Andre Corsini); lasting influence of Masaccio on, 95; "lush historiography" of, 93–94; painting and themes of the frescoes in, 92, 92n6, 101, 104; realism of the frescoes in, 103–104; as a school of art history, 95–97
Brancusi, Constantin, 225
Braque, Georges, 227, 228, 229, 241
Bredekamp, Hors, 98
Bremmer, H. P., 230, 231
Bressani, Martin, 60
Bronzino (Agnolo di Cosimo), 171
Brown, Lancelot, 170
Brown, Thomas, 191
Brühl, Maria Theresa, 183, 183n17
Bruin, Claas, 237
Bruno, Giordano, 169
Buchloh, Benjamin, 259–260, 261, 266
Buonarroti, Michelangelo, 171
Burckhardt, Jacob, 104–105, 166
burial customs, Roman, 41–42
Bush, The (van Ruisdael), 218, 218n41
Byzantium, 100

calendar illuminations, 137–138
Calvin, John, 33, 174; and the privileging of the ear over the eye, 129
Calvinism: and art, 33–34, 160; and the formation of the Dutch character, 151–152. *See also* Neo-Calvinism
Camille, Michael, 83
Canaletto (Giovanni Antonio Canal), 171
"Candide" (Voltaire), 170
Cardinal Richelieu (de Champaigne [1760]), 169–170
Carmean, E. A., 249
Carmelite Order, 92, 93, 99, 100–101, 101–102, 103, 104; Marian altar of, 101
Carracci, Annibale, 199
cartography, 140; innovations in and the development of landscape painting, 112
Cathedral of Notre-Dame (Paris), 59–60
Celestial Hierarchy (Pseudo-Dionysius), 64
Chain Pier, Brighton (Constable), 202
Champa, Kermit, 233
Chardin, Jean-Baptiste-Siméon, 171, 173
Charles VI (king of France), 77
Chartres Cathedral (c. 1194–1220), 72; experience of the approach into, 67–68; labyrinths of, 70–71; nave of, *58*, sculptural program of, 62–63; stained glass of, 67, 68, 68n24
Children's Games (Pieter Bruegel the Elder [1559–1560]), 143
Christ, Alice, 52n40, 55n51
Christ Asleep during the Tempest (Delacroix), 221
Christianity, 43–44, 109, 208–209, 266; legalization of in the Roman Empire, 44, 48; and the visual arts, 20
Christians, and participation in society, 33
City of God (Augustine), 118, 119
Clark, T. J., 246, 253
Clement of Alexandria, 42
Cleve, Joos van, 112
Coates, Robert M., 250n41

Columbus, Christopher, 169
Constable, Abram, 193
Constable, John, 26; artistic reputation of, 193; copies of van Ruisdael made by, 199–200; distrust of radicalism, 205; exhibition paintings of, 203; inner vision of, 202; landscapes as a vehicle of expression for, 204; loss of his wife and best friend, 203–204; statements of concerning landscape painting, 204–205; visual perception of, 199
Constantine, 48, 55
Constantinople, city plan of, 37
Corsini, Nicolò, 102
Corsinio, Andre, 106. See also *Vita*, of Blessed Andre Corsini,
cosmology, and everyday life, 83–84
Cowper, William, 195–196
Coyote: I Like America and America Likes Me (Joseph Beuys [1974]), *254*, 255, 255n1, 259, 260, 266; expression of creative freedom in, 268; influence of Native American mythology on, 265; lack of Christian imagery in, 264–265; political vision of, 262–263; therapeutic action of, 261; use of the coyote in, 263, 265
Cranach, Lucas (the Elder), 129–131, 130n20, 133, 171
creation, as ordered by God's sovereign decree, 32–33
Cross in the Mountains. See *Tetschen Altar* (Friedrich [1808])
Crucifixion, The (Allegory of Redemption), 129–130
Cubism, 227–230, 231, 234–235, 241
Cutler, Anthony, 98
cynicism, 18

da Carcano, Michele, 128
da Vinci, Leonardo, 94, 168
Dance, The (Antoine Watteau [1717–1718]), *164*, 165, 176
David, Jacques Louis, 171, 173
de Bles, Herri met, 112
de Champaigne, Philippe, 169
de Duve, Thierry, 262, 262n25
de Guevara, Felipe, 113
de Selve, Georges, 125–126, 127, 131
De Stijl, 230, 234
de Voragine, Jacobus, 115
de Vries, Lyckle, 157
Dedham Vale (Constable [1828]), *192*, 193; framing of trees and sky, 201–202; treatment of the foliage in, 196–197
Delacroix, Eugène, 171, 212, 221, 222; repainting of the *Massacre of Scios*, 203
Delaunay, Robert, 225, 242
della Mirandola, Pico, 168
Demosthenes, 50
der Blaue Reiter ("the Blue Rider") art group, 242
der Leck, Bart van, 230
Descartes, René, 170
d'Etaples, Lefèvre, 126
die Brücke ("the bridge") art group, 242
Dinkler, Erich, 48
"Discourses" (Descartes), 170
Doesburg, Theo van, 230
Dominican Order, 99

Doryphoros (Polykleitos), 37
dualism, 19
Dunthorne, John, 200
Dürer, Albrecht, 112, 124; engraving of the fall of
    Adam and Eve, 117
Dutch War of Independence, 161–162

Eckstein, Nicholas, 103
Edict of Milan (A.D. 313), 42
Eighty Years' War, 157, 161n26
Eire, Carlos, 128
Elkins, James, 91, 96–97n38, 99, 166; on the
    history of the interpretation of the Brancacci
    question, 97; on Renaissance art history, 93
Entretiens sur l'architecture (*Lectures on Architecture*
    [Viollet-le-Duc]), 59
Erasmus, 124, 128
Eriugena, 71
essentialism, 246
Eusebius, 65
Evolution (P. Mondrian [1911]), 233, 235
Expressionism, 252. *See also* Abstract
    Expressionism; German Expressionists
"externalization of piety," 128

Falkenburg, Reindert, 118, 142–143
"Fatti di Masolino e di Masaccio" (Longhi), 96
Favier, Jean, 70
Fielding, Henry, 171
Fish, Stanley, 92
Fisher, John, 194–195, 199; death of, 203–204
Florence, 104
Florensky, Pavel, 105, 105–106n104
Floris, Frans, 144
Flowering Apple Tree. See Bloeiende Appelboom (Piet
    Mondrian [1912])
Fragonard, Jean-Honoré, 170, 173
Francis I (king of France), 125, 126, 174
Franciscan Order, 99
Franklin, Benjamin, 169
Free University, Amsterdam (Vrije Universiteit), 15
Freedberg, David, 131
French Ambassadors, The (Hans Holbein [1533]),
    122, 123–124; Holbein's skill at work in
    the presentation of the two main subjects,
    127–128; main scene of, 126–127; and the
    process of secularization, 133–134; symbolism
    of the anamorphic skull in, 130–131
Friedrich, Casper David, 181; defense of his
    Tetschen Altar, 187–188; emphasis on common
    landscape features in a work of art, 186; impor-
    tance of Langham to, 194
Frost, George, 196, 197–198
Fuchs, Rudi, 235–236
funerary art, Christian. *See* sarcophagi, Christian

Gage, John, 67
Gainsborough, Thomas, 169, 173, 196
Ganymede, 83, 85
Garden of Love, The (Rubens), 174
Gassel, Lucas, 112
Gauguin, Paul, 36, 171, 220, 220nn47–48, 241
Gay, John, 171
Georgics (Virgil), 141
Gereformeerde Church (Amsterdam), 231

German Expressionists, 241, 242
Gibson, Walter, 141
Gillot, Claude, 174
Giltaij, Jeroen, 156
Gipfelkreuz crucifix ("summit cross"), 181–182,
    185, 189–190
Glebe Farm, The (Constable [1830]), 194
Gloomy Day, The (Pieter Bruegel the Elder [1565]),
    137, 148
God, 109, 158, 166, 187, 265; communion with,
    72; as "divine darkness," 71; as the "Light of
    Lights," 63; sovereignty of, 32–33, 166, 230
Goethe, Johann Wolfgang von, 68
Gogh, Theo van, 207, 211, 211n16
Gogh, Vincent van, 195, 207, 212n17, 216n32; in
    Arles, 215–216, 217, 241; on an artist's respon-
    sibility, 212–213; on becoming an artist as a
    moral choice, 213–214; as a Buddhist, 209n4;
    conception of a person as a pilgrim, 216; corre-
    spondence of, 207, 207n2, 209, 209n6, 209n8,
    210–211, 210n12, 214n27; experimentation
    of with Impressionist and Pointillist methods,
    220–221; first artwork of, 212; influence of
    Delacroix on, 221, 221nn49–53; influence
    of Rembrandt on, 218–219; influence of van
    Ruisdael on, 216–218; myths of concerning
    the sale of his paintings, 211n16; in Paris,
    219–220; relationship between the Bible and
    works of art in his life, 209–210, 213n23;
    relationship between Christianity and art in
    his life, 207–209, 213–214; relationship with
    Gauguin, 220n47; on Rembrandt, 221n51;
    theory concerning his separation of faith and
    art, 208n3
Gogh-Bonger, Johanna van, 208n3
Golden Legend, The (de Voragine), 92, 115–116
Gombrich, E. H., 111
Gothic architecture/Gothic revival, 60–62, 61n7;
    and Scholasticism, 60, 61; and sensory experi-
    ence, 62, 64–65
Gothic cathedrals/churches: alienation of the
    beholder of from the material world itself,
    71–72; experience of music in, 68–70; experi-
    ence of in relation to theological currents,
    63–64; in the Île-de-France, 62; labyrinths of,
    70–71, 71n32; nave of, 62; as the prime vehicle
    for redemption, 62
"Gothic Glass: Two Aspects of a Dionysian
    Aesthetic" (Gage), 67
Gottlieb, Adolph, 243, 246; on the abstractness
    of his painting, 247; and the "realism of our
    time," 247–248
Goyen, Jan van, 24n5, 35–36, 217
Graham, John, 243–244n14, 252
Gray Apple Tree (P. Mondrian), 228–229, 235, 237
Great Themes in Art (Walford), 18, 23, 36, 61, 62,
    86, 123, 149, 151, 166, 178, 225, 239, 240;
    achievement of, 275; categorical framework
    of, 167; spirituality, the self, nature, and the
    city as the great themes of art in, 165; on van
    Ruisdael's style of painting, 24n5
Greenberg, Clement, 244–245, 249, 252; critiques
    of his formalist views of Pollock, 246
Gregorian chant, 69–70, 69nn27–28
Greuze, Jean-Baptiste, 171

Gustav IV (king of Sweden), 183

"Hans Rookmaaker's 'Four Freedoms' and Christian Art" (Walford), 15n1, 32
Harvesters, The (Pieter Bruegel the Elder [1565]), 137, 148
Hauser, Arnold, 166
Haymaking (Pieter Bruegel the Elder [1565]), 137, 148
Haywain, The (Constable [1821]), 203
Heckel, Erich, 241, 242
Hegel, G. W. F., 91, 91n4, 96
Henry VIII (king of England), 125, 126
Hervey, Mary, 125
Hobbes, Thomas, 170
Hogarth, William, 169, 171, 172, 173
Holbein, Hans, 124–125; power of his images, 132; time spent in London, 125
Holy Spirit, 34, 129
Hoving, Kirsten, 249
Hugh of Saint Victor, 64, 65
Hugo, Victor, 214, 215
Huizinga, Johan, 75
Hulsker, Jan, 212
human drama paintings, critical and financial advantages of, 24
Hume, David, 170
Hunters in the Snow (Pieter Bruegel the Elder [1565]), *136*, 137–138; composition and subject matter of, 138, 145–146; and the context of providence in, 148–149; depiction of Saint Hubert in, 142–143; depiction of the woman hauling firewood in, 147; and devotional contemplation, 142; foreign elements included in, 146; how Niclaes Jongelinck may have viewed the panting, 146–147, 148; image of the pig in, 138, 138n5; importance of tree lines in, 146; original context of, 139; as part of a series of landscapes (the *Months*), 137, 138–139, 147–149; scope and perspective of, 140–141; spiritual perception of in the context of the yearly calendar, 141–142
Hussites, 76
Huygens, Constantijn, 28–29, 236
Huys, Pieter, 113

I Like America. See *Coyote: I Like America and America Likes Me* (Joseph Beuys [1974])
iconoclasm, 33, 124, 131, 152, 157, 158; Calvinist iconoclasm, 156; iconoclastic impulses, 133
iconography, humanist, 177
icons, 93n11; aesthetic demerits of, 4
images, 131–134, 160–161; effect of the Protestant Reformation on the use of symbols/images in churches, 157–158, 157n16; expectations viewers bring to images, 131–132; suppression of, 131
Imitation of Christ, The (à Kempis), 216
Impressionism, 252
In Praise of Folly (Erasmus), 124
Ingres, Jean Auguste Dominique, 171
Interior of Saint Odulphus Church, Assendelft (Pieter Saenredam [1649]), *150*, 151, 152–153, 154n6; as a "Calvinist altarpiece," 161; and the church itself as a memento mori, 159; as a

commission of the De Jonge family, 161n25; depiction of the choir in, 159; detailed realism and geometrically organized space in, 153–154; elapsed time between preliminary drawings for and the completed painting, 154, 154n6; importance of the orientation of the church in, 156; interconnected personal details placed in the painting by the artist, 153; and the liturgical significance of the church, 156–157; method of perspective used in, 155; realism and the viewers of the painting, 154–155; role of selective naturalism in, 155–156; use of light in, 153n3, 159–160, 160n21
Isis Unveiled (Blavatsky), 232

Jacob van Ruisdael and the Perception of Landscape (Walford), 23–24, 109, 123, 200–201, 217n38, 275
Jacobs, Fredrika, 98
Janson, H. W., 105
January, a page from *Les Très Riches Heures du Duc de Berry* (Limbourg brothers [1413–1416]), *74*, 76; allusion of to the Hundred Years' War, 83; attribution of, 79; banquet scene of, 81–82; broad themes of, 80; chariot of Apollo in, 85, 86; cosmology and the connection with people's everyday lives in, 83–84; depiction of a bishop in, 81, 81nn23–24; depiction of royal privilege, wealth, and power in, 81, 82, 86–87; depiction of the Trojan War in, 80–81, 82–83; feast scene of depicted as the literal radiance of Jean, Duke of Berry, 85–86; as a "feudal display" of wealth, 86–87; identity of Jean, Duke of Berry in, 79–80; ideological aim of the calendar cycle in, 87; image of Aquarius in, 83, 85; innumerable *joyaux* throughout, 86; layering of disparate settings in, 80; role of the zodiacal calendar in, 80, 82, 83–84; temporal displacement in, 83; transformation of Jean, Duke of Berry, into a Christ-like figure in, 88
Jay, Martin, 97
Jean of Dinteville, 125–126, 127, 130–131
Jean of France, Duke of Berry, 77, 77n8, 79. See also *January,* a page from *Les Très Riches Heures du Duc de Berry* (Limbourg brothers [1413–1416])
Jesus Christ, 114, 143, 166, 187, 230; comparison of to the sun, 189; crucifixion of, 188; incarnation of, 62, 265; monogram of His victory over death, 44; portrayal of in Christian art, 44
Joachim of Fiore, 65
Job, depictions of, 51–52, 51n34
John (apostle), visionary experience of, 65–66
John of France, Duke of Berry, 77. See also *January,* a page from *Les Très Riches Heures du Duc de Berry* (Limbourg brothers [1413–1416])
Johnsen, William, 97
Jonghelinck, Niclaes, 139, 144–145, 146, 148
Jonghelinck, Thomas, 144
Jung, Carl, 243, 252
Jupiter, 83

Kandinsky, Wassily, 225, 233, 240, 242, 253; break of with representation, 242

Kaprow, Alan, 250
Katherine of Aragon, 126
Kirchner, Ernst Ludwig, 241, 242
Klimt, Gustav, 171
Kodera, Tsukasa, 219
Koerner, Joseph Leo, 130, 130n20
Kosegarten, Gotthard, 182
Kühn, Gottlieb Christian, 182
Kuspit, Donald, 260–262; on artistic action, 260;
    on "subjective realism," 261
Kuyper, Abraham, 33, 231; on Calvinism's role
    in art history, 33–34, 33n39; as a champion
    of art, 33; on the meaning of beauty and
    harmony, 34–35, 35n41; on the responsibility
    of the artist, 34

labyrinths, 70–71, 71n32
l'Académie royale de peinture et de sculpture, 175
landscape painting, 109, 110n5, 236; development
    of as a specific genre of painting, 111–112,
    111n6; "golden age" of Dutch landscape
    painting, 35; and the landscape as subject, 24;
    origins of, 109–112; perception of in seven-
    teenth-century Netherlands, 27–28; reception
    of, 110–111; and theatrical backdrops in
    ancient Greece and Rome, 110; uninhabited
    landscapes, 25n6
Landscape Room, Holkham Hall, 197
Landscape with a Goatherd and Goats (Lorrain), 198
Landscape with Hagar and the Angel (Lorrain
    [1646]), 197–198, 201
Landscape with Saint Jerome (Joachim Patinir
    [1520]), 108, 112; association of his suffering
    in with that of Christ, 114; as a devotional
    image, 119; flora depicted in, 118; and the
    idea of Contemptus mundi (condemnation of
    the world), 119–120; representation of Jerome
    in, 113–114; rugged terrain depicted in, 115;
    symbolism of the cardinal's robe and the life-
    less branch in, 114, 114n13; symbolism of the
    doves and dovecote in, 118–119; symbolism
    of the goat depicted in, 116–117; symbolism
    of Jerome's status as one of the four Latin
    Fathers of the church in, 114–115; symbolism
    of the owl and the yellow parrot depicted in,
    117; symbolism of rabbits representing carnal
    knowledge in, 117–118; symbolism of salaman-
    ders representing deception in, 117
Langhorne, Elizabeth, 249, 252
Leaping Horse, The (Constable [1826]), 203
Lectures on Calvinism (Kuyper), 33
Lectures on Fine Art (Hegel), 91
Leibniz, Gottfried Wilhelm, 169
LeMée, Katharine, 69, 69n29
Les Fêtes Vénitiennes, 176–177, 178
Letter on Toleration (Locke), 169
Limbourg, Herman, 76–77
Limbourg, Johan, 76–77
Limbourg, Paul, 76–77, 79
Lippi, Filippino, 96
Lives of the Artists (Vasari), 95, 96
"living paintings," 100
Locke, John, 169
Longhi, Pietro, 171
Longhi, Roberto, 96, 96–97n38

Lorrain, Claude, 197–198, 201, 204; composition
    system of, 198; Reynolds's opinion of, 198–199
Louis XIII (king of France), 174
Louis XIV (king of France), 169, 174
Louis XV (king of France), 173
Luther, Martin, 125, 128, 129, 159
lye, added to sarcophagus, 41n3

MacGregor, Neil, 130
Machiavelli, 168
Madame Pompadour, 170, 173
Madame de Pompadour (Boucher), 169
Madonna Enthroned, 101–102
Maguire, Henry, 52n39
Malevich, Kasimir, 240, 243
Mander, Karel van, 27–28, 27–28n15
Mandijn, Jan, 113
Manetti, Antonio, 94
Maniura, Robert, 98
MANRESA (Beuys [1966]), 265
Marc, Franz, 242
Marie de Medici cycle of paintings (Rubens), 174
Marino, Eugenio, 105n99
Mary Countess Howe (Gainsborough [1765]),
    169–170
Masaccio, 92, 92n6, 96, 97, 101, 105; death of, 94;
    as the inventor of perspective, 104; naturalis-
    tic paintings of, 106; realism of his frescoes,
    103–104; sterling reputation of, 94–95, 95n25
Masolino, 92, 92n6, 96, 101, 103; naturalistic
    paintings of, 106
Massys, Quentin, 112
Master of the Female Half-Lengths, 112
Mennekes, Friedhelm, 263, 264, 265
Michael, Erika, 127
Michelangelo, 95, 102, 105–106n104, 106, 169,
    171
Middle Ages, the, 156; the Black Death in, 86;
    importance of images in, 128–129; and late
    medieval cosmology, 83–84; music and music
    theory in, 68, 69; Scholasticism in, 60, 61,
    61n8; waning of, 75–76
Milanesi, Gaëtano, 96
Millet, Jean-François, 212, 213
Milliner, Matthew, 20
Milton, John, 174, 205
Mitchell, W. J. T., 131
Modern Art and the Death of Culture (Rookmaaker),
    35
Moderne Kunst Kring (Modern Art Circle),
    227–228, 233
Modernism, 18, 242, 272, 273
"Modernist Painting" (Greenberg), 245
Mondrian, Frits, 231
Mondrian, Piet, 225–226, 236–237, 240, 242–243;
    Calvinist upbringing of, 231–232; Christian
    commissions of, 231–232; continuity between
    his early and late work, 235–236; formal char-
    acteristics of his art, 226–227; friendship of
    with Catholics, 232; "iconic" Mondrian style,
    230; influence of Cubism on, 227–230; influ-
    ence of on modernist art, 226; intentions of in
    his Cubist tree paintings, 234–235; as a mem-
    ber of the Moderne Kunst Kring (Modern Art
    Circle), 227–228; and the "Plastic Essence"

(Neo-Plasticism), 232, 243n11; productivity of during World War I, 230; views on Cubism and Futurism, 231

Monet, Claude, 26, 240–241, 244n25, 252, 252n48

Months (series of landscape paintings by Pieter Bruegel the Elder [1565]), 137, 138–139, 142; and daily life in the countryside surrounding Antwerp, 143–144; as faithful renderings of the countryside surrounding Antwerp, 140; the series considered as a whole, 147–149

More, Thomas, 125

Moses, 66

Moxey, Keith, 127–128; on the portrait in painting and religious practice, 130–131

Mr. and Mrs. Andrews (Gainsborough [1749]), 170

musical mirrors, 69

Mystical Ark, The (Richard of Saint Victor), 64

Nagel, Alexander, 93, 93n11, 98, 101; on early Christocentric imagery, 102

Namuth, Hans, 244

Nattier, Jean-Marc, 169

naturalism, 36; selective naturalism, 27–28, 155–156, 217–218

nature: as the "art of God," 191, 191n42; as "God's landscape painting," 29; as "God's second book of revelation," 29; theosophical view of, 232–233

Naval Battle in the Bay of Naples (Pieter Bruegel the Elder [1556]), 140

Neo-Calvinism, 28, 32, 33; and the concept of art, 38; and the concept of themes, 37–38

Neoclassical Academy, 173

Netherlandish Proverbs (Pieter Bruegel the Elder [1559]), 143

Netherlands, the, 27, 157; neutrality of in World War I, 230; profusion of art and visual representation in the seventeenth century, 160

Netherlands Reformed Churches, 29, 155; Confession of Faith of, 200

Neumann, Johann Balthasar, 169, 173

New Testament, 43, 56

Newman, Barnett, 243

Newton, John, 195

Nolde, Emil, 241

Oecolampadius, Johannes, 125

Old Church Tower at Nuenen, The (V. van Gogh), 214–215

Old Testament, 43, 55–56

"On Fairy-Stories" (Tolkien), 266–267

"On Taste" (Hume), 170

Order of the Golden Fleece, 82

Organization for Direct Democracy through Referendum (Free People's Initiative) June, 1971 (Beuys), 262

Ossorio, Alfonso, 249

Ostade, Isaac van, 217

painting: "action painting," 244, 245–246, 251, 253; internal logic of, 154

Panofsky, Erwin, 61, 105, 105n99, 105–106n104, 166; on perspective and religious art, 106

Paradise Lost (Milton), 174

Pater, Nicolas Lancret Jean-Baptiste, 175–176

Patinir, Joachim, 109, 112; attention to detail needed in viewing his landscapes, 118; death of, 112; emulation of his style by other painters, 112–113

Paul (apostle): death of, 54, 54n47; depictions of, 44, 48–49, 51, 53–54; Paul's comparison of Adam to Christ, 52, 52n41

Peace of the Church (A.D. 313), 42

Peace of Westphalia (1648), 183

Peasant Dance, The (Pieter Bruegel the Elder [1567]), 143

Peasant Wedding Feast, The (Pieter Bruegel the Elder [1567]), 143

period dynamics, 172, 172n13

Peter (apostle), depictions of, 44, 48, 50–51, 92

Peter Walking on the Waves (Runge), 183

Philip the Bold, Duke of Burgundy, 77

Philip the Good, 82

Philonenko, M., 51–52n37

Philosophy of Art (von Schelling), 68

Picasso, Pablo, 227, 228, 229, 241

Pierozzi, Antonino, 104

Pilgrimage à Cythara (Watteau), 175, 175n17

Pilgrim's Progress, The (Bunyan), 216

pluralism, 18

Pollock, Jackson, 171, 226, 246; and "action painting," 244, 245–246, 251; approach to his art as influenced by Monet, 244n15; break of with the picturing function of art, 240, 244–245; and church design, 249–252; imagery used by, 243–244; interest of in Jung, 243–244n14; and the relationship between matter and spirit, 252; and spiritual expression, 248–249

Poor Richard's Almanac, 169

Poot, Hubert Kornelisz, 29

Pope, Alexander, 171

postmodernism, 18

Potato Eaters, The (V. van Gogh), 219

Poussin, Nicolas, 177

Prague Art Academy, 183

Protestant Reformation, 124–125, 126n7, 157

Protestants, 133, 157–158

Pseudo-Dionysius, 64; negative theology of, 67

putti (bare infants), 46, 182

radicalism, 205

"Rape of the Lock" (Pope), 171

Rappard, Anthon van, 213

rationalism, 169

Red Tree, The (P. Mondrian [1909]), 225, 226, 227

Reinagle, Ramsey Richard, 200

relativism, 18

Renaissance, the, 98–99, 104, 105, 127, 168–169, 227; the Northern Renaissance, the, 76; the "Renaissance popes," 169; Walford's view of, 106–107

Renoir, Pierre-Auguste, 171

Return of the Herd (Pieter Bruegel the Elder [1565]), 137, 147, 148

Reynolds, Joshua, 170; opinion of Lorrain, 198–199

Rhenanus, Beatus, 124

Richard of Saint Victor, 64, 65; on the four modes of seeing, 64–65; on John's revelation, 65–66

Rijn, Rembrandt van, 30, 210, 212, 218–219, 221, 222
Rinuccini, 94
Robertson, Andrew, 205
Rococo Enlightenment, the, 169–170, 175, 176, 177; lyrical escapism of Rococo art, 172; and the Neoclassical Academy, 173; unifying cultural dynamic of, 170–171, 172, 172n13
Rodman, Selden, 246, 247
Romaine, James, 20
Roman Catholics, 157–158
Romanticism, 272
Rome/Roman Empire: as the center for sarcophagus carving, 41–42; and landscape painting, 110, 111; legalization of Christianity in, 44; political instability in, 42–43
Rookmaaker, Hans, 15, 20, 166, 272, 273; appreciation of Dutch landscape painting, 35–36; death of, 17; differences with Walford, 19; friendship with Walford, 15–16; influence of on Walford, 35–37, 37n48; topics of as an art critic, 36
Rosenberg, Harold, 244, 251, 253; on the existential in art, 245–246
Rosenthal, Mark, 259–260, 261
Rothko, Mark, 243; on whether his paintings were abstracts, 246–247
Rouault, Georges, 225
Royal Academy Schools, 199, 200
Rubens, Peter Paul, 171, 174
Ruisdael, Jacob van, 17–18, 26–27, 199–200, 217–218, 222, 236–237; baptism of, 29, 29n23; as an interior decorator, 27; pictorial naturalism of, 27; religious environment in which he worked (Reformed Calvinism), 28–29, 29n23; reputation of as a landscape painter, 24; ruins as a recurring motif in his art, 34n40; selective naturalism of, 27–28, 29; style of, 24n5, 25; technical mastery of, 27
"Ruisdael in Provence" (Blotkamp), 217
Rumohr, Friedrich Wilhelm Basilius von, 96, 97, 186; criticism of the *Tetschen Altar*, 186–187
Runge, Philipp Otto, 183
Rupert of Deutz, 65
Ruysdael, Salomon van, 24

Saenredam, Pieter Jansz, 151, 152, 156–157; ambivalence of concerning the Catholic past and Protestant present in which he lived, 159n18; Calvinism of, 157; depiction of churches by, 158–159, 158n17; drawings of, 160n22; gravestone of, 153n4
Saint Bavo Kerk, 201
Saint Hubert, 142–143
Saint Jerome, 113; self-flagellation of, 117; and the wounded lion, 115–116. See also *Landscape with Saint Jerome* (Joachim Patinir [1520])
Saint Jerome in the Wilderness (Pieter Bruegel the Elder [1555–1560]), 146
Saint Laurent, Yves, 226
Santa Maria del Carmine, 92
Santa Maria Maggiore, 101
sarcophagi: *lenos* (tub-shaped sarcophagus), 45n13; "passion sarcophagi," 47, 47nn18–19; two-

tiered columnar sarcophagus, 46n16. *See also* sarcophagi, Christian
sarcophagi, Christian, 42, 48; Abraham and Isaac motifs carved on, 44; biblical themes carved on, 42; depictions of Pilate on, 49, 49n16; horizontal format of, 42; iconographic design in early Christian sarcophagi, 45; Jonah motifs carved on, 43, 43n7, 44; third-century Christian preference for Old Testament carvings on, 43; "Two Brothers" frieze sarcophagus, 49
Sarcophagus of Junius Bassus (A.D. 359), *40, 41,* 41n1, 45n14, 55–56; Adam, Eve, and Daniel scenes on, 52–53, 53n42, 53n46; Bosio's engraving of, 52n40; composition of the central axis, 47–48; depiction of Abraham sacrificing Isaac on, 49–50; depiction of Christ before Pilate on, 49; depiction of Christ enthroned above Caelus on, 48–49; discovery of, 53; as an example of "passion sarcophagi," 47; façade of, 45–46; five scenes on the lower level of, 51–53; general format of, 46; images of Peter and Paul carved on, 44, 50–51, 53–54; inscription identifying Junius Bassus on, 54–55, 55n50; lower central scene of, 49–50; *orant* (praying) figure on, 53; sacrifice theme of, 50
scenae frons (stone stage), 46
Schelfhout, Lodewijk, 228
Schelling, Friedrich von, 68
Schmarsow, August, 96
Secret Doctrine, The (Blavatsky), 232
Secular Age, A (Taylor), 72
secularism/secularization, 133–134, 265–266
Serlio, Sebastiano, 144–145
"Seventeenth-century Dutch art: Christian art?" (Rookmaaker), 36
similitude, 84
Sistine Madonna (Raphael), 184
Slive, Seymour, 27, 31
Smith, David, 133
Smith, J. T., 200
Smith, Tony, 249
Sower with Setting Sun (Vincent van Gogh [1888]), *206,* 207, 207n1, 211, 217, 218; disguised symbolism in, 219; employment of color in, 220–221; and the halo in, 219
Spectator Papers, 169
Spiegel, H. L., 28–29, 236
Spinoza, Baruch, 169
Spiritual in Art, The: Abstract Painting 1890–1985 (exhibition catalog), 233
Spoor, Cornelius, 232
Stachelhaus, Heiner, 256
Steen, Jan, 172
Steiner, Rudolf, 232; and the concept of the "Christ impulse," 263–264
Stokstad, Marilyn, 48
Stracciabende, Pellegrina, 102, 103
Sufism, 166
Summers, David, 110
Swing, The (Fragonard), 170

Tattler, 169
Taylor, Charles, 72
Tempest, The (Shakespeare), 174

Testament of Job (Greek midrash), 51–52n37, 52
Tetschen Altar (Friedrich [1808]), *180*, 181–182, 182n6; gilded frame of, 182; as a *Gipfelkreuz* crucifix ("summit cross"), 181–182, 185, 189–190; initial commission of, 182–183; purchase of by Count Franz Anton von Thun-Hohenstein, 183–184; as a religious altar piece, 184–185; symbolic program of the frame in, 190–191; symbolic religious truths in, 185–186; use of light in, 188–189
Teuffel, Gardner von, 100
Thausing, Moritz, 96
theosophy, 232–233; view of nature, 232–233
Thunø, Erik, 99–100
Tiepolo, Giovanni Battista, 171
Tiger Hunt (Delacroix [1854]), 37
Tisdale, Caroline, 257
Titian (Tiziano Vecellio), 169, 171
Tolkien, J. R. R., 257; and the conception of myth, 266–268
Toorop, Jan, 234
Toulouse-Lautrec, Henri, 220
Trecento frescoes, 101
Trees (P. Mondrian), 228, 234–235
Très Riches Heures du Duc de Berry: centrality of the calendar to, 78–79, 141–142; perspective structuring of, 78; as primarily a devotional, 77–78. See also *January*, a page from *Les Très Riches Heures du Duc de Berry* (Limbourg brothers [1413–1416])
Trexler, Richard, 98, 99n53
Trinity (Masaccio [1425–1427]), 105
Turner, J. M. W., 193
"typiconic idioms," 172, 172n9, 174–175
typology, 43

van, von. *See next element of name*
Vasari, Giorgio, 94–95, 95n29, 98, 100, 106
Verdon, Timothy, 105
Vermeer, Johannes, 172
View of Haarlem from the Dunes at Overeen (van Ruisdael [1660s]), *22*, 24n5, 201, 217–218, 217n37; coherence of, 26; composition of, 26; orchestration of the viewer's position in, 26–27; rich visual detail of, 25–26; use of light in, 30; as a visual depiction of God's provident direction revealed in nature and human activity, 30
villa decoration, 144–145
Vincent Van Gogh: Between Heaven and Earth: The Landscapes (Mendes Bürgi, Zimmer, and Feilchenfeldt), 215
Viollet-le-Duc, Eugène Emmanuel, 2–3, 66–67, 72; as a champion of Gothic architecture, 60–61
Vita (Life), of Blessed Andre Corsini, 102–104
Vitruvius, 145
Vulgate, the, 113–114

Walford, John, *14*, 15, 27n12, 31n32, 41, 123, 149, 151, 156, 178, 199, 235, *270*, 271, 277–278; anxiety and discouragement of, 276; blog of ("Only Connect"), 19; British wit of, 274; at Cambridge University, 17–18, 32, 272; as champion of quality art in the church, 19–20; development of an art history curriculum by, 274–275; development of his Neo-Calvinist

perspective on art, 17; differences with Hans Rookmaaker, 19; on Dutch landscape painting in the seventeenth century, 155, 236–237; emphasis of on the content of von Ruisdael's art, 27; faith of, 37; friendship with Rookmaaker, 15–16; influence of Rookmaaker on, 35–37, 37n48; love of photography, 276; on P. Mondrian, 225–226; opinion of *The French Ambassadors*, 123–124, 134; opinion of Gothic cathedrals, 61, 63, 68; opinion of Monet's *Poplars*, 240; opinion of the *Tetschen Altar*, 185; persona of, 275–276; potential of in the art field, 16; presence of on the Internet, 277; on Renaissance art, 106–107; as a student at the Free University, 15–16, 32, 272; studying of the Scriptures by, 16–17; understanding of art and theology as natural partners, 273; at Wheaton College, 18, 271–275; on the work of Delaunay, 242. *See also* Walford, John, art/historical methodology of
Walford, John, art/historical methodology of, 23–24, 23n2; categories (spirituality, the self, nature, the city) of his art methodology, 165–166, 168; on the city and art, 167; and the "contemplative mode of perception," 30–31; criticism of iconographic decoding in art history, 31–32; on the formal features ("line, shape, mass, light, color, texture, and space") one needs in observing art, 166; on image and perception, 154; on light ("light-beams") as an image of divine providence, 29–30; meaning-directed method of, 123; on nature and art, 167; "perception" method of, 36; on selective naturalism as a creative method, 27–28, 155–156, 217–218; on the self and art, 167; on spirituality in the observance of art, 166, 225–226; stress of on the continuity of being-ness, 37; on the strong or weakly formed work of art, 167–168
Waning of the Middle Ages, The: A Study of the Forms of Life, Thought, and Art in France and in the Netherlands in the XIVth and XVth Centuries (Huizinga), 75
Water Lilies (Monet [1914–1926]), 244n15
Watteau, Jean-Antoine, 174, 175–176; perception of, 177
Weintraub, Linda, 262–263
Welsh, Robert, 233
West, Benjamin, 194
White on White (Malevich), 243
William of Orange, 162, 162n27
Wölfflin, Heinrich, 166
Wood, Christopher, 93, 93n11, 101
Wordsworth, William, 195
Worley, Taylor, 264, 265
Wormser, J. A., 231

Zeitung für die elegante Welt (*Journal for the Elegant World*), 186
Zen, 166
Zeno of Verona, 51, 51n36
Zeus, 44, 48